Scientific Computing with Python 3

An example-rich, comprehensive guide for all of your Python computational needs

Claus Führer

Jan Erik Solem

Olivier Verdier

BIRMINGHAM - MUMBAI

Scientific Computing with Python 3

First published: December 2016

Production reference: 1141216

Published by Packt Publishing Ltd.
Livery Place
35 Livery Street
Birmingham
B3 2PB, UK.
ISBN 978-1-78646-351-7

www.packtpub.com

Credits

Authors

Claus Führer

Jan Erik Solem

Olivier Verdier

Reviewers

 Helmut Podhaisky

Commissioning Editor

Veena Pagare

Acquisition Editor

Sonali Vernekar

Content Development Editor

Aishwarya Pandere

Technical Editor

Karan Thakkar

Copy Editor

Vikrant Phadkay

Sneha Singh

Project Coordinator

Nidhi Joshi

Proofreader

Safis Editing

Indexer

Mariammal Chettiyar

Graphics

Disha Haria

Production Coordinator

Arvindkumar Gupta

About the Authors

Claus Führer is a professor of scientific computations at Lund University, Sweden. He has an extensive teaching record that includes intensive programming courses in numerical analysis and engineering mathematics across various levels in many different countries and teaching environments. Claus also develops numerical software in research collaboration with industry and received Lund University's Faculty of Engineering Best Teacher Award in 2016.

Jan Erik Solem is a Python enthusiast, former associate professor, and currently the CEO of Mapillary, a street imagery computer vision company. He has previously worked as a face recognition expert, founder and CTO of Polar Rose, and computer vision team leader at Apple. Jan is a World Economic Forum technology pioneer and won the Best Nordic Thesis Award 2005-2006 for his dissertation on image analysis and pattern recognition. He is also the author of "Programming Computer Vision with Python" (O'Reilly 2012).

Olivier Verdier began using Python for scientific computing back in 2007 and received a PhD in mathematics from Lund University in 2009. He has held post-doctoral positions in Cologne, Trondheim, Bergen, and Umeå and is now an associate professor of mathematics at Bergen University College, Norway.

About the Reviewer

Helmut Podhaisky works in the Institute of Mathematics at the Martin Luther University in Halle-Wittenberg, where he teaches mathematics and scientific computing. He has co-authored a book on numerical methods for ordinary differential equations as well as several research papers on numerical methods. For work and fun, he uses Python, Fortran, Octave, Mathematica, and Haskell.

www.PacktPub.com

For support files and downloads related to your book, please visit www.PacktPub.com.

Did you know that Packt offers eBook versions of every book published, with PDF and ePub files available? You can upgrade to the eBook version at www.PacktPub.com and as a print book customer, you are entitled to a discount on the eBook copy. Get in touch with us at service@packtpub.com for more details.

At www.PacktPub.com, you can also read a collection of free technical articles, sign up for a range of free newsletters and receive exclusive discounts and offers on Packt books and eBooks.

https://www.packtpub.com/mapt

Get the most in-demand software skills with Mapt. Mapt gives you full access to all Packt books and video courses, as well as industry-leading tools to help you plan your personal development and advance your career.

Why subscribe?

- Fully searchable across every book published by Packt
- Copy and paste, print, and bookmark content
- On demand and accessible via a web browser

Acknowledgement

We want to acknowledge the competent and helpful comments and suggestions by Helmut Podhaisky, Halle University, Germany. To have such a partner in the process of writing a book is a big luck and chance for the authors.

We would also like to express our gratitude towards the reviewers of the first edition of this book, [7], Linda Kann, KTH Stockholm, Hans Petter Langtangen, Simula Research Laboratory, and Alf Inge Wang, NTNU Trondheim.

A book has to be tested in teaching. And here we had fantastic partners: the teaching assistants from the course "Beräkningsprogramering med Python" during the years and the colleagues involved in teaching: Najmeh Abiri, Christian Andersson, Dara Maghdid, Peter Meisrimel, Fatemeh Mohammadi, Azahar Monge, Anna-Maria Persson, Alexandros Sopasakis, Tony Stillfjord, Lund University. Najmeh Abiri also tested most of the Jupyter notebook material which you find on the book's webpage.

A book has not only to be written, it has to be published, and in this process Aishwarya Pandere and Karan Thakkar, PACKT Publishing, were always constructive, friendly and helpful partners bridging different time zones and different text processing tools. Thanks.

Claus Führer, Jan-Erik Solem, Olivier Verdier Lund, Bergen 2016

Table of Contents

Preface   1

Chapter 1: Getting Started   11

    Installation and configuration instructions   12

        Installation   12

        Anaconda   13

        Configuration   14

        Python Shell   14

        Executing scripts   15

        Getting Help   15

        Jupyter – Python notebook   15

    Program and program flow   16

        Comments   17

        Line joining   17

    Basic types   18

        Numbers   18

        Strings   18

        Variables   19

        Lists   19

        Operations on lists   20

        Boolean expressions   20

    Repeating statements with loops   21

        Repeating a task   21

        Break and else   22

    Conditional statements   22

    Encapsulating code with functions   23

    Scripts and modules   24

        Simple modules – collecting functions   24

        Using modules and namespaces   25

    Interpreter   25

    Summary   26

Chapter 2: Variables and Basic Types   27

    Variables   27

    Numeric types   28

        Integers   29

Plain integers	29
Floating point numbers	30
Floating point representation	30
Infinite and not a number	31
Underflow – Machine Epsilon	32
Other float types in NumPy	33
Complex numbers	34
Complex Numbers in Mathematics	34
The j notation	34
Real and imaginary parts	35
Booleans	37
Boolean operators	37
Boolean casting	38
Automatic Boolean casting	39
Return values of and and or	39
Boolean and integer	40
Strings	40
Operations on strings and string methods	42
String formatting	43
Summary	44
Exercises	44
Chapter 3: Container Types	49
Lists	49
Slicing	50
Strides	52
Altering lists	53
Belonging to a list	53
List methods	54
In–place operations	54
Merging lists – zip	55
List comprehension	55
Arrays	56
Tuples	58
Dictionaries	58
Creating and altering dictionaries	59
Looping over dictionaries	60
Sets	60
Container conversions	62
Type checking	63
Summary	64

Exercises	64

Chapter 4: Linear Algebra – Arrays | 67 |

Overview of the array type	67
Vectors and matrices	67
Indexing and slices	69
Linear algebra operations	69
Solving a linear system	70
Mathematical preliminaries	71
Arrays as functions	71
Operations are elementwise	71
Shape and number of dimensions	72
The dot operations	73
The array type	75
Array properties	75
Creating arrays from lists	76
Accessing array entries	77
Basic array slicing	77
Altering an array using slices	79
Functions to construct arrays	79
Accessing and changing the shape	80
The shape function	80
Number of dimensions	81
Reshape	81
Transpose	83
Stacking	84
Stacking vectors	84
Functions acting on arrays	85
Universal functions	85
Built-in universal functions	85
Create universal functions	86
Array functions	88
Linear algebra methods in SciPy	89
Solving several linear equation systems with LU	89
Solving a least square problem with SVD	91
More methods	92
Summary	93
Exercises	93

Chapter 5: Advanced Array Concepts | 97 |

| **Array views and copies** | 97 |
| Array views | 97 |

Slices as views	98
Transpose and reshape as views	98
Array copy	99
Comparing arrays	99
Boolean arrays	99
Checking for equality	100
Boolean operations on arrays	101
Array indexing	102
Indexing with Boolean arrays	102
Using where	103
Performance and Vectorization	104
Vectorization	105
Broadcasting	106
Mathematical view	106
Constant functions	107
Functions of several variables	108
General mechanism	108
Conventions	110
Broadcasting arrays	110
The broadcasting problem	110
Shape mismatch	112
Typical examples	113
Rescale rows	113
Rescale columns	113
Functions of two variables	113
Sparse matrices	115
Sparse matrix formats	116
Compressed sparse row	116
Compressed Sparse Column	118
Row-based linked list format	118
Altering and slicing matrices in LIL format	119
Generating sparse matrices	119
Sparse matrix methods	120
Summary	121
Chapter 6: Plotting	123
Basic plotting	123
Formatting	129
Meshgrid and contours	132
Images and contours	136
Matplotlib objects	138
The axes object	139

Modifying line properties	140
Annotations	141
Filling areas between curves	142
Ticks and ticklabels	144
Making 3D plots	145
Making movies from plots	149
Summary	150
Exercises	151

Chapter 7: Functions	153
Basics	153
Parameters and arguments	154
Passing arguments – by position and by keyword	154
Changing arguments	155
Access to variables defined outside the local namespace	156
Default arguments	157
Beware of mutable default arguments	158
Variable number of arguments	158
Return values	160
Recursive functions	161
Function documentation	163
Functions are objects	164
Partial application	164
Using Closures	165
Anonymous functions – the lambda keyword	165
The lambda construction is always replaceable	166
Functions as decorators	167
Summary	168
Exercises	169

Chapter 8: Classes	171
Introduction to classes	172
Class syntax	173
The __init__ method	173
Attributes and methods	174
Special methods	176
Reverse operations	178
Attributes that depend on each other	180
The property function	181
Bound and unbound methods	182
Class attributes	182

Class methods	183
Subclassing and inheritance	185
Encapsulation	188
Classes as decorators	189
Summary	192
Exercises	192

Chapter 9: Iterating — 195

The for statement	195
Controlling the flow inside the loop	196
Iterators	197
Generators	198
Iterators are disposable	199
Iterator tools	199
Generators of recursive sequences	201
Arithmetic geometric mean	201
Convergence acceleration	203
List filling patterns	205
List filling with the append method	205
List from iterators	205
Storing generated values	206
When iterators behave as lists	207
Generator expression	207
Zipping iterators	208
Iterator objects	209
Infinite iterations	210
The while loop	210
Recursion	211
Summary	212
Exercises	212

Chapter 10: Error Handling — 215

What are exceptions?	215
Basic principles	217
Raising exceptions	217
Catching exceptions	218
User-defined exceptions	220
Context managers — the with statement	221
Finding Errors: Debugging	223
Bugs	223
The stack	223

The Python debugger	224
Overview – debug commands	226
Debugging in IPython	227
Summary	228

Chapter 11: Namespaces, Scopes, and Modules — 229

Namespace	229
Scope of a variable	230
Modules	232
Introduction	232
Modules in IPython	234
The IPython magic command	234
The variable __name__	234
Some useful modules	235
Summary	235

Chapter 12: Input and Output — 237

File handling	237
Interacting with files	237
Files are iterable	239
File modes	239
NumPy methods	240
savetxt	240
loadtxt	240
Pickling	241
Shelves	242
Reading and writing Matlab data files	243
Reading and writing images	243
Summary	244

Chapter 13: Testing — 245

Manual testing	245
Automatic testing	246
Testing the bisection algorithm	247
Using unittest package	249
Test setUp and tearDown methods	250
Parameterizing tests	251
Assertion tools	253
Float comparisons	253
Unit and functional tests	255
Debugging	256

Test discovery	256
Measuring execution time	256
Timing with a magic function	257
Timing with the Python module timeit	258
Timing with a context manager	259
Summary	260
Exercises	260

Chapter 14: Comprehensive Examples
263

Polynomials	263
Theoretical background	263
Tasks	265
The polynomial class	266
Newton polynomial	270
Spectral clustering	272
Solving initial value problems	276
Summary	280
Exercises	280

Chapter 15: Symbolic Computations - SymPy
281

What are symbolic computations?	281
Elaborating an example in SymPy	283
Basic elements of SymPy	285
Symbols – the basis of all formulas	285
Numbers	286
Functions	286
Undefined functions	287
Elementary Functions	288
Lambda – functions	289
Symbolic Linear Algebra	290
Symbolic matrices	291
Examples for Linear Algebra Methods in SymPy	292
Substitutions	294
Evaluating symbolic expressions	296
Example: A study on the convergence order of Newton's Method	297
Converting a symbolic expression into a numeric function	299
A study on the parameter dependency of polynomial coefficients	299
Summary	301

Appendix: References
303

Index
307

Preface

Python can be used for more than just general-purpose programming. It is a free, open source language and environment that has tremendous potential for use within the domain of scientific computing. This book presents Python in tight connection with mathematical applications and demonstrates how to use various concepts in Python for computing purposes, including examples with the latest version of Python 3. Python is an effective tool to use when coupling scientific computing and mathematics and this book will teach you how to use it for linear algebra, arrays, plotting, iterating, functions, polynomials, and much more.

What this book covers

Chapter 1, *Getting Started*, addresses the main language elements of Python without going into detail. Here we make a brief tour through all. It is a good starting point for those who want to start directly. It is a quick reference for those readers who want in a later chapter understand an example which uses might use constructs like functions before functions were explained in deep .

Chapter 2, *Variables and Basic Types*, presents the most important and basic types in Python. Float is the more important datatype in scientific computing together with the special numbers nan and inf. Booleans, integers, complex, and strings are other basic datatypes, which will be used throughout this book.

Chapter 3, *Container Types*, explains how to work with container types, mainly lists. Dictionaries and tuples will be explained as well as indexing and looping, through container objects. Occasionally, one uses even sets as a special container type.

Chapter 4, *Linear Algebra*, works with the most important objects in linear algebra--vectors and matrices. This book chooses NumPy array as the central tool for describing matrices and even higher order tensors. Arrays have many advanced features and allows also for universal functions acting on matrices or vectors elementwise. The book emphasizes on array indexing, slices, and the dot product as the basic operation in most computing tasks. Some linear algebra examples are worked out to demonstrate the use of SciPy's submodule linalg.

Chapter 5, *Advanced Array Concepts,* explains some more advanced aspects of arrays. The difference between array copies and views is explained extensively as views make programs using arrays very fast but are often a source for errors, which are hard to debug. The use of Boolean arrays to write effective, compact, and readable code is shown and demonstrated. Finally, the technique of array broadcasting-- a unique feature of NumPy arrays -- is explained by its analogy to operations performed on functions.

Chapter 6, *Plotting,* shows how to make plots, mainly classical x/yplots but also 3D plots and histograms. Scientific computing requires good tools for visualizing the results. Python's module matplotlib is introduced starting from the handy plotting commands in its submodule pyplot. Finetuning and modifying plots becomes possible by creating graphical objects such as axes. We show how attributes of these objects can be changed and annotations can be made.

Chapter 7, *Functions,* form the fundamental building block in programming, which is probably nearest to underlying mathematical concepts. Function definition and function calls are explained as the different ways to set function arguments. Anonymous lambda functions are introduced and used in various examples throughout the book.

Chapter 8, *Classes,* defines objects as instances of classes, which we provide with methods and attributes. In mathematics, class attributes often depend on each other, which requires special programming techniques for setter and getter functions. Basic mathematical operations such as + can be defined for special mathematic datatypes. Inheritance and abstraction are mathematical concepts which are reflected by object oriented programming. We demonstrate the use of inheritance by a simple solver class for ordinary differential equations.

Chapter 9, *Iterating,* presents iteration using loops and iterators. There is now a chapter in this book without loops and iterations, but here we come to principles of iterators and create own generator objects. In this chapter, you learn why a generator can be exhausted and how infinite loops can be programmed. Python's module itertools is a useful companion for this chapter.

Chapter 10, *Error Handling,* covers errors and exceptions and how to find and fix them. An error or an exception is an event, which breaks the execution of a program unit. This chapter shows what to do then, that is, how an exception can be handled. You learn to define your own exception classes and how to provide valuable information, which can be used for catching these exceptions. Error handling is more than printing an error message.

Chapter 11, *Namespaces, Scopes and Modules,* covers Python modules. What are local and global variables? When is a variable known and when is it unknown to a program unit? This is discussed in this chapter. A variable can be passed to a function by a parameter list or tacitly injected by making use of its scope. When should this technique be applied and when not? This chapter tries to give an answer to this central question.

Chapter 12, *Input and Output,* covers some options for handling data files. Data files are used for storing and providing data for a given problem, often large scale measurements. This chapter describes how this data can be accessed and modified using different formats.

Chapter 13, *Testing,* focuses on testing for scientific programming. The key tool is unittest, which allows for automatic testing and parametrized tests. By considering the classical bisection algorithm in numerical mathematics, we exemplify different steps to design meaningful tests, which as a side effect also deliver a documentation of the use of a piece of code. Careful testing provides test protocols which can be later helpful when debugging a complex code often written by many different programmers.

Chapter 14, *Comprehensive Examples,* presents some comprehensive and longer examples together with a brief introduction to the theoretical background and their complete implementation. These examples make use of all constructs shown in the book so far and put them in a larger and more complex context. They are open for extensions by the reader.

Chapter 15, *Symbolic Computations - SymPy,* speaks about symbolic computations. Scientific computing is mainly numeric computations with inexact data and approximative results. This is contrasted by symbolic computations often formal manipulation, which aims for exact solutions in a closed form expression. In this last chapter of the book, we introduce this technique in Python, which is often used for deriving and verifying theoretically mathematical models and numerical results. We emphasize on high precision floating point evaluation of symbolic expressions.

What you need for this book

You would need Pyhon3.5 or higher, SciPy, NumPy, Matplotlib, IPython shell (we recommend strongly to install Python and its packages through Anaconda). The examples of the book do not have any special hardware requirements on memory and graphics.

Who this book is for

This book is the outcome of a course on Python for scientific computing which is taught at Lund University since 2008. The course expanded over the years, and condensed versions of the material were taught at universities in Cologne, Trondheim, Stavanger, Soran, Lappeenranta and also in computation oriented companies.

Our belief is that Python and its surrounding scientific computing ecosystem — SciPy, NumPY and matplotlib — represent a tremendous progress in scientific computing environment. Python and the aforementioned libraries are free and open source. What's more, is a modern language featuring all the bells and whistles that this adjective entails: object oriented programming, testing, advanced shell with IPython, etc. When writing this book we had two groups of readers in mind:

- The reader who chooses Python as his or her first programming language will use this book in a teacher-led course. The book guides into the different topics and offers background reading and experimenting. A teacher typically selects and orders the material from this book in such a way, that it fits to the specific learning outcomes of an introductory course.
- The reader who already has some experience in programming, and some taste for scientific computing or mathematics will use this book as a companion when diving into the world of Scipy and Numpy. Programming in Python can be quite different from programming in MATLAB, say. The book wants to point out the "pythonic" way of programming, which makes programming a pleasure.

Our goal is to explain the steps to get started with Python in the context of scientific computing. The book may be read either from the first page to the last, or by picking the bits that seem most interesting. Needless to say, as improving one's programming skills requires considerable practice, it is highly advisable to experiment and play with the examples and the exercises in the book.

We hope that the readers will enjoy programming with Python, SciPy, NumPY and matplotlib as much as we do.

Python vs Other Languages

When it comes to deciding what language to use for a book on scientific computing many factors come in to play. The learning threshold of the language itself is important for newcomers, here scripting languages usually provide the best options. A wide range of modules for numerical computing is necessary, preferably with a strong developer community. If these core modules are built on a well-tested, optimized foundation of fast libraries like e.g. LAPACK, even better. Finally, if the language is also usable in a wider setting and a wider range of applications, the chance of the reader using the skills learned from this book outside an academic setting is greater. Therefore the choice of Python was a natural one.

In short, Python is

- free and open source
- a scripting language, meaning that it is interpreted
- a modern language (object oriented, exception handling, dynamic typing etc.)
- concise, easy to read and quick to learn
- full of freely available libraries, in particular scientific ones (linear algebra, visualization tools, plotting, image analysis, differential equations solving, symbolic computations, statistics etc.)
- useful in a wider setting: scientific computing, scripting, web sites, text parsing, etc.
- widely used in industrial applications

There are other alternatives to Python. Some of them and the differences to Python are listed here.

Java, C++ : Object oriented, compiled languages. More verbose and low level compared to Python. Few scientific libraries.

C, FORTRAN : Low level compiled languages. Both languages are extensively used in scientific computing, where computational time matters. Nowadays these languages are often combined with Python *wrappers*.

PHP, Ruby, other interpreted languages. PHP is web oriented. Ruby is as flexible as Python but has few scientific libraries.

MATLAB, Scilab, Octave : MATLAB is a tool for matrix computation that evolved for scientific computing. The scientific library is huge. The language features are not as developed as those of Python. Neither free nor open source. SciLab and Octave are open source tools which are syntactically similar to MATLAB.

Haskell : Haskell is a modern functional language and follows different programming paradigms than Python. There are some common constructions like list comprehension. Haskell is rarely used in scientific computing. See also [12].

Other Python literature

Here we give some hints to literature on Python which can serve as complementary sources or as texts for parallel reading. Most introductory books on Python are devoted to teach this language as a general purpose tool. One excellent example which we want to mention here explicitly is [19]. It explains the language by simple examples, e.g. object oriented programming is explained by organizing a pizza bakery.

There are very few books dedicated to Python directed towards scientific computing and engineering. Among these few books we would like to mention the two books by Langtangen which combine scientific computing with the modern "pythonic" view on programming, [16,17].

This "pythonic" view is also the guiding line of our way of teaching programming of numerical algorithms. We try to show how many well-established concepts and constructions in computer science can be applied to problems within scientific computing. The pizza-bakery example is replaced by Lagrange polynomials, generators become time stepping methods for ODEs, and so on.

Finally we have to mention the nearly infinite amount of literature on the web. The web was also a big source of knowledge when preparing this book. Literature from the web often covers things that are new, but can also be totally outdated. The web also presents solutions and interpretations which might contradict each other. We strongly recommend to use the web as additional source, but we consider a "traditional" textbook with the web resources "edited" as the better entry point to a rich new world.

Conventions

In this book, you will find a number of text styles that distinguish between different kinds of information. Here are some examples of these styles and an explanation of their meaning.

Code words in text, database table names, folder names, filenames, file extensions, pathnames, and user input are shown as follows: "install additional packages with `conda install` within your virtual environment"

A block of code is set as follows:

```
from scipy import *
from matplotlib.pyplot import *
```

Any command-line input or output is written as follows:

```
jupyter notebook
```

New terms and **important words** are shown in bold. Words that you see on the screen, for example, in menus or dialog boxes, appear in the text like this: "The **Jupyter notebook** is a fantastic tool for demonstrating your work."

Warnings or important notes appear in a box like this.

Tips and tricks appear like this.

Reader feedback

Feedback from our readers is always welcome. Let us know what you think about this book-what you liked or disliked. Reader feedback is important for us as it helps us develop titles that you will really get the most out of. To send us general feedback, simply e-mail feedback@packtpub.com, and mention the book's title in the subject of your message. If there is a topic that you have expertise in and you are interested in either writing or contributing to a book, see our author guide at www.packtpub.com/authors.

Customer support

Now that you are the proud owner of a Packt book, we have a number of things to help you to get the most from your purchase.

Downloading the example code

You can download the example code files for this book from your account at http://www.packtpub.com. If you purchased this book elsewhere, you can visit http://www.packtpub.com/support and register to have the files e-mailed directly to you.

You can download the code files by following these steps:

1. Log in or register to our website using your e-mail address and password.
2. Hover the mouse pointer on the **SUPPORT** tab at the top.
3. Click on **Code Downloads & Errata**.
4. Enter the name of the book in the **Search** box.
5. Select the book for which you're looking to download the code files.
6. Choose from the drop-down menu where you purchased this book from.
7. Click on **Code Download**.

Once the file is downloaded, please make sure that you unzip or extract the folder using the latest version of:

- WinRAR / 7-Zip for Windows
- Zipeg / iZip / UnRarX for Mac
- 7-Zip / PeaZip for Linux

The code bundle for the book is also hosted on GitHub at https://github.com/PacktPublishing/Scientific-Computing-with-Python-3. We also have other code bundles from our rich catalog of books and videos available at https://github.com/PacktPublishing/. Check them out!

Downloading the color images of this book

We also provide you with a PDF file that has color images of the screenshots/diagrams used in this book. The color images will help you better understand the changes in the output. You can download this file from https://www.packtpub.com/sites/default/files/downloads/ScientificComputingwithPython3_ColorImages.pdf.

Errata

Although we have taken every care to ensure the accuracy of our content, mistakes do happen. If you find a mistake in one of our books-maybe a mistake in the text or the code-we would be grateful if you could report this to us. By doing so, you can save other readers from frustration and help us improve subsequent versions of this book. If you find any errata, please report them by visiting http://www.packtpub.com/submit-errata, selecting your book, clicking on the **Errata Submission Form** link, and entering the details of your errata. Once your errata are verified, your submission will be accepted and the errata will be uploaded to our website or added to any list of existing errata under the Errata section of that title.

To view the previously submitted errata, go to https://www.packtpub.com/books/content/support and enter the name of the book in the search field. The required information will appear under the **Errata** section.

Piracy

Piracy of copyrighted material on the Internet is an ongoing problem across all media. At Packt, we take the protection of our copyright and licenses very seriously. If you come across any illegal copies of our works in any form on the Internet, please provide us with the location address or website name immediately so that we can pursue a remedy.

Please contact us at copyright@packtpub.com with a link to the suspected pirated material.

We appreciate your help in protecting our authors and our ability to bring you valuable content.

Questions

If you have a problem with any aspect of this book, you can contact us at questions@packtpub.com, and we will do our best to address the problem.

1
Getting Started

In this chapter, we will give a brief overview of the principal syntactical elements of Python. Readers who have just started learning programming are guided through the book in this chapter. Every topic is presented here in a *how-to* way and will be explained later in the book in a deeper conceptual manner and will also be enriched with many applications and extensions.

Readers who are already familiar with another programming language will come across, in this chapter, the Python way of doing classical language constructs. It offers them a quick start to Python programming.

Both types of readers are encouraged to take this chapter as a brief guideline when zigzagging through the book. However, before we start we have to make sure that everything is in place and you have the correct version of Python installed together with the main modules for Scientific Computing and tools, such as a good editor and a shell, which helps in code developing and testing.

Read the following section, even if you already have access to a computer with Python installed. You might want to adjust things to have a working environment conforming to the presentation in this book.

Installation and configuration instructions

Before diving into the subject of the book you should have all the relevant tools installed on your computer. We will give you some advice and recommend tools that you might want to use. We only describe public domain and free tools.

Installation

There are currently two major versions of Python; the *2.x* branch and the new *3.x* branch. There are language incompatibilities between these branches and one has to be aware of which one to use. This book is based on the *3.x* branch, considering the language up to release *3.5*.

For this book you need to install the following:

- The interpreter: Python *3.5* (or later)
- The modules for scientific computing: SciPy with NumPy
- The module for graphical representation of mathematical results: matplotlib
- The shell: IPython
- A Python related editor: Spyder (refer to the following *Figure 1.1, Spyder*), Geany

The installation of these is eased by the so-called distribution packages. We recommend that you use Anaconda. The default screen of Spyder consists of an editor window on left, a console window in the lower right corner which gives access to an IPython shell and a help window in the upper right corner as shown in the following figure:

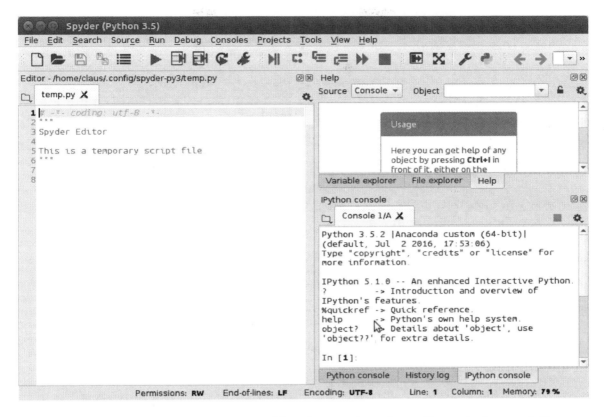

Figure 1.1: The default screen of Spyder consists of an editor window on left, a console window in the lower right corner which gives access to an IPython shell and a help window in the upper right corner.

Anaconda

Even if you have Python pre-installed on your computer, we recommend that you create your personal Python environment that allows you to work without the risk of accidentally affecting the software on which your computer's functionality might depend. With a virtual environment, such as Anaconda, you are free to change language versions and install packages without the unintended side-effects.

If the worst happens and you screw things up totally, just delete the Anaconda directory and start again. Running the Anaconda installer will install Python, a Python development environment and editor (Spyder), the shell IPython, and the most important packages for numerical computations, for example SciPy, NumPy, and matplotlib.

You can install additional packages with `conda install` within your virtual environment created by Anaconda (refer for official documentation from [2]).

Configuration

Most Python codes will be collected in files. We recommend that you use the following header in all your Python files:

```
from scipy import *
from matplotlib.pyplot import *
```

With this, you make sure that all standard modules and functions used in this book, such as SciPy, are imported. Without this step, most of the examples in the book would raise errors. Many editors, such as Spyder, provide the possibility to create a template for your files. Look for this feature and put the preceding header into a template.

Python Shell

The Python shell is good but not optimal for interactive scripting. We therefore recommend using IPython instead (refer to [26] for the official documentation). IPython can be started in different ways:

- In a terminal shell by running the following command: `ipython`

- By directly clicking on an icon called Jupyter QT Console

- When working with Spyder you should use an IPython console (refer to *Figure 1.1, Spyder*).

Executing scripts

You often want to execute the contents of a file. Depending on the location of the file on your computer, it is necessary to navigate to the correct location before executing the contents of a file.

- Use the command `cd` in IPython in order to move to the directory where your file is located.
- To execute the contents of a file named `myfile.py`, just run the following command in the IPython shell

```
run myfile
```

Getting Help

Here are some tips on how to use IPython:

- To get help on an object, just type `?` after the object's name and then `return`.
- Use the arrow keys to reuse the last executed commands.
- You may use the *Tab* key for completion (that is, you write the first letter of a variable or method and IPython shows you a menu with all the possible completions).
- Use *Ctrl+D* to quit.
- Use IPython's magic functions. You can find a list and explanations by applying `%magic` on the command prompt.

You can find out more about IPython in its online documentation, [15].

Jupyter – Python notebook

The Jupyter notebook is a fantastic tool for demonstrating your work. Students might want to use it to make and document homework and exercises and teachers can prepare lectures with it, even slides and web pages.

If you have installed Python via Anaconda, you already have everything for Jupyter in place. You can invoke the notebook by running the following command in the terminal window:

```
jupyter notebook
```

A browser window will open and you can interact with Python through your web browser.

Program and program flow

A program is a sequence of statements that are executed in a top-down order. This linear execution order has some important exceptions:

- There might be a conditional execution of alternative groups of statements (blocks), which we refer to as branching.
- There are blocks that are executed repetitively, which is called looping (refer to the following *Figure 1.2, Program flow*).
- There are function calls that are references to another piece of code, which is executed before the main program flow is resumed. A function call breaks the linear execution and pauses the execution of a program unit while it passes the control to another unit–a function. When this gets completed, its control is returned to the calling unit.

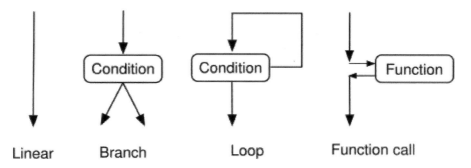

Figure 1.2: Program flow

Python uses a special syntax to mark blocks of statements: a keyword, a colon, and an indented sequence of statements, which belong to the block (refer to the following *Figure 1.3, Block command*).

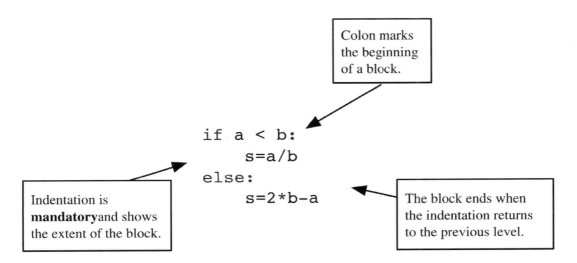

Figure 1.3: Block command

Comments

If a line in a program contains the symbol #, everything following on the same line is considered as a comment:

```
# This is a comment of the following statement
a = 3  # ... which might get a further comment here
```

Line joining

A backslash \ at the end of the line marks the next line as a continuation line, that is, explicit line joining. If the line ends before all the parentheses are closed, the following line will automatically be recognized as a continuation line, that is, implicit line joining.

Basic types

Let's go over the basic data types that you will encounter in Python.

Numbers

A number may be an integer, a real number, or a complex number. The usual operations are:

- addition and subtraction, + and –
- multiplication and division, * and /
- power, **

Here is an example:

```
2 ** (2 + 2) # 16
1j ** 2 # -1
1. + 3.0j
```

The symbol for complex numbers

j is a symbol to denote the imaginary part of a complex number. It is a syntactic element and should not be confused with multiplication by a variable. More on complex numbers can be found in section *Numeric Types* of `Chapter 2`, *Variables and Basic Types*.

Strings

Strings are sequences of characters, enclosed by simple or double quotes:

```
'valid string'
"string with double quotes"
"you shouldn't forget comments"
'these are double quotes: ".." '
```

You can also use triple quotes for strings that have multiple lines:

```
"""This is
a long,
long string"""
```

Variables

A variable is a reference to an object. An object may have several references. One uses the assignment operator = to assign a value to a variable:

```
x = [3, 4] # a list object is created
y = x # this object now has two labels: x and y
del x # we delete one of the labels
del y # both labels are removed: the object is deleted
```

The value of a variable can be displayed by the print function:

```
x = [3, 4] # a list object is created
print(x)
```

Lists

Lists are a very useful construction and one of the basic types in Python. A Python list is an ordered list of objects enclosed by square brackets. One can access the elements of a list using zero-based indexes inside square brackets:

```
L1 = [5, 6]
L1[0] # 5
L1[1] # 6
L1[2] # raises IndexError
L2 = ['a', 1, [3, 4]]
L2[0] # 'a'
L2[2][0] # 3
L2[-1] # last element: [3,4]
L2[-2] # second to last: 1
```

Indexing of the elements starts at zero. One can put objects of any type inside a list, even other lists. Some basic list functions are as follows:

- `list(range(n))}` creates a list with n elements, starting with zero:

  ```
  print(list(range(5))) # returns [0, 1, 2, 3, 4]
  ```

- `len` gives the length of a list:

  ```
  len(['a', 1, 2, 34]) # returns 4
  ```

- `append` is used to append an element to a list:

```
L = ['a', 'b', 'c']
L[-1] # 'c'
L.append('d')
L # L is now ['a', 'b', 'c', 'd']
L[-1] # 'd'
```

Operations on lists

- The operator + concatenates two lists:

```
L1 = [1, 2]
L2 = [3, 4]
L = L1 + L2 # [1, 2, 3, 4]
```

- As one might expect, multiplying a list with an integer concatenates the list with itself several times:

> `n*L` is equivalent to making *n* additions.

```
L = [1, 2]
3 * L # [1, 2, 1, 2, 1, 2]
```

Boolean expressions

A Boolean expression is an expression that may have the value `True` or `False`. Some common operators that yield conditional expressions are as follow:

- Equal, ==
- Not equal, !=
- Less than, Less than or equal to, < , <=
- Greater than, Greater than or equal to, > , >=

One combines different Boolean values with or and and.

The keyword not , gives the logical negation of the expression that follows. Comparisons can be chained so that, for example, x < y < z is equivalent to x < y and y < z. The difference is that y is only evaluated once in the first example.

In both cases, z is not evaluated at all when the first condition, x < y, evaluates to False:

```
2 >= 4  # False
2 < 3 < 4 # True
2 < 3 and 3 < 2 # False
2 != 3 < 4 or False # True
2 <= 2 and 2 >= 2 # True
not 2 == 3 # True
not False or True and False # True!
```

Precedence rules
The <, >, <=, >=, !=, and == operators have higher precedence than not . The operators and, or have the lowest precedence. Operators with higher precedence rules are evaluated before those with lower.

Repeating statements with loops

Loops are used to repetitively execute a sequence of statements while changing a variable from iteration to iteration. This variable is called the index variable. It is successively assigned to the elements of a list, (refer to Chapter 9, *Iterating*):

```
L = [1, 2, 10]
for s in L:
    print(s * 2) # output: 2 4 20
```

The part to be repeated in the for loop has to be properly indented:

```
for elt in my_list:
    do_something
    something_else
print("loop finished") # outside the for block
```

Repeating a task

One typical use of a for loop is to repeat a certain task a fixed number of times:

```
n = 30
for iteration in range(n):
    do_something # this gets executed n times
```

Break and else

The `for` statement has two important keywords: `break` and `else`. `break` quits the `for` loop even if the list we are iterating is not exhausted:

```
for x in x_values:
    if x > threshold:
      break
    print(x)
```

The finalizing `else` checks whether the `for` loop was `broken` with the `break` keyword. If it was not broken, the block following the `else` keyword is executed:

```
for x in x_values:
    if x > threshold:
        break
else:
    print("all the x are below the threshold")
```

Conditional statements

This section covers how to use conditions for branching, breaking, or otherwise controlling your code. A conditional statement delimits a block that will be executed if the condition is true. An optional block, started with the keyword `else` will be executed if the condition is not fulfilled (refer to *Figure 1.3*, *Block command* diagram). We demonstrate this by printing |x|, the absolute value of *x*:

$$|x| = \begin{cases} x & \text{if} \quad x \geq 0 \\ -x & \text{otherwise} \end{cases}$$

The Python equivalent is as follows:

```
x = ...
if x >= 0:
    print(x)
else:
    print(-x)
```

Any object can be tested for the truth value, for use in an `if` or `while` statement. The rules for how the truth values are obtained are explained in section Boolean of `Chapter 2`, *Variables and Basic Types*.

Encapsulating code with functions

Functions are useful for gathering similar pieces of code in one place. Consider the following mathematical function:

$$x \mapsto f(x) := 2x + 1$$

The Python equivalent is as follows:

```
def f(x):
    return 2*x + 1
```

In Figure 1.4 *Anatomy of a function* the elements of a function block are explained.

- The keyword `def` tells Python we are defining a function.
- `f` is the name of the function.
- `x` is the argument, or input of the function.
- What is after `return` is called the output of the function.

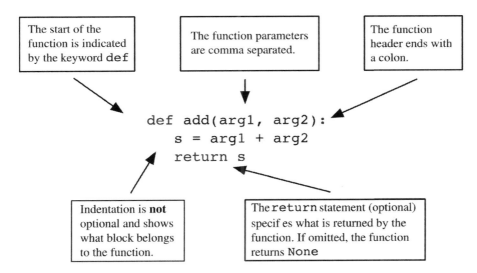

Figure 1.4: Anatomy of a function

Once the function is defined, it can be called using the following code:

```
f(2)  # 5
f(1)  # 3
```

Scripts and modules

A collection of statements in a file (which usually has a `py` extension), is called a script. Suppose we put the contents of the following code into a file named `smartscript.py`:

```
def f(x):
    return 2*x + 1
z = []
for x in range(10):
    if f(x) > pi:
        z.append(x)
    else:
        z.append(-1)
print(z)
```

In a Python or IPython shell, such a script can then be executed with the `exec` command after opening and reading the file. Written as a one-liner it reads:

```
exec(open('smartscript.py').read())
```

The IPython shell provides the magic command `%run` as a handy alternative way to execute a script:

```
%run smartscript
```

Simple modules – collecting functions

Often one collects functions in a script. This creates a module with additional Python functionality. To demonstrate this, we create a module by collecting functions in a single file, for example `smartfunctions.py`:

```
def f(x):
    return 2*x + 1
def g(x):
    return x**2 + 4*x - 5
def h(x):
    return 1/f(x)
```

- These functions can now be used by any external script or directly in the IPython environment.
- Functions within the module can depend on each other.
- Grouping functions with a common theme or purpose gives modules that can be shared and used by others.

Again, the command `exec(open('smartfunctions.py').read())` makes these functions available to your IPython shell (note that there is also the IPython magic function `run`). In Python terminology, one says that they are put into the actual namespace.

Using modules and namespaces

Alternatively, the modules can be imported by the command `import`. It creates a named namespace. The command `from` puts the functions into the general namespace:

```
import smartfunctions
print(smartfunctions.f(2))       # 5

from smartfunctions import g     #import just this function
print(g(1)) # 0

from smartfunctions import *     #import all
print(h(2)*f(2))                 # 1.0
```

Import

The commands `import` and `from` import the functions only once into the respective namespace. Changing the functions after the import has no effect for the current Python session. More on modules can be found in section *Modules* of `Chapter 11`, *Namespaces, Scopes and Modules*.

Interpreter

The Python interpreter executes the following steps:

- First, run the syntax.
- Then execute the code line by line.
- Code inside a function or class declaration is *not* executed (but checked for syntax).

```
def f(x):
    return y**2
a = 3    # here both a and f are defined
```

You can run the preceding program because there are no syntactical errors. You get an error only when you call the function f.

```
f(2) # error, y is not defined
```

Summary

In this chapter, we briefly addressed the main language elements of Python without going into detail.

You should now be able to start playing with small pieces of code and to test different program constructs. All this is intended as an appetizer for the following chapters in which we will give you the details, examples, exercises, and more background information.

2
Variables and Basic Types

In this chapter, we will present the most important and basic types in Python. What is a type? It is a set consisting of data content, its representation, and all possible operations. Later in this book, we will make this definition much more precise, when we introduce the concepts of a class in Chapter 8, *Classes*.

Variables

Variables are references to Python objects. They are created by assignments, for example:

```
a = 1
diameter = 3.
height = 5.
cylinder = [diameter, height] # reference to a list
```

Variables take names that consist of any combination of capital and small letters, the underscore _ , and digits. A variable name must not start with a digit. Note that variable names are case sensitive. A good naming of variables is an essential part of documenting your work, so we recommend that you use descriptive variable names.

Python has some *reserved keywords*, which cannot be used as variable names (refer to following table, *Table 2.1*). An attempt to use such a keyword as variable name would raise a syntax error.

and	as	assert	break	class	continue	def	del
elif	else	except	exec	False	finally	for	from
global	if	import	in	is	lambda	None	nonlocal
not	or	pass	raise	return	True	try	while
yield							

Table 2.1: Reserved Python keywords.

As opposed to other programming languages, variables require no type declaration. You can create several variables with a multiple assignment statement:

```
a = b = c = 1    # a, b and c get the same value 1
```

Variables can also be altered after their definition:

```
a = 1
a = a + 1 # a gets the value 2
a = 3 * a    # a gets the value 6
```

The last two statements can be written by combining the two operations with an assignment directly by using increment operators:

```
a += 1   # same as a = a + 1
a *= 3   # same as a = 3 * a
```

Numeric types

At some point, you will have to work with numbers, so we start by considering different forms of numeric types in Python. In mathematics, we distinguish between natural numbers ($\mathbb{N}$), integers ($\mathbb{Z}$), rational numbers ($\mathbb{Q}$), real numbers ($\mathbb{R}$) and complex numbers ($\mathbb{C}$). These are infinite sets of numbers. Operations differ between these sets and may even not be defined. For example, the usual division of two numbers in $\mathbb{Z}$ might not result in an integer — it is not defined on $\mathbb{Z}$.

In Python, like many other computer languages, we have numeric types:

- The numeric type int, which is at least theoretically the entire $\mathbb{Z}$
- The numeric type float, which is a finite subset of $\mathbb{R}$ and
- The numeric type complex, which is a finite subset of $\mathbb{C}$

Finite sets have a smallest and a largest number and there is a minimum spacing between two numbers; refer to the section on *Floating Point Representation* for further details.

Integers

The simplest numerical type is the integer type.

Plain integers

The statement k = 3 assigns the variable k to an integer.

Applying an operation of the type +, −, or * to integers returns an integer. The division operator, //, returns an integer, while / may return a float:

```
6 // 2   # 3
7 // 2   # 3
7 / 2    # 3.5
```

The set of integersin Python is unbounded; there is no largest integer. The limitation here is the computer's memory rather than any fixed value given by the language.

 If the division operator (/) in the example returns 3, you might not have installed the correct Python version.

Floating point numbers

If you execute the statement a = 3.0 in Python, you create a floating-point number (Python type: float). These numbers form a subset of rational numbers, $\mathbb{Q}$.

Alternatively the constant could have been given in exponent notation as a = 30.0e-1 or simply a = 30.e-1. The symbol e separates the exponent from the mantissa, and the expression reads in mathematical notation $a = 30.0 \times 10^{-1}$. The name *floating-point number* refers to the internal representation of these numbers and reflects the floating position of the decimal point when considering numbers over a wide range.

Applying the elementary mathematical operations +, −, *, and / to two floating-point numbers or to an integer and a floating-point number returns a floating-point number. Operations between floating-point numbers rarely return the exact result expected from rational number operations:

```
0.4 - 0.3 # returns 0.10000000000000003
```

This facts matters, when comparing floating point numbers:

```
0.4 - 0.3 == 0.1 # returns False
```

Floating point representation

Internally, floating-point numbers are represented by four quantities: the sign, the mantissa, the exponent sign, and the exponent:

$$\text{sign}(x)\left(x_0 + x_1\beta^{-1} + \ldots + x_{t-1}\beta^{-(t-1)}\right)\beta^{(e)|e|}$$

with $\beta \in \mathbb{N}$ and $x_0 \neq 0$, $0 \leq x_i \leq \beta$

$x_0 \ldots x_{t-1}$ is called the mantissa, β the basis and e the exponent $|e| \leq U$. t is called the mantissa length. The condition $x_0 \neq 0$ makes the representation unique and saves, in the binary case ($\beta = 2$), one bit.

There exist two-floating point zeros +0 and -0, both represented by the mantissa 0.

On a typical Intel processor, $\beta = 2$. To represent a number in the float type 64 bits are used, namely 2 bits for the signs, $t = 52$ bits for the mantissa and 10 bits for the exponent $|e|$. The upper bound U for the exponent is consequently $2^{10} - 1 = 1023$.

With this data the smallest positiverepresentable number is

$fl_{min} = 1.0 \times 2^{-1023} \approx 10^{-308}$ and the largest is $fl_{max} = 1.111...1 \times 2^{1023} \approx 10^{308}$.

Note that floating-point numbers are not equally spaced in $[0, fl_{max}]$. There is in particular a gap at zero (refer to [29]). The distance between 0 and the first positive number is 2^{-1023}, while the distance between the first and the second is smaller by a factor $2^{-52} \approx 2.2 \times 10^{-16}$. This effect, caused by the normalization $x_0 \neq 0$, is visualized in *Figure 2.1*.

This gap is filled equidistantly with subnormal floating-point numbers to which such a result is rounded. Subnormal floating-point numbers have the smallest possible exponent and do not follow the convention that the leading digit x_0 has to differ from zero; refer to [13].

Infinite and not a number

There are in total $2(\beta - 1)\beta^{t-1}(2U + 1) + 1$ floating-point numbers. Sometimes a numerical algorithm computes floating-point numbers outside this range.

This generates number over- or underflow. In SciPy the special floating-point number `inf` is assigned to overflow results:

```
exp(1000.)  # inf
a = inf
3 - a    # -inf
3 + a    # inf
```

Working with `inf` may lead to mathematically undefined results. This is indicated in Python by assigning the result another special floating-point number, `nan`. This stands for not-a-number, that is, an undefined result of a mathematical operation:

```
a + a # inf
a - a # nan
a / a # nan
```

There are special rules for operations with `nan` and `inf`. For instance, `nan` compared to anything (even to itself) always returns `False`:

```
x = nan
x < 0 # False
x > 0 # False
x == x # False
```

See *Exercise 4* for some surprising consequences of the fact that `nan` is never equal to itself.

The float `inf` behaves much more as expected:

```
0 < inf      # True
inf <= inf   # True
inf == inf   # True
-inf < inf   # True
inf - inf    # nan
exp(-inf)    # 0
exp(1 / inf)  # 1
```

One way to check for `nan` and `inf` is to use the `isnan` and `isinf` functions. Often, one wants to react directly when a variable gets the value `nan` or `inf`. This can be achieved by using the NumPy command `seterr`. The following command

```
seterr(all = 'raise')
```

would raise an error if a calculation were to return one of those values.

Underflow – Machine Epsilon

Underflow occurs when an operation results in a rational number that falls into the gap at zero; refer to *Figure 2.1*.

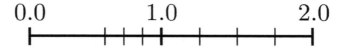

Figure 2.1: The floating point gap at zero, here t = 3, U = 1

The *machine epsilon* or rounding unit is the largest number ε such that float$(1.0 + \varepsilon) = 1.0$.

Note that $\varepsilon \approx \beta^{1-t}/2 = 1.1102 \times 10^{-16}$ on most of today's computers. The value that is valid on the actual machine you are running your code on is accessible using the following command:

```
import sys
sys.float_info.epsilon # 2.220446049250313e-16 (something like that)
```

The variable `sys.float_info` contains more information about the internal representation of the float type on your machine.

The function `float` converts other types to a floating-point number—if possible. This function is especially useful when converting an appropriate string to a number:

```
a = float('1.356')
```

Other float types in NumPy

NumPy also provides other float types, known from other programming languages as double-precision and single-precision numbers, namely `float64` and `float32`:

```
a = pi           # returns 3.141592653589793
a1 = float64(a)  # returns 3.1415926535897931
a2 = float32(a)  # returns 3.1415927
a - a1           # returns 0.0
a - a2           # returns -8.7422780126189537e-08
```

The second last line demonstrates that a and a1 do not differ in accuracy. In the first two lines, they only differ in the way they are displayed. The real difference in accuracy is between a and its single-precision counterpart, a2.

The NumPy function `finfo` can be used to display information on these floating-point types:

```
f32 = finfo(float32)
f32.precision   # 6 (decimal digits)
f64 = finfo(float64)
f64.precision   # 15 (decimal digits)
f = finfo(float)
f.precision     # 15 (decimal digits)
f64.max         # 1.7976931348623157e+308 (largest number)
f32.max         # 3.4028235e+38 (largest number)
help(finfo)     # Check for more options
```

Complex numbers

Complex numbers are an extension of the real numbers frequently used in many scientific and engineering fields.

Complex Numbers in Mathematics

Complex numbers consist of two floating-point numbers, the real part a of the number and its imaginary part b. In mathematics, a complex number is written as $z=a+bi$, where i defined by $i^2 = -1$ is the imaginary unit. The conjugate complex counterpart of z is $\bar{z} = a - bi$.

If the real part a is zero, the number is called an imaginary number.

The j notation

In Python, imaginary numbers are characterized by suffixing a floating-point number with the letter j, for example, z = 5.2j. A complex number is formed by the sum of a floating-point number and an imaginary number, for example, z = 3.5 + 5.2j.

While in mathematics the imaginary part is expressed as a product of a real number b with the imaginary unit i, the Python way of expressing an imaginary number is not a product: j is just a suffix to indicate that the number is imaginary.

This is demonstrated by the following small experiment:

```
b = 5.2
z = bj    # returns a NameError
z = b*j   # returns a NameError
z = b*1j  # is correct
```

The method `conjugate` returns the conjugate of z:

```
z = 3.2 + 5.2j
z.conjugate() # returns (3.2-5.2j)
```

Real and imaginary parts

One may access the real and imaginary parts of a complex number z using the `real` and `imag` attributes. Those attributes are read-only:

```
z = 1j
z.real          # 0.0
z.imag          # 1.0
z.imag = 2      # AttributeError: readonly attribute
```

It is not possible to convert a complex number to a real number:

```
z = 1 + 0j
z == 1          # True
float(z)        # TypeError
```

Interestingly, the `real` and `imag` attributes as well as the conjugate method work just as well for complex arrays (Chapter 4, *Linear Algebra – Arrays*). We demonstrate this by computing the Nth roots of unity which are $z_k = e^{i 2\pi k/N}$, $k = 0, \ldots, N-1$, that is, the N solutions of the equation $z^N = 1$:

```
N = 10
# the following vector contains the Nth roots of unity:
unity_roots = array([exp(1j*2*pi*k/N) for k in range(N)])
# access all the real or imaginary parts with real or imag:
axes(aspect='equal')
plot(unity_roots.real, unity_roots.imag, 'o')
allclose(unity_roots**N, 1) # True
```

The resulting figure (*Figure 2.2*) shows the roots of unity together with the unit circle. (For more details on how to make plots, refer `Chapter 6`, *Plotting*.)

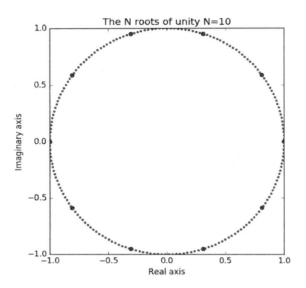

Figure 2.2: Roots of unity together with a unit circle

It is of course possible to mix the previous methods, as illustrated by the following examples:

```
z = 3.2+5.2j
(z + z.conjugate()) / 2.    # returns (3.2+0j)
((z + z.conjugate()) / 2.).real    # returns 3.2
(z - z.conjugate()) / 2.    # returns 5.2j
((z - z.conjugate()) / 2.).imag    # returns 5.2
sqrt(z * z.conjugate())    # returns (6.1057350089894991+0j)
```

Booleans

Boolean is a datatype named after *George Boole* (1815-1864). A Boolean variable can take only two values, True or False. The main use of this type is in logical expressions. Here are some examples:

```
a = True
b = 30 > 45    # b gets the value False
```

Boolean expressions are often used in conjunction with the if statement:

```
if x > 0:
   print("positive")
else:
   print("nonpositive)
```

Boolean operators

Boolean operations are performed using the and, or, and not keywords in Python:

```
True and False # False
False or True # True
(30 > 45) or (27 < 30) # True
not True # False
not (3 > 4) # True
```

The operators follow some precedence rules (refer to section *Executing scripts* in Chapter 1, *Getting started*) which would make the parentheses in the third line and in the last obsolete (it is a good practice to use them anyway to increase the readability of your code). Note that the and operator is implicitly chained in the following Boolean expressions:

```
a < b < c      # same as: a < b and b < c
a == b == c    # same as: a == b and b == c
```

Rules of Conversion to Booleans:

Bool	False	True
`string`	"	'not empty'
`number`	0	≠
`list`	[]	[...] (not empty)
`tuple`	()	(..,..) (not empty)
`array`	array([])	array([a]) (a ≠ 0)
`array`	array([0])	
`array`	Exception raised if array contains more than one element	

Table 2.2 : Rule of conversion to Boolean

Boolean casting

Most objects Python may be converted to Booleans; this is called *Boolean casting*. The built-in function `bool` performs that conversion. Note that most objects are cast to `True`, except 0, the empty tuple, the empty list, the empty string, or the empty array. These are all cast to `False`.

It is *not* possible to cast arrays into Booleans unless they contain no or only one element; this is explained further in `Chapter 5`, *Advanced Array Concepts*. The previous table contains summarized rules for Boolean casting. Some usage examples:

```
bool([])    # False
bool(0)    # False
bool(' ')    # True
bool('')    # False
bool('hello')    # True
bool(1.2)    # True
bool(array([1]))    # True
bool(array([1,2]))    # Exception raised!
```

Automatic Boolean casting

Using an `if` statement with a non-Boolean type will cast it to a Boolean. In other words, the following two statements are always equivalent:

```
if a:
    ...
if bool(a): # exactly the same as above
    ...
```

A typical example is testing whether a list is empty:

```
# L is a list
if L:
    print("list not empty")
else:
    print("list is empty")
```

An empty array, list, or tuple will return `False`. You can also use a variable in the `if` statement, for example, an integer:

```
# n is an integer
if n % 2:
    print("n is odd")
else:
    print("n is even")
```

Note that we used `%` for the modulo operation, which returns the remainder of an integer division. In this case, it returns 0 or 1 as the remainder after modulo 2.

In this last example, the values 0 or 1 are cast to `bool`. Boolean operators `or`,`and`, and `not` will also implicitly convert some of their arguments to a Boolean.

Return values of and and or

Note that the operators`and` and `or` do not necessarily produce Boolean values. The expression x and y is equivalent to:

```
def and_as_function(x,y):
    if not x:
        return x
    else:
        return y
```

And the expression `x or y` is equivalent to:

```
def or_as_function(x,y):
    if x:
        return x
    else:
        return y
```

Interestingly, this means that when executing the statement `True or x`, the variable `x` need not even be defined! The same holds for `False and x`.

Note that, unlike their counterparts in mathematical logic, these operators are no longer commutative in Python. Indeed, the following expressions are not equivalent:

```
[1] or 'a' # produces [1]
'a' or [1] # produces 'a'
```

Boolean and integer

In fact, Booleans and integers are the same. The only difference is in the string representation of 0 and 1 which is in the case of Booleans `False` and `True` respectively. This allows constructions like this (for the format method refer section on *string formatting*):

```
def print_ispositive(x):
    possibilities = ['nonpositive', 'positive']
    return "x is {}".format(possibilities[x>0])
```

We note for readers already familiar with the concept of subclasses, that the type `bool` is a subclass of the type `int` (refer to Chapter 8, *Classes*). Indeed, all four inquiries `isinstance(True, bool)`, `isinstance(False, bool)`, `isinstance(True, int)`, and `isinstance(False, int)` return the value `True` (refer to section *Type Checking* in Chapter 3, *Container Types*).

Even rarely used statements such as `True+13` are syntactically correct.

Strings

The type `string` is a type used for text:

```
name = 'Johan Carlsson'
child = "Åsa is Johan Carlsson's daughter"
book = """Aunt Julia
        and the Scriptwriter"""
```

A string is enclosed either by single or double quotes. If a string contains several lines, it has to be enclosed by three double quotes """ or three single quotes ' ' '.

Strings can be indexed with simple indexes or slices (refer to `Chapter 3`, *Container Types*, for a comprehensive explanation on slices):

```
book[-1] # returns 'r'
book[-12:] # returns 'Scriptwriter'
```

Strings are immutable; that is, items cannot be altered. They share this property with tuples. The command `book[1] = 'a'` returns:

```
TypeError: 'str' object does not support item assignment
```

The string '\n' is used to insert a line break and 't' inserts a horizontal tabulator (TAB) into the string to align several lines:

```
print('Temperature:\t20\tC\nPressure:\t5\tPa')
```

These strings are examples of *escape sequences*. Escape sequences always start with a backslash, \ . A multi line string automatically includes escape sequences:

```
a="""
A multiline
example"""
a #  returns '\nA multiline \nexample'
```

A special escape sequence is " ", which represents the backslash symbol in text:

```
latexfontsize="\\tiny"
```

The same can be achieved by using a raw string instead:

```
latexfs=r"\tiny"   # returns "\tiny"
latexfontsize == latexfs  # returns True
```

Note that in raw strings, the backslash remains in the string and is used to escape some special characters:

```
r"\"\"   # returns '\\"'
r"\\"    # returns '\\\\'
r"\"     # returns an error
```

Operations on strings and string methods

Addition of strings means concatenation:

```
last_name = 'Carlsson'
first_name = 'Johanna'
full_name = first_name + ' ' + last_name
                             # returns 'Johanna Carlsson'
```

Multiplication is just repeated addition:

```
game = 2 * 'Yo' # returns 'YoYo'
```

When strings are compared, lexicographical order applies and the uppercase form precedes the lowercase form of the same letter:

```
'Anna' > 'Arvi' # returns false
'ANNA' < 'anna'  # returns true
'10B' < '11A'    # returns true
```

Among the variety of string methods, we will mention here only the most important ones:

- **Splitting a string**: This method generates a list from a string by using a single or multiple blanks as separators. Alternatively, an argument can be given by specifying a particular string as a separator:

  ```
  text = 'quod erat      demonstrandum'
  text.split() # returns ['quod', 'erat', 'demonstrandum']
  table = 'Johan;Carlsson;19890327'
  table.split(';') # returns ['Johan','Carlsson','19890327']
  king = 'CarlXVIGustaf'
  king.split('XVI')  # returns ['Carl','Gustaf']
  ```

- **Joining a list to a string**: This is the reverse operation of splitting:

  ```
  sep = ';'
  sep.join(['Johan','Carlsson','19890327'])
  # returns 'Johan;Carlsson;19890327'
  ```

- **Searching in a string**: This method returns the first index in the string, where a given search substring starts:

  ```
  birthday = '20101210'
  birthday.find('10') # returns 2
  ```

  If the search string is not found, the return value of the method is -1 .

String formatting

String formatting is done using the `format` method:

```
course_code = "NUMA21"
print("This course's name is {}".format(course_code))
# This course's name is NUMA21
```

The function `format` is a string method; it scans the string for the occurrence of placeholders, which are enclosed by curly brackets. These placeholders are replaced in a way specified by the argument of the format method. How they are replaced depends on the format specification defined in each `{}` pair. Format specifications are indicated by a colon, `":"`, as their prefix.

The format method offers a range of possibilities to customize the formatting of objects depending on their types. Of particular use in scientific computing are the formatting specifiers for the `float` type. One may choose either the standard with `{:f}` or the exponential notation with `{:e}`:

```
quantity = 33.45
print("{:f}".format(quantity)) # 33.450000
print("{:1.1f}".format(quantity)) # 33.5
print("{:.2e}".format(quantity)) # 3.35e+01
```

The format specifiers allow to specify the rounding precision (digits following the decimal point in the representation). Also the total number of symbols including leading blanks to represent the number can be set.

In this example, the name of the object that gets its value inserted is given as an argument to the format method. The first `{}` pair is replaced by the first argument and the following pairs by the subsequent arguments. Alternatively, it may also be convenient to use the key-value syntax:

```
print("{name} {value:.1f}".format(name="quantity",value=quantity))
# prints "quantity 33.5"
```

Here, two values are processed, a string `name` without a format specifier and a float `value` that is printed in fixed point notation with one digit after the decimal point. (We refer to the complete reference documentation for more details on *string formatting*, [34]).

Braces in the string

Sometimes, a string might contain a pair of curly braces, which should not be considered as placeholders for a `format` method. In that case, double braces are used:

```
r"we {} in LaTeX \begin{{equation}}".format('like')
```

This returns the following string: `'we like in LaTeX \\begin{equation}'`.

Summary

In this chapter, you met the basic data types in Python and saw the corresponding syntax elements. We will work mostly with numeric types such as integers, floats and complex.

Booleans are needed for setting conditions, and by using strings, we often communicate results and messages.

Exercises

Ex. 1 → Check whether $x = 2.3$ is a zero of the function:

$$f(x) = x^2 + 0.25x - 5.$$

Ex. 2 → According to de Moivre's formula, the following holds:

$$(\cos x + i \sin x)^n = \cos nx + i \sin nx \qquad n \in \mathbb{Z}, \quad x \in \mathbb{R}.$$

Choose numbers n and x and verify that formula in Python.

Ex. 3 → Complex numbers. Verify Euler's formula in the same way:

$$e^{ix} = \cos x + i \sin x \qquad x \in \mathbb{R}.$$

Ex. 4 → Suppose we are trying to check the convergence of a diverging sequence (here the sequence is defined by the recursive relation $u_{n+1} = 2u_n$ and $u_0 = 1.0$):

```
u = 1.0 # you have to use a float here!
uold = 10.
for iteration in range(2000):
    if not abs(u-uold) > 1.e-8:
        print('Convergence')
        break # sequence has converged
    uold = u
    u = 2*u
else:
    print('No convergence')
```

1. Since the sequence does not converge, the code should print the `No convergence` message. Execute it to see what happens.

2. What happens if you replace the line:

   ```
   if not abs(u-uold) > 1.e-8
   ```

   with:

   ```
   if abs(u-uold) < 1.e-8
   ```

   It should give exactly the same result, shouldn't it? Run the code again to see what happens.

3. What happens if you replace *u=1.0* by *u=1* (without decimal point). Run the code to check your predictions.

4. Explain the unexpected behavior of this code. The key to understand what happens is that `inf` evaluates to `nan`, and the comparison of `nan` with anything else is returns always the value `False`.

Ex. 5 → An implication $C = (A \Rightarrow B)$ is a Boolean expression that is defined as

- *C* is `True` if *A* is `False` or *A* and *B* are both `True`
- *C* is `False` otherwise

Write a Python function `implication(A, B)`.

Ex. 6 → This exercise is to train Boolean operations. Two binary digits (bits) are added by using a logical device called a **half adder**. It produces a carry bit (the digit of the next higher value) and the sum as defined by the following table, and half adder circuit.

p	q	sum	carry
1	1	0	1
1	0	1	0
0	1	1	0
0	0	0	0

Definition of the half adder operation

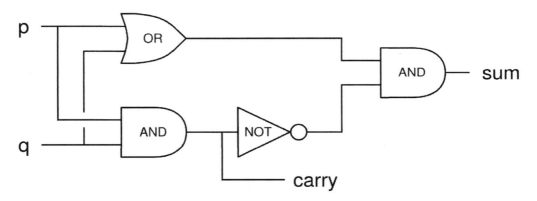

Figure 2.3: A half adder circuit

A full adder consists of two half adders and sums up two bits and an additional carry bit on the input (refer to the following figure):

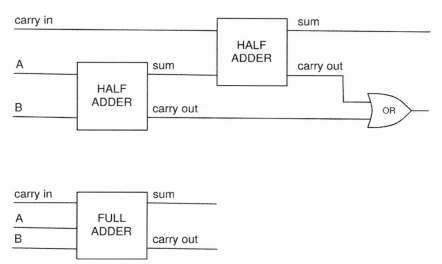

Figure 2.4: A full adder circuit

Write a function that implements a half adder and another that implements a full adder. Test these functions.

3

Container Types

Container types are used to group objects together. The main difference between the different container types is the way individual elements are accessed and how operations are defined.

Lists

A list is, as the name hints, a list of objects of any kind:

```
L = ['a' 20.0, 5]
M = [3,['a', -3.0, 5]]
```

The individual objects are enumerated by assigning each element an index. The first element in the list gets index 0. This zero-based indexing is frequently used in mathematical notation. Consider the usual indexing of coefficients of a polynomial.

The index allows us to access the following objects:

```
L[1] # returns 20.0
L[0] # returns 'a'
M[1] # returns ['a',-3.0,5]
M[1][2] # returns 5
```

The bracket notation here corresponds to the use of subscripts in mathematical formulas. L is a simple list, while M itself contains a list so that one needs two indexes to access an element of the inner list.

A list containing subsequent integers can easily be generated by the command range:

```
L=list(range(4)) # generates a list with four elements: [0, 1, 2 ,3]
```

A more general use is to provide this command with start, stop, and step parameters:

```
L=list(range(17,29,4)) # generates [17, 21, 25]
```

The command `len` returns the length of the list:

```
len(L) # returns 3
```

Slicing

Slicing a list between `i` and `j` creates a new list containing the elements starting at `index` `i` and ending just before `j`.

For slicing, a range of indexes has to be given. `L[i:j]` means create a list by taking all elements from `L` starting at `L[i]` until `L[j-1]`. In other words, the new list is obtained by removing the first `i` elements from `L` and taking the next `j-i` elements (for $j > i \geq 0$). See the following figure (*Figure 3.1*) for more examples:

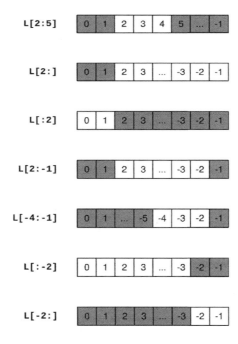

Figure 3.1: Some typical slicing situations

Here, `L[i:]` means remove the *i* first elements, `L[:i]` means take only the first *i* elements, and similarly, `L[:-i]` means remove the last *i* elements, and `L[-i:]` means take only the last *i* elements. This may be combined in `L[i:-j]` to remove the first *i* and the last *j* elements:

```
L = ['C', 'l', 'o', 'u', 'd', 's']
L[1:5] # remove one element and take four from there:
# returns ['l', 'o', 'u', 'd']
```

One may omit the first or last bound of the slicing:

```
L = ['C', 'l', 'o', 'u','d', 's']
L[1:] # ['l', 'o', 'u', 'd','s']
L[:5] # ['C', 'l', 'o','u','d']
L[:] # the entire list
```

Python allows the use of negative indexes for counting from the right. In particular, the element `L[-1]` is the last element in the list `L`.

Some list indexing descriptions:

- `L[i:]` amounts to taking all elements except the *i* first ones
- `L[:i]` amounts to taking the first *i* elements
- `L[-i:]` amounts to taking the last *i* elements
- `L[:-i]` amounts to taking all elements except the *i* last ones

Here is an example:

```
L = ['C', 'l', 'o', 'u', 'd', 's']
L[-2:] # ['d', 's']
L[:-2] # ['C', 'l', 'o','u']
```

Omitting one index in the range corresponds to half-open intervals in $\mathbb{R}$. The half-open interval (∞, a) means, take all numbers strictly lower than a; this is similar to the syntax `L[:j]`.

Out of-bound slices
Notice that you never get index errors with out-of-bound slices. Possibly, you may obtain empty lists.

Here is an example:

```
L = list(range(4)) # [0, 1, 2, 3]
L[4] # IndexError: list index out of range
L[1:100] # same as L[1:]
L[-100:-1] # same as L[:-1]
L[-100:100] # same as L[:]
L[5:0] # empty list []
L[-2:2] # empty list []
```

Be careful when using variables in indexing that may become negative, since it changes the slice completely. This might lead to unexpected results:

```
a = [1,2,3]
 for iteration in range(4):
    print(sum(a[0:iteration-1]))
```

The result is 3, 0, 1, 3 while one expects 0, 0, 1, 3.

Strides

When computing slices, one may also specify a stride, which is the length of the step from one index to the other. The default stride is one. Here is an example:

```
L = list(range(100))
L[:10:2] # [0, 2, 4, 6, 8]
L[::20] # [0, 20, 40, 60, 80]
L[10:20:3] # [10, 13, 16, 19]
```

Note that the stride may also be negative:

```
L[20:10:-3] # [20, 17, 14, 11]
```

It is also possible to create a new list that is reversed, using a negative stride (find about reverse method in section *In-place operations*):

```
L = [1, 2, 3]
R = L[::-1] # L is not modified
R # [3, 2, 1]
```

Altering lists

Typical operations on lists are insertion and deletion of elements and list concatenation. With the slicing notation, list insertion and deletion become obvious; deletion is just replacing a part of a list by an empty list [ ]:

```
L = ['a', 1, 2, 3, 4]
L[2:3] = [] # ['a', 1, 3, 4]
L[3:] = [] # ['a', 1, 3]
```

Insertion means replacing an empty slice with the list to be inserted:

```
L[1:1] = [1000, 2000] # ['a', 1000, 2000, 1, 3]
```

Two lists are concatenated by the plus operator + :

```
L = [1, -17]
M = [-23.5, 18.3, 5.0]
L + M # gives [1, -17, 23.5, 18.3, 5.0]
```

Concatenating a list n times with itself motivates the use of the multiplication operator *:

```
n = 3
n * [1.,17,3] # gives [1., 17, 3, 1., 17, 3, 1., 17, 3]
[0] * 5 # gives [0,0,0,0,0]
```

There is no arithmetic operations on list, such as elementwise summation or division. For such operations we use arrays (refer to section *Array*).

Belonging to a list

One may use the keywords in and not in to determine whether an element belongs to a list or not which is similar to $\in$ and $\notin$ in mathematics:

```
L = ['a', 1, 'b', 2]
'a' in L # True
3 in L # False
4 not in L # True
```

List methods

Some useful methods of the `list` type are collected in the following *Table 3.1*:

Command	Action
`list.append(x)`	Add x to the end of the list.
`list.expand(L)`	Expand the list by the elements of the list L.
`list.insert(i,x)`	Insert x at position i.
`list.remove(x)`	Remove the first item from the list whose value is x.
`list.count(x)`	The number of times x appears in the list.
`list.sort()`	Sort the items of the list, in place.
`list.reverse()`	Reverse the elements of the list, in place.
`list.pop()`	Remove the last element of the list, in place.

Table 3.1: Methods of the datatype list

There are two ways list methods can act:

- They can directly alter the list, that is, in-place operations.
- They produce a new object.

In–place operations

All methods that result in a list are in-place operating methods, for example, `reverse`:

```
L = [1, 2, 3]
L.reverse() # the list
L is now reversed
L # [3, 2, 1]
```

Be aware of in-place operations. One might be tempted to write:

```
L=[3, 4, 4, 5]
newL = L.sort()
```

This is correct Python. But it results in a possibly unintended alternation of L in a variable `newL` having the value `None`. The reason is that `sort` operates in-place.

Here we demonstrate in-place operating methods:

```
L = [0, 1, 2, 3, 4]
L.append(5) # [0, 1, 2, 3, 4, 5]
L.reverse() # [5, 4, 3, 2, 1, 0]
L.sort() # [0, 1, 2, 3, 4, 5]
L.remove(0) # [1, 2, 3, 4, 5]
L.pop() # [1, 2, 3, 4]
L.pop() # [1, 2, 3]
L.extend(['a','b','c']) # [1, 2, 3, 'a', 'b', 'c']
```

L is altered. The `count` method is an example of a method that generates a new object:

```
L.count(2) # returns 1
```

Merging lists – zip

A particularly useful function for lists is `zip`. It can be used to merge two given lists into a new list by pairing the elements of the original lists. The result is a list of tuples (refer section *Tuples* for more information):

```
ind = [0,1,2,3,4]
color = ["red", "green", "blue", "alpha"]
list(zip(color,ind)) # gives [('red', 0), ('green', 1),
                               ('blue', 2), ('alpha', 3)]
```

This example also demonstrates what happens if the lists have different lengths. The length of the zipped list is the shorter of the two input lists.
`zip` creates a special iterable object that can be turned into a list by applying the `list` function, as in the preceding example. Refer to section *Iterators* in `Chapter 9`, *Iterating*, for more details on iterable objects.

List comprehension

A convenient way to build up lists is by using the list comprehension construct, possibly with a condition inside. The syntax of a list comprehension is:

```
[<expr> for <variable> in <list>]
```

or more generally:

```
[<expr> for <variable> in <list> if <condition>]
```

Here is an example:

```
L = [2, 3, 10, 1, 5]
L2 = [x*2 for x in L] # [4, 6, 20, 2, 10]
L3 = [x*2 for x in L if 4 < x <= 10] # [20, 10]
```

It is possible to have several `for` loops inside a list comprehension:

```
M = [[1,2,3],[4,5,6]]
flat = [M[i][j] for i in range(2) for j in range(3)]
# returns [1, 2, 3, 4, 5, 6]
```

This is of particular interest when dealing with arrays.

Set notation

List comprehension is closely related to the mathematical notation for sets. Compare: $L_2 = \{2x; \; x \in L\}$ and `L2 = [2*x for x in L]`. One big difference though, is that lists are ordered while sets aren't (Refer, section *Sets* for more information).

Arrays

The NumPy package offers arrays, which are container structures for manipulating vectors, matrices, or even higher order tensors in mathematics. In this section, we point out the similarities between arrays and lists. But arrays deserve a broader presentation, which will be given in `Chapter 4`, *Linear Algebra – Arrays*, and `Chapter 5`, *Advanced Array Concepts*.

Arrays are constructed from lists by the function `array` :

```
v = array([1.,2.,3.])
A = array([[1.,2.,3.],[4.,5.,6.]])
```

To access an element of a vector, we need one index, while an element of a matrix is addressed by two indexes:

```
v[2]      # returns 3.0
A[1,2]    # returns 6.0
```

At first glance, arrays are similar to lists, but be aware that they are different in a fundamental way, which can be explained by the following points:

- Access to array data corresponds to that of lists, using square brackets and slices. They may also be used to alter the array:

```
M = array([[1.,2.],[3.,4.]])
v = array([1., 2., 3.])
v[0] # 1
v[:2] # array([1.,2.])
M[0,1] # 2
v[:2] = [10, 20] # v is now array([10., 20., 3.])
```

- The number of elements in a vector, or the number of rows of a matrix, is obtained by the function `len` :

```
len(v) # 3
```

- Arrays store only elements of the same numeric type (usually `float` or `complex` but also `int`). Refer to section *Array properties* in `Chapter` 4, *Liner Algebra – Arrays*, for more information.
- The operations +, *, /, and – are all elementwise. The `dot` function and, in Python versions ≥ 3.5, the infix operator @ are used for the scalar product and the corresponding matrix operations.
- Unlike lists, there is no `append` method for arrays. Nevertheless, there are special methods to construct arrays by stacking smaller size arrays (Refer to section *Stacking* in `Chapter` 4, *Linear Algebra – Arrays*, for more information.). A related point is that arrays are not elastic as lists; one cannot use slices to change their length.
- Vector slices are views; that is, they may be used to modify the original array. Refer to section *Array views and copies* in `Chapter` 5, *Advanced Array Concepts*, for more information.

Tuples

A tuple is an immutable list. Immutable means that it cannot be modified. A tuple is just a comma-separated sequence of objects (a list without brackets). To increase readability, one often encloses a tuple in a pair of parentheses:

```
my_tuple = 1, 2, 3      # our first tuple
my_tuple = (1, 2, 3)    # the same
my_tuple = 1, 2, 3,     # again the same
len(my_tuple) # 3, same as for lists
my_tuple[0] = 'a'    # error! tuples are immutable
```

The comma indicates that the object is a tuple:

```
singleton = 1,    # note the comma
len(singleton)    # 1
```

Tuples are useful when a group of values goes together; for example, they are used to return multiple values from functions (refer to section *Returns Values* in Chapter 7, *Functions*. One may assign several variables at once by unpacking a list or tuple:

```
a, b = 0, 1 # a gets 0 and b gets 1
a, b = [0, 1] # exactly the same effect
(a, b) = 0, 1 # same
[a,b] = [0,1] # same thing
```

The swapping trick
Use packing and unpacking to swap the contents of two variables:
```
a, b = b, a
```

To summarize:

- Tuples are nothing other than immutable lists with a notation without brackets.
- In most cases, lists may be used instead of tuples.
- The notation without parentheses is convenient but dangerous. You should use parentheses when you are not sure:

```
a, b = b, a # the swap trick; equivalent to:
(a, b) = (b, a)
# but
1, 2 == 3, 4 # returns (1, False, 4)
(1, 2) == (3, 4) # returns False
```

Dictionaries

Lists, tuples, and arrays are ordered sets of objects. The individual objects are inserted, accessed, and processed according to their place in the list. On the other hand, dictionaries are unordered sets of pairs. One accesses dictionary data by keys.

Creating and altering dictionaries

For example, we may create a dictionary containing the data of a rigid body in mechanics, as follows:

```
truck_wheel = {'name':'wheel','mass':5.7,
               'Ix':20.0,'Iy':1.,'Iz':17.,
               'center of mass':[0.,0.,0.]}
```

A key/data pair is indicated by a colon, :. These pairs are comma separated and listed inside a pair of curly brackets, {}.

Individual elements are accessed by their keys:

```
truck_wheel['name']    # returns 'wheel'
truck_wheel['mass']    # returns 5.7
```

New objects are added to the dictionary by creating a new key:

```
truck_wheel['Ixy'] = 0.0
```

Dictionaries are also used to provide parameters to a function (refer to section *Parameters and arguments* in `Chapter 7`, *Functions*, for further information). Keys in a dictionary can be, among others, strings, functions, tuples with immutable elements, and classes. Keys cannot be lists or arrays. The command `dict` generates a dictionary from a list with key/value pairs:

```
truck_wheel = dict([('name','wheel'),('mass',5.7),('Ix',20.0),
               ('Iy',1.), ('Iz',17.),
               ('center of mass',[0.,0.,0.])])
```

The `zip` function may come in handy in this context (refer to section *Merging List*).

Looping over dictionaries

There are mainly three ways to loop over dictionaries:

- By keys:

```
for key in truck_wheel.keys():
    print(key) # prints (in any order) 'Ix', 'Iy', 'name',...
```

    or equivalently:

```
for key in truck_wheel:
    print(key) # prints (in any order) 'Ix', 'Iy', 'name',...
```

- By value:

```
for value in truck_wheel.value():
    print(value)
        # prints (in any order) 1.0, 20.0, 17.0, 'wheel', ...
```

- By item, that is, key/value pairs:

```
for item in truck_wheel.items():
    print(item)
        # prints (in any order) ('Iy', 1.0), ('Ix, 20.0),...
```

Please, refer to section *Shelves* in `Chapter 12`, *Input and Output*, for a special dictionary object for file access.

Sets

Sets are containers that share properties and operations with sets in mathematics. A mathematical set is a collection of distinct objects. Here are some mathematical set expressions:

$$A = \{1, 2, 3, 4\},\ B = \{5\},\ C = A \cup B,\ D = A \cap C,\ E = C \backslash A,\ 5 \in C$$

And their Python counterparts:

```
A = {1,2,3,4}
B = {5}
C = A.union(B)    # returns set([1,2,3,4,5])
D = A.intersection(C)    # returns set([1,2,3,4])
E = C.difference(A)    # returns set([5])
5 in C    # returns True
```

Sets contain an element only once, corresponding to the aforementioned definition:

```
A = {1,2,3,3,3}
B = {1,2,3}
A == B # returns True
```

And a set is unordered; that is, the order of the elements in the set is not defined:

```
A = {1,2,3}
B = {1,3,2}
A == B # returns True
```

Sets in Python can contain all kinds of hashable objects, that is, numeric objects, strings, and Booleans.

There are `union` and `intersection` methods:

```
A={1,2,3,4}
A.union({5})
A.intersection({2,4,6}) # returns set([2, 4])
```

Also, sets can be compared using the methods `issubset` and `issuperset` :

```
{2,4}.issubset({1,2,3,4,5}) # returns True
{1,2,3,4,5}.issuperset({2,4}) # returns True
```

Empty set

An empty set is defined in Python by `empty_set=set([])` and not by `{}`, which would define an empty dictionary!

Container conversions

We summarize in the following *Table 3.2* the most important properties of the container types presented so far. Arrays will be treated in `Chapter 4`, *Linear Algebra – Arrays*.

Type	Access	Order	Duplicate values	Mutability
List	index	yes	yes	yes
Tuple	index	yes	yes	no
Dictionary	key	no	yes	yes
Set	no	no	no	yes

Table 3.2 : Container Types

As you can see in the previous table, there is a difference in accessing container elements, and sets and dictionaries are not ordered.

Due to the different properties of the various container types, we frequently convert one type to another:

Container Types	Syntax
List → Tuple	`tuple([1,2,3])`
Tuple → List	`list((1,2,3))`
List, Tuple → Set	`set([1,2,3]), set((1,2,3))`
Set → List	`list({1,2,3})`
Dictionary → List	`{'a':4}.values()`
List → Dictionary	–

Type checking

The direct way to see the type of a variable is to use the `type` command:

```
label = 'local error'
type(label) # returns str
x = [1, 2] # list
type(x) # returns list
```

However, if you want to test for a variable to be of a certain type, you should use `isinstance` (instead of comparing the types with `type`):

```
isinstance(x, list) # True
```

The reason for using `isinstance` becomes apparent after having read `Chapter 8`, *Classes*, and in particular the concept of subclassing and inheritance in section *Subclassing and Inheritance* in `Chapter 8`, *Classes*. In short, often different types share some common properties with some basic type. The classical example is the type `bool`, which is derived by subclassing from the more general type `int`. In this situation, we see how the command `isinstance` can be used in a more general way:

```
test = True
isinstance(test, bool) # True
isinstance(test, int) # True
type(test) == int # False
type(test) == bool # True
```

So, in order to make sure that the variable `test` is as good as an integer (the particular type may be irrelevant), you should check that it is an instance of `integer`:

```
if isinstance(test, int):
    print("The variable is an integer")
```

Type checking

Python is not a typed language. What that means is that objects are identified by what they can do rather than what they are. For instance, if you have a string manipulating function that acts on an object by using the `len` method, then your function will probably be useful for any objects implementing that method.

So far, we have come across different types: `float`, `int`, `bool`, `complex`, `list`, `tuple`, `module`, `function`, `str`, `dict`, and `array`.

Summary

In this chapter, you learned to work with container types, mainly lists. It is important to know how to fill these containers and how to access their content. We saw that there is access by position or by keyword.

We will meet the important concept of slicing again in the next chapter on arrays. These are containers specially designed for mathematical operations.

Exercises

Ex. 1 → Execute the following statements:

```
L = [1, 2]
L3 = 3*L
```

1. What is the content of L3?

2. Try to predict the outcome of the following commands:

```
L3[0]
L3[-1]
L3[10]
```

3. What does the following command do?

```
L4 = [k**2 for k in L3]
```

4. Concatenate L3 and L4 to a new list L5.

Ex. 2 → Use the `range` command and a list comprehension to generate a list with 100 equidistantly spaced values between 0 and 1.

Ex. 3 → Assume that the following signal is stored in a list:

```
L = [0,1,2,1,0,-1,-2,-1,0]
```

What is the outcome of:

```
L[0]
L[-1]
L[:-1]
L + L[1:-1] + L
L[2:2] = [-3]
L[3:4] = []
L[2:5] = [-5]
```

Do this exercise by inspection only, that is, without using your Python Shell.

Ex. 4 → Consider the Python statements:

```
L = [n-m/2 for n in range(m)]
ans = 1 + L[0] + L[-1]
```

and assume that the variable m has been previously assigned an integer value. What is the value of ans? Answer this question without executing the statements in Python.

Ex. 5 → Consider the recursion formula:

$$u_{n+3} = u_{n+2} + ha\left(\frac{23}{12}u_{n+2} - \frac{4}{3}u_{n+1} + \frac{5}{12}u_n\right)$$

with $n = 0,\ldots, 1000$, $h = 1/1000$, and $a = -0.5$.

1. Create a list u. Store in its first three elements e^0, e^{ha}, and e^{2ha}. These represent the starting values u_0, u_1, and u_2 in the given formula. Build up the complete list from the recursion formula.
2. Construct a second list, td, in which you store the values nh, with $n = 0, \ldots, 1000$. Plot td versus u (refer section *Basic plotting* in Chapter 6, *Plotting*, for more information). Make a second plot in which you plot the difference, that is, $|e^{at_n} - u_n|$, where t_n represents the values inside the vector td. Set axis labels and a title.

The recursion is a multistep formula to solve the differential equation $u' = au$ with the initial value $u(0) = u_0 = 1$. u_n approximates $u(nh) = e^{anh}u_0$.

Ex. 6 → Let *A* and *B* be sets. The set (A \ B) ∪ (B \ A) is called the symmetric difference of the two sets. Write a function that performs this operation. Compare your results to the result of the command:

```
A.symmetric_difference(B).
```

Ex. 7 → Verify in Python the statement that the empty set is a subset of any set.

Ex. 8 → Study other operations on sets. You find a complete list of those by using the command completion feature of IPython. In particular, study the `update` and `intersection_update` methods. What is the difference between `intersection` and `intersection_update`?

4
Linear Algebra – Arrays

Linear algebra is one of the essential building blocks of computational mathematics. The objects of linear algebra are vectors and matrices. The package NumPy includes all the necessary tools to manipulate those objects.

The first task is to build matrices and vectors, or to alter existing ones by slicing. The other main task is the `dot` operation, which embodies most of the linear algebra operations (scalar product, matrix-vector product, and matrix-matrix product). Finally, various methods are available to solve linear problems.

Overview of the array type

For the impatient, here is how to use arrays in a nutshell. Be aware though that the behavior of arrays may be surprising at first, so we encourage you to read on after this introductory section.

Vectors and matrices

Creating vectors is as simple as using the function `array` to convert a list to an array:

```
v = array([1.,2.,3.])
```

The object `v` is now a vector that behaves much like a vector in linear algebra. We have already emphasized the differences with the list object in Python (refer to section *Arrays* in `Chapter 3`, *Containers Type*). Here are some illustrations of the basic linear algebra operations on vectors:

```
# two vectors with three components
v1 = array([1., 2., 3.])
```

```
v2 = array([2, 0, 1.])

# scalar multiplications/divisions
2*v1 # array([2., 4., 6.])
v1/2 # array([0.5, 1., 1.5])

# linear combinations
3*v1 # array([ 3., 6., 9.])
3*v1 + 2*v2 # array([ 7., 6., 11.])

# norm
from scipy.linalg import norm
norm(v1) # 3.7416573867739413
# scalar product
dot(v1, v2) # 5.
v1 @ v2 # 5 ; alternative formulation
```

Note that all basic arithmetic operations are performed elementwise:

```
# elementwise operations:
v1 * v2 # array([2., 0., 3.])
v2 / v1 # array([2.,0.,.333333])
v1 - v2 # array([-1., 2., 2.])
v1 + v2 # array([ 3., 2., 4.])
```

Some functions act elementwise on arrays as well:

```
cos(v1) # cosine, elementwise: array([ 0.5403,
                            -0.4161, -0.9899])
```

This subject will be covered in the section *Functions Acting on Arrays*.

A matrix is created in a similar way to a vector, but from a list of lists instead:

```
M = array([[1.,2],[0.,1]])
```

Vectors are no column – and no row matrices
The n vector, an $n \times 1$, and a $1 \times n$ matrix are three different objects even if they contain the same data.

To create a row matrix containing the same data as the vector v = array([1., 2., 1.]), we do this:

```
R = array([[1.,2.,1.]]) # notice the double brackets:
                        # this is a matrix
shape(R)                # (1,3): this is a row matrix
```

The corresponding column matrix is obtained by the method `reshape`:

```
C = array([1., 2., 1.]).reshape(3, 1)
shape(C) # (3,1): this is a column matrix
```

Indexing and slices

Indexing and slicing are similar to that of a list. The main difference is that there may be several indexes or slices when the array is a matrix. The subject will be covered in depth in section *Array indexing;* here, we just give some illustrating examples of indexing and slicing:

```
v = array([1., 2., 3])
M = array([[1., 2],[3., 4]])

v[0] # works as for lists
v[1:] # array([2., 3.])

M[0, 0] # 1.
M[1:] # returns the matrix array([[3., 4]])
M[1] # returns the vector array([3., 4.])

# access
v[0] # 1.
v[0] = 10

# slices
v[:2] # array([10., 2.])
v[:2] = [0, 1] # now v == array([0., 1., 3.])
v[:2] = [1, 2, 3] # error!
```

Linear algebra operations

The essential operator that performs most of the usual operations of linear algebra is the Python function `dot`. It is used for matrix-vector multiplications:

```
dot(M, v) # matrix vector multiplication; returns a vector
M @ v # alternative formulation
```

It may be used to compute a scalar product between two vectors:

```
dot(v, w) # scalar product; the result is a scalar
v @ w # alternative formulation
```

Lastly, it is used to compute matrix-matrix products:

```
dot(M, N) # results in a matrix
M @ N # alternative formulation
```

Solving a linear system

If A is a matrix and b is a vector, you can solve the linear equation:

$$Ax = b$$

Using the `solve` method, which has this syntax:

```
from scipy.linalg import solve
x = solve(A, b)
```

For example, we want to solve:

$$\begin{cases} x_1 + 2x_2 & = 1 \\ 3x_1 + 4x_2 & = 4 \end{cases}$$

Here is the solution for the preceding equation:

```
from scipy.linalg import solve
A = array([[1., 2.], [3., 4.]])
b = array([1., 4.])
x = solve(A, b)
allclose(dot(A, x), b) # True
allclose(A @ x, b) # alternative formulation
```

The command `allclose` is used here to compare two vectors. If they are close enough to each other, this command returns `True`. Optionally a tolerance value can be set. For more methods related to linear equations systems, refer to section *Linear algebra methods in SciPy*.

Mathematical preliminaries

In order to understand how arrays work in NumPy, it is useful to understand the mathematical parallel between accessing tensor (matrix and vector) elements by indexes and evaluating mathematical functions by providing arguments. We also cover in this section the generalization of the dot product as a reduction operator.

Arrays as functions

Arrays may be considered from several different points of view. We believe that the most fruitful one in order to understand arrays is that of functions of several variables.

For instance, selecting a component of a given vector in $\mathbb{R}^n$ may just be considered a function from the set of $\mathbb{N}_n$ to $\mathbb{R}$, where we define the set:

$$\mathbb{N}_n := \{0, 1, \ldots, n-1\}$$

Here the set $\mathbb{N}_n$ has n elements. The Python function `range` generates $\mathbb{N}_n$.

Selecting an element of a given matrix, on the other hand, is a function of two parameters, taking its value in $\mathbb{R}$. Picking a particular element of an $m \times n$ matrix may thus be considered a function from $\mathbb{N}_m \times \mathbb{N}_n$ to $\mathbb{R}$.

Operations are elementwise

NumPy arrays are essentially treated as mathematical functions. This is in particular true for operations. Consider two functions, f and g, defined on the same domain and taking real values. The product $f g$ of those two functions is defined as the pointwise product, that is:

$$(fg)(x) := f(x)g(x)$$

Note that this construction is possible for any operation between two functions. For an arbitrary operation defined on two scalars, which we denote here by $\star$, we could define $f \star g$ as follows:

$$(f \star g)(x) := f(x) \star g(x)$$

This innocuous remark allows us to understand NumPy's stance on operations; all operations are elementwise in arrays. For instance, the product between two matrices m and n is defined, as with functions, as follows:

$$(mn)_{ij} := m_{ij} n_{ij}$$

Shape and number of dimensions

There is a clear distinction between a:

- **Scalar**: Function with no arguments
- **Vector**: Function with one argument
- **Matrix**: Function with two arguments
- **Higher order tensor**: Function with more than two arguments

In what follows, the number of dimensions is the number of arguments of a function. The shape corresponds essentially to the domain of definition of a function.

For instance, a vector of size n is a function from the set $\mathbb{N}_n$ to $\mathbb{R}$. As a result, its domain of definition is $\mathbb{N}_n$. Its shape is defined as the singleton $(n,)$. Similarly, a matrix of size $m \times n$ is a function defined on $\mathbb{N}_m \times \mathbb{N}_m$. The corresponding shape is simply the pair (m, n). The shape of an array is obtained by the numpy.shape function, and the number of dimensions by the numpy.ndim function.

The dot operations

Treating arrays as functions, although very powerful, completely neglects the linear algebra structures we are familiar with, that is, matrix-vector and matrix-matrix operations. Fortunately, these linear algebra operations may all be written in a similar unified form:

The vector-vector operation:

$$s = \sum_i x_i y_i$$

The matrix-vector operation:

$$y_i = \sum_j A_{ij} x_j$$

The matrix-matrix operation:

$$C_{ij} = \sum_k A_{ik} B_{kj}$$

The vector-matrix operation:

$$y_j = \sum_i x_i A_{ij}$$

The essential mathematical concept is that of reduction. For a matrix-vector operation, the reduction is given by:

$$\sum_j A_{ij} x_j$$

In general, a reduction operation defined between two tensors T and U of respective number of dimensions m and n may be defined as:

$$(T \cdot U)_{i_1,\ldots,i_{m-1},j_2,\ldots,j_n} := \sum_k T_{i_1,\ldots,i_{m-1},k} U_{k,j_2,\ldots,j_n}$$

Clearly, the shapes of the tensors must be compatible for that operation to make any sense. This requirement is familiar for matrix-matrix multiplication. The multiplication *M N* of matrices *M* and *N* only makes sense if the number of columns of *M* equals the number of rows of *N*.

Another consequence of the reduction operation is that it produces a new tensor with $m + n - 2$ dimensions. In the following table, we gather the output of the reduction operation for the familiar cases involving matrices and vectors:

T_1=tensor(ndim)	T_2=tensor(ndim)	(T_1 T_2)(ndim)
matrix(2)	vector(1)	vector(1)
matrix(2)	matrix(2)	matrix(2)
vector (1)	vector(1)	scalar(0)
vector(1)	matrix(2)	vector(1)

Table 4.1: Output of the reduction operation for the familiar cases involving matrices and vectors

In Python, all reduction operations are performed using the dot function:

```
angle = pi/3
M = array([[cos(angle), -sin(angle)],
           [sin(angle), cos(angle)]])
v = array([1., 0.])
y = dot(M, v)
```

As in mathematical textbooks, also in modern Python (Version 3.5 and higher), the dot product is sometimes preferred to be written in its operator form, dot (M, v), or by using the more handy infix notation, M @ v. From now on we stick to the operator form; you can modify the examples if the other form is preferred.

Elementwise versus matrix multiplication
The multiplication operator * is always elementwise. It has nothing to do with the dot operation. Even if *A* is a matrix and *v* is a vector, *A*v* is still a legal operation.
The matrix-vector multiplication is performed using the dot function.
Refer to section *Broadcasting* of Chapter 5, *Advanced Array Concepts*, for more information.

The array type

The objects used to manipulate vectors, matrices, and more general tensors in NumPy are called arrays. In this section, we examine their essential properties, how to create them, and how to access their information.

Array properties

Arrays are essentially characterized by three properties, which is given in the following table (*Table 4.2*):

Name	Description
shape	It describes how the data should be interpreted, as a vector, a matrix or as a higher order tensor, and it gives the corresponding dimension. It is accessed with the shape attribute.
dtype	It gives the type of the underlying data (float, complex, integer, and so on).
strides	This attribute specifies in which order the data should be read. For instance, a matrix could be stored in memory contiguously column by column (the FORTRAN convention), or row by row (the C convention). The attribute is a tuple with the numbers of bytes that have to be skipped in memory to reach the next row and the number of bytes to be skipped to reach the next column. The strides attribute even allows for a more flexible interpretation of the data in memory, which is what makes array views possible.

Table 4.2 : Properties of Arrays

Consider the following array:

```
A = array([[1, 2, 3], [3, 4, 6]])
A.shape   # (2, 3)
A.dtype   # dtype('int64')
A.strides # (24, 8)
```

Its elements have type 'int64'; that is, they use 64 bits or 8 bytes in memory. The complete array is stored in memory row-wise. The distance from A[0, 0] to the first element in the next row A[1, 0] is thus 24 bytes (three matrix elements) in memory. Correspondingly, the distance in memory between A[0,0] and A[0,1] is 8 bytes (one matrix element). These values are stored in the attribute strides .

Creating arrays from lists

The general syntax to create an array is the function `array`. The syntax to create a real vector would be:

```
V = array([1., 2., 1.], dtype=float)
```

To create a complex vector with the same data:

```
V = array([1., 2., 1.], dtype=complex)
```

When no type is specified, the type is guessed. The `array` function chooses the type that allows storing of all the specified values:

```
V = array([1, 2]) # [1, 2] is a list of integers
V.dtype # int
V = array([1., 2]) # [1., 2] mix float/integer
V.dtype # float
V = array([1. + 0j, 2.]) # mix float/complex
V.dtype # complex
```

Silent type conversion

NumPy silently casts floats into integers, which might give unexpected results:

```
a = array([1, 2, 3])
a[0] = 0.5
a # now: array([0, 2, 3])
```

The same often unexpected array type casting happens from complex to float.

Array and Python parentheses

As we have noticed in section *Program and program flow* in Chapter 1, *Getting Started*, Python allows a line break when some opening brace or parenthesis is not closed. This allows a convenient syntax for array creation, which makes it more pleasing to the human eye:

```
# the identity matrix in 2D
Id = array([[1., 0.], [0., 1.]])
# Python allows this:
Id = array([[1., 0.],
            [0., 1.]])
# which is more readable
```

Accessing array entries

Array entries are accessed by indexes. In contrast to vector coefficients two indexes are needed to access matrix coefficients. These are given in one pair of brackets. This distinguishes the array syntax from a list of lists. There, two pairs of brackets are needed to access elements.

```
M = array([[1., 2.],[3., 4.]])
M[0, 0] # first row, first column: 1.
M[-1, 0] # last row, first column: 3.
```

Basic array slicing

Slices are similar to those of lists except that there might now be in more than one dimension:

- `M[i,:]` is a vector filled by the row *i* of *M*.
- `M[:,j]` is a vector filled by the column *i* of *M*.
- `M[2:4,:]` is a slice of `2:4` on the rows only.
- `M[2:4,1:4]` is a slice on rows and columns.

The result of matrix slicing is given in the following figure (*Figure 4.1*):

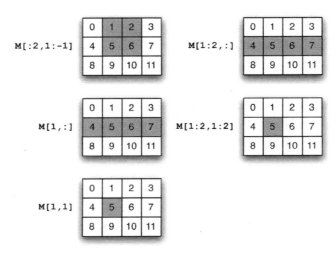

Figure 4.1: The result of matrix slicing

Omitting a dimension

If you omit an index or a slice, NumPy assumes you are taking rows only. M[3] is a vector that is a view on the third row of *M* and M[1:3] is a matrix that is a view on the second and third rows of *M*.

Changing the elements of a slice affects the entire array:

```
v = array([1., 2., 3.])
v1 = v[:2] # v1 is array([1., 2.])
v1[0] = 0. # if v1 is changed ...
v # ... v is changed too: array([0., 2., 3.])
```

General slicing rules are given in the following table (*Table 4.3*):

Access	ndim	Kind
index, index	0	scalar
slice, index	1	vector
index, slice	1	vector
slice, slice	2	matrix

Table 4.3: General Slicing Rules

The results of slicing operations for an array M of shape *(4, 4)* are given in the following table (*Table 4.4*):

Access	Shape	ndim	Kind
M[:2, 1:-1]	*(2, 2)*	2	matrix
M[1, :]	*(4,)*	1	vector
M[1, 1]	*( )*	0	scalar
M[1:2, :]	*(1, 4)*	2	matrix
M[1:2, 1:2]	*(1, 1)*	2	matrix

Table 4.4: Result of slicing operation for an array M of shape (4,4)

Altering an array using slices

You may alter an array using slices or by direct access. The following changes only one element in a 5 × 3 matrix M:

```
M[1, 3] = 2.0 # scalar
```

But we may change one full row of the matrix:

```
M[2, :] = [1., 2., 3.] # vector
```

We may also replace a full submatrix:

```
M[1:3, :] = array([[1., 2., 3.],[-1.,-2., -3.]])
```

There is a distinction between a column matrix and a vector. The following assignment with a column matrix returns no error
```
M[1:4, 2:3] = array([[1.],[0.],[-1.0]])
```
while the assignment with a vector returns a `Value Error`
```
M[1:4, 2:3] = array([1., 0., -1.0]) #  error
```

The general slicing rules are shown in *Table 4.2*. The matrices and vectors in the preceding examples must have the right size to fit into matrix *M*. You may also make use of the broadcasting rules (for more information, refer to section *Broadcasting* of `Chapter 5`, *Advanced Array Concepts*) to determine the allowed size of the replacement arrays. If the replacement array does not have the right shape, a `ValueError` exception will be raised.

Functions to construct arrays

The usual way to set up an array is via a list. But there are also a couple of convenient methods for generating special arrays, which are given in the following table (*Table 4.5*):

Methods	Shape	Generates
`zeros((n,m))`	*(n,m)*	Matrix filled with zeros
`ones((n,m))`	*(n,m)*	Matrix filled with ones
`diag(v,k)`	*(n,n)*	(Sub-, super-) diagonal matrix from a vector *v*
`random.rand(n,m)`	*(n,m)*	Matrix filled with uniformly distributed random numbers in (0,1)

arange(n)	*(n,)*	First *n* integers
linspace(a,b,n)	*(n,)*	Vector with *n* equispaced points between *a* and *b*

Table 4.5: Commands to create arrays

These commands may take additional arguments. In particular, the commands `zeros`, `ones`, and `arange` take `dtype` as an optional argument. The default type is `float`, except for `arange`. There are also methods such as `zeros_like` and `ones_like`, which are slight variants of the preceding ones. For instance, the `zeros_like(A)` method is equivalent to `zeros(shape(A))`.

Here is the `identity` function, which constructs an identity matrix of a given size:

```
I = identity(3)
```

The command is identical to:

```
I = array([[ 1.,  0.,  0.],
           [ 0.,  1.,  0.],
           [ 0.,  0.,  1.]])
```

Accessing and changing the shape

The number of dimensions is what distinguishes a vector from a matrix. The **shape** is what distinguishes vectors of different sizes, or matrices of different sizes. In this section, we examine how to obtain and change the shape of an array.

The shape function

The shape of a matrix is the tuple of its dimensions. The shape of an n × m matrix is the tuple (n, m). It can be obtained by the `shape` function:

```
M = identity(3)
shape(M)  # (3, 3)
```

For a vector, the shape is a singleton containing the length of that vector:

```
v = array([1., 2., 1., 4.])
shape(v)  # (4,) <- singleton (1-tuple)
```

An alternative is to use the array attribute `shape`, which gives the same result:

```
M = array([[1.,2.]])
shape(M) # (1,2)
M.shape # (1,2)
```

However, the advantage of using `shape` as a function is that this function may be used on scalars and lists as well. This may come in handy when code is supposed to work with both scalars and arrays:

```
shape(1.) # ()
shape([1,2]) # (2,)
shape([[1,2]]) # (1,2)
```

Number of dimensions

The number of dimensions of an array is obtained with the function `numpy.ndim` or using the array attribute `ndarray.ndim`:

```
ndim(A) # 2
A.ndim # 2
```

Note that the number of dimensions, given by the function `ndim`, of a tensor `T` (a vector, matrix, or higher order tensor) is always equal to the length of its shape:

```
T = zeros((2,2,3)) # tensor of shape (2,2,3); three dimensions
ndim(T) # 3
len(shape(T)) # 3
```

Reshape

The method `reshape` gives a new view of the array, with a new shape, without copying the data:

```
v = array([0,1,2,3,4,5])
M = v.reshape(2,3)
shape(M) # returns (2,3)
M[0,0] = 10 # now v[0] is 10
```

Reshape does not copy

Reshape does not create a new array. It rather gives a new view on the existing array. In the preceding example, changing one element of M would automatically result in a change in the corresponding element in v. When this behavior is not acceptable, you need to copy the data.

The various effects of the `reshape` method on an array defined by `arange(6)` are given in the following figure :

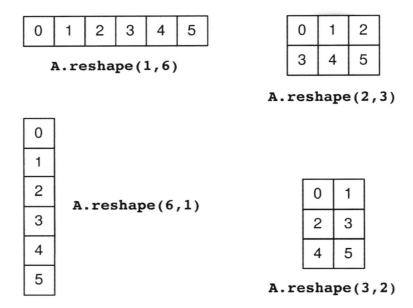

Figure 4.2: The various effects of the reshape method on an array defined by arange(6)

If one tries to reshape an array with a shape that does not multiply to the original shape, an error is raised:

```
ValueError: total size of new array must be unchanged.
```

Sometimes, it is convenient to specify only one shape parameter and let Python determine the other in such a way that it multiplies to the original shape. This is done by setting the free shape parameter -1:

```
v = array([1, 2, 3, 4, 5, 6, 7, 8])
M = v.reshape(2, -1)
shape(M) # returns (2, 4)
M = v.reshape(-1, 2)
shape(M) # returns (4,2 )
M = v.reshape(3,- 1) # returns error
```

Transpose

A special form of reshaping is transposing. It just switches the two shape elements of the matrix. The transpose of a matrix A is a matrix B such that:

$$B_{ij} = A_{ji}$$

Which is resolved in the following way:

```
A = ...
shape(A) # 3,4

B = A.T # A transpose
shape(B) # 4,3
```

Transpose does not copy

Transposition is very similar to reshaping. In particular, it does not copy the data either and just returns a view on the same array:

```
A= array([[ 1., 2.],[ 3., 4.]])
B=A.T
A[1,1]=5.
B[1,1] # 5
```

Transposing a vector makes no sense since vectors are tensors of one dimension, that is, functions of one variable. NumPy will, however, comply and return exactly the same object:

```
v = array([1., 2., 3.])
v.T # exactly the same vector!
```

What you have in mind when you want to transpose a vector is probably to create a row or column matrix. This is done using `reshape`:

```
v.reshape(-1, 1)  # column matrix containing v
v.reshape(1, -1)  # row matrix containing v
```

Stacking

The universal method to build matrices from a couple of (matching) submatrices is `concatenate`. Its syntax is:

```
concatenate((a1, a2, ...), axis = 0)
```

This command stacks the submatrices vertically (on top of each other) when `axis=0` is specified. With the `axis=1` argument, they are stacked horizontally, and this generalizes according to arrays with more dimensions. This function is called by several convenient functions, as follows:

- `hstack`: Used to stack matrices horizontally
- `vstack`: Used to stack matrices vertically
- `columnstack`: Used to stack vectors in columns

Stacking vectors

One may stack vectors row-wise or column-wise using `vstack` and `column_stack`, as illustrated in the following figure:

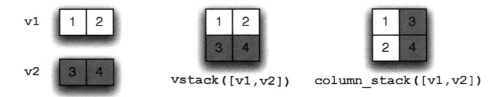

hstack would produce the concatenation of v1 and v2.

Let us consider the symplectic permutation as an example for vector stacking:
We have a vector of size *2n*. We want to perform a symplectic transformation of a vector with an even number of components, that is, exchange the first half with the second half of the vector with sign change:

$$(x_1, x_2, \ldots, x_n, x_{n+1}, \ldots, x_{2n}) \mapsto (x_{n+1}, \ldots, x_{2n}, -x_1, \ldots, -x_n)$$

This operation is resolved in Python as follows:

```
# v is supposed to have an even length.
def symp(v):
    n = len(v) // 2 # use the integer division //
    return hstack([v[-n:], -v[:n]])
```

Functions acting on arrays

There are different types of functions acting on arrays. Some act elementwise, and they return an array of the same shape. Those are called universal functions. Other array functions return an array of a different shape.

Universal functions

Universal functions are functions that act elementwise on arrays. They thus have an output array that has the same shape as the input array. These functions allow us to compute the result of a scalar function on a whole array at once.

Built-in universal functions

A typical example is the cos function (the one provided by NumPy):

```
cos(pi)  # -1
cos(array([[0, pi/2, pi]]))  # array([[1, 0, -1]])
```

Note that universal functions work on arrays in a componentwise manner. This is also true for operators, such as multiplication or exponent:

```
2 * array([2, 4]) # array([4, 8])
array([1, 2]) * array([1, 8]) # array([1, 16])
array([1, 2])**2 # array([1, 4])
2**array([1, 2]) # array([1, 4])
array([1, 2])**array([1, 2]) # array([1, 4])
```

Create universal functions

Your function will automatically be universal if you use only universal functions in it. If, however, your function uses functions that are not universal, you might get scalar results, or even an error, when trying to apply them on an array:

```
def const(x):
    return 1
const(array([0, 2])) # returns 1 instead of array([1, 1])
```

Another example is the following:

```
def heaviside(x):
    if x >= 0:
        return 1.
    else:
        return 0.

heaviside(array([-1, 2])) # error
```

The expected behaviour would be that the heaviside function applied to a vector [a, b] would return [heaviside(a), heaviside(b)]. Alas, this does not work because the function always returns a scalar, no matter the size of the input argument. Besides, using the function with an array input would raise an exception. The NumPy function vectorize allows us to quickly solve this problem:

```
vheaviside = vectorize(heaviside)
vheaviside(array([-1, 2])) # array([0, 1]) as expected
```

A typical application of this method is its use when plotting a function:

```
xvals = linspace(-1, 1, 100)
plot(xvals, vectorize(heaviside)(xvals))
axis([-1.5, 1.5, -0.5, 1.5])
```

The following graph shows the heaviside function:

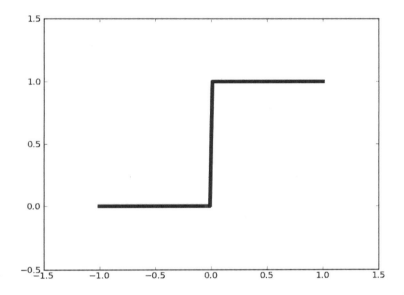

 The `vectorize` function does not improve performance. It provides only a convenient way to quickly transform a function, so that it operates elementwise on list and arrays.

Array functions

There are a number of functions acting on arrays that do not act componentwise. Examples of such functions are `max`, `min`, and `sum`. These functions may operate on the whole matrix, row-wise, or column-wise. When no argument is provided, they act on the whole matrix. Suppose A is the following matrix:

1	2	3	4
5	6	7	8

The `sum` function acting on that matrix returns a scalar:

```
sum(A)  # 36
```

The command has an optional parameter, `axis` . It allows us to choose along which axis to perform the operation. For instance, if the axis is *0*, it means that the sum should be computed along the first axis. The sum along axis *0* of an array of shape *(m, n)* will be a vector of length *n*.

Suppose we compute the sum of A along the axis 0:

```
sum(A, axis=0)  # array([ 6, 8, 10, 12])
```

This amounts to computing the sum on the columns:

1	2	3	4
5	6	7	8

The result is a vector:

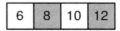

Now suppose we compute the sum along the axis *1*:

```
A.sum(axis=1)  # array([10, 26])
```

This amounts to computing the sum on the rows:

1	2	3	4
5	6	7	8

The result is a vector:

Linear algebra methods in SciPy

SciPy offers a large range of methods from numerical linear algebra in its `scipy.linalg` module. Many of these methods are Python wrapping programs from `LAPACK`, a collection of well-approved FORTRAN subroutines used to solve linear equation systems and eigenvalue problems. Linear algebra methods are the core of any method in scientific computing, and the fact that SciPy uses wrappers instead of pure Python code makes these central methods extremely fast. We present in detail here how two linear algebra problems are solved with SciPy to give you a flavour of this module.

Solving several linear equation systems with LU

Let A be an $n \times n$ matrix and $b_1, b_2, \ldots, b_k$ be a sequence of n-vectors. We consider the problem to find n vectors x_i such that:

$$Ax_i = b_i$$

We assume that the vectors b_i are not known simultaneously. In particular, it is quite a common situation that the ith problem has to be solved before b_{i+1} becomes available.

LU factorization is a way to organize the classical Gauss elimination method in such a way that the computation is done in two steps:

- A factorization step of the matrix A to get matrices in triangular form
- A relatively cheap backward and forward elimination step that works on the b_i's and benefits from the more time-consuming factorization step

The method also uses the fact that if P is a permutation matrix such that PA is the original matrix with its rows permuted.

The two systems

$$Ax = b \quad \text{and} \quad PAx = Pb$$

have the same solution.

LU factorization finds a permutation matrix P, a lower triangular matrix L, and an upper triangular matrix U such that:

$$PA = LU \quad \text{or equivalently} \quad A = PLU.$$

Such a factorization always exists. Furthermore, L can be determined in such a way that $L_{ii} = 1$. Thus, the essential data from L that has to be stored is L_{ij} with $i > j$. Consequently, L and U can be stored together in an $n \times n$ array, while the information about the permutation matrix P just requires an n integer vector – the pivot vector.

In SciPy, there are two methods to compute the *LU* factorization. The standard one is `scipy.linalg.lu`, which returns the three matrices L, U, and P. The other method is `lu_factor`. That is the method we describe here, because it will be conveniently used later in combination with `lu_solve`:

```
import scipy.linalg as sl
[LU,piv] = sl.lu_factor(A)
```

Here, the A matrix is factorized and an array with the information about L and U is returned, together with the pivot vector. With this information, the system can be solved by performing row interchanges of the vectors b_i according to the information stored in the pivot vector, backward substitution using U, and finally forward substitution using L. This is bundled in Python, in the `lu_solve` method. The following code snippet shows how the system $Ax_i = b_i$ is solved once the *LU* factorization is performed and its results stored in the tuple (LU, piv):

```
import scipy.linalg as sl
xi = sl.lu_solve((LU, piv), bi)
```

Solving a least square problem with SVD

A linear equation system $Ax = b$, with A being an $m \times n$ matrix and $m > n$, is called an overdetermined linear system. In general it has no classical solution and one seeks a vector $x^* \in \mathbb{R}^n$ with the property:

$$\| \underbrace{Ax^* - b}_{=:r} \|_2 = \min_{x \in \mathbb{R}^n} \|Ax - b\|_2.$$

Here, $\| \cdot \|$ denotes the Euclidean vector norm $\|v\|_2 = \sqrt{\sum_{i=1}^n v_i^2}$.

This problem is called a least square problem. A stable method to solve it is based on factorizing $A = U\Sigma V^T$, with U being a $m \times m$ orthogonal matrix, V a $n \times n$ orthogonal matrix, and $\Sigma = (\sigma_{ij})$ an $m \times n$ matrix with the property $\sigma_{ij} = 0$ for all $i \neq j$. This factorization is called a **singular value decomposition (SVD)**.

We write,

$$\Sigma = \begin{bmatrix} \Sigma_1 \\ 0 \end{bmatrix}$$

with a diagonal $n \times n$ matrix Σ_1. If we assume that A has full rank, then Σ_1 is invertible and it can be shown that, $x^* = V \begin{bmatrix} \Sigma_1^{-1} & 0 \end{bmatrix} U^T b$. If we split $U = [U_1 \ U_2]$ with U_1 being an $m \times n$ submatrix, then the preceding equation can be simplified to $x^* = V\Sigma_1^{-1} U_1^T b$.

SciPy provides a function called `svd`, which we use to solve this task:

```
import scipy.linalg as sl
[U1, Sigma_1, VT] = sl.svd(A, full_matrices = False,
                           compute_uv = True)
xast = dot(VT.T, dot(U1.T, b) / Sigma_1)
r = dot(A, xast) - b # computes the residual
nr = sl.norm(r, 2) # computes the Euclidean norm of r
```

The keyword `full_matrices` says that only the portion U_1 of U needs to be computed. As one often uses `svd` to compute only singular values, σ_{ii}, we have to explicitly demand the computation of U and V by using the keyword `compute_uv`. The SciPy function `scipy.linalg.lstsq` solves the least square problem similarly by using a singular value decomposition.

More methods

In the examples so far, you met a couple of methods for computational tasks in linear algebra, for example, `solve`. Most common methods are available after the command `import scipy.linalg as sl` is executed. We refer to their documentation for further reference. Some linear algebra functions of the `scipy.linalg` module are given in the following table (*Table 4.6*):

Methods	Description (matrix methods)
`sl.det`	Determinant of a matrix
`sl.eig`	Eigenvalues and eigenvectors of a matrix
`sl.inv`	Matrix inverse
`sl.pinv`	Matrix pseudoinverse
`sl.norm`	Matrix or vector norm
`sl.svd`	Singular value decomposition
`sl.lu`	LU decomposition
`sl.qr`	QR decomposition
`sl.cholesky`	Cholesky decomposition
`sl.solve`	Solution of a general or symmetric linear system: $Ax = b$
`sl.solve.banded`	The same for banded matrices
`sl.lstsq`	Least squares solution

Table 4.6: Linear algebra functions of the **scipy.linalg** module

Execute `import scipy.linalg as sl` first.

Summary

In this chapter, we worked with the most important objects in linear algebra – vectors and matrices. For this, we learned how to define arrays and we met important array methods. A smaller section demonstrated how to use modules from `scipy.linalg` to solve central tasks in linear algebra.

Exercises

Ex. 1 → Consider a 4 × 3 matrix M:

$$\begin{bmatrix} 1 & 2 & 3 \\ 4 & 5 & 6 \\ 7 & 8 & 9 \\ 10 & 11 & 12 \end{bmatrix}$$

1. Construct this matrix in Python using the function `array`.
2. Construct the same matrix using the function `arange` followed by a suitable reshape.
3. What is the result of the expression `M[2,:]` ? What is the result of the similar expression `M[2:]`?

Ex. 2 → Given a vector x, construct in Python the following matrix:

$$V = \begin{bmatrix} x_0^5 & x_0^4 & \cdots & x_0^1 & x_0^0 \\ x_1^5 & x_1^4 & \cdots & x_1^1 & x_1^0 \\ & & \vdots & & \\ x_5^5 & x_5^4 & \cdots & x_5^1 & x_5^0 \end{bmatrix}$$

Here, x_i are the components of the vector x (numbered from zero). Given a vector y, solve in Python the linear equation system $Va = y$. Let the components of a be denoted by a_i, $i = 0, ...,$ 5. Write a function `poly`, which has a and z as input and which computes the polynomial:

$$p(z) = \sum_{i=0}^{5} a_{5-i} z^i$$

Plot this polynomial and depict in the same plot the points (x_i, y_i) as small stars. Try your code with the vectors:

- $x = (0.0, 0.5, 1.0, 1.5, 2.0, 2.5)$
- $y = (-2.0, 0.5, -2.0, 1.0, -0.5, 1.0)$

Ex. 3 → The matrix V in *Ex. 2* is called a Vandermonde matrix. It can be set up in Python directly by the command `vander`. Evaluating a polynomial defined by a coefficient vector can be done with the Python command `polyval`. Repeat *Ex. 2* by using these commands.

Ex. 4 → Let u be a one dimensional array. Construct another array ξ with values $\xi_i = (u_i + u_{i+1} + u_{i+2})/3$. In statistics, this array is called the moving average of u. In approximation theory, it plays the role as the Greville abscissae of cubic splines. Try to avoid the use of for loops in your script.

Ex. 5 →

1. Construct from the matrix V given in *Ex. 2* a matrix A by deleting V's first column.
2. Form the matrix $B = (A^T A)^{-1} A^T$.
3. Compute $c = B y$ with y from *Ex. 2*.
4. Use c and `polyval` to plot the polynomial defined by c. Plot in the same picture again the points (x_i, y_i).

Ex. 6 → *Ex. 5* describes the least square method. Repeat that exercise but use SciPy's `scipy.linalg.lstsq` method instead.

Ex. 7 → Let v be a vector written in its coordinate form as a 3×1 matrix $[1\ \text{-}1\ 1]^T$. Construct the projection matrices:

$$P = \frac{vv^{\mathrm{T}}}{v^{\mathrm{T}}v} \qquad \text{and} \qquad Q = I - P.$$

Show experimentally that v is an eigenvector for both matrices P and Q. What are the corresponding eigenvalues?

Ex. 8 → In numerical linear algebra the $m \times m$ matrix A with the property

$$A_{ij} = \begin{cases} 0 & \text{if } i < j \text{ and } j \neq m \\ 1 & \text{if } i = j \text{ or } j = m \\ -1 & \text{otherwise} \end{cases}$$

is used as an example for an extreme growth-factor, when performing *LU* factorization.

Set up this matrix in Python for various m, compute its *LU* factorization using the command `scipy.linalg.lu` and derive experimentally a statement about the growth factor

$$\rho = \frac{\max_{ij} |U_{ij}|}{\max_{ij} |A_{ij}|}$$

in relation to m.

5
Advanced Array Concepts

In this chapter, we will explain some more advanced aspects of arrays. First, we will cover the notion of an array view, followed by Boolean arrays and how to compare arrays. We briefly describe indexing and vectorization, explain sparse arrays, and some special topics such as broadcasting.

Array views and copies

In order to control precisely how memory is used, NumPy offers the concept of view of an array. Views are smaller arrays that share the same data as a larger array. This works just like a reference to one single object (refer to section *Basic Types* in `Chapter 1`, *Getting Started*).

Array views

The simplest example of a view is given by a slice of an array:

```
M = array([[1.,2.],[3.,4.]])
v = M[0,:] # first row of M
```

The preceding slice is a view of M. It shares the same data as M. Modifying v will modify M as well:

```
v[-1] = 0.
v # array([[1.,0.]])
M # array([[1.,0.],[3.,4.]]) # M is modified as well
```

It is possible to access the object that owns the data using the array attribute `base`:

```
v.base # array([[1.,0.],[3.,4.]])
v.base is M # True
```

If an array owns its data, the attribute base is none :

```
M.base # None
```

Slices as views

There are precise rules on which slices will return views and which ones will return copies. Only basic slices (mainly index expressions with :) return views, whereas any advanced selections (such as slicing with a Boolean) will return a copy of the data. For instance, it is possible to create new matrices by indexing with lists (or arrays):

```
a = arange(4) # array([0.,1.,2.,3.])
b = a[[2,3]] # the index is a list [2,3]
b # array([2.,3.])
b.base is None # True, the data was copied
c = a[1:3]
c.base is None # False, this is just a view
```

In the preceding example, the array b is not a view, whereas the array c, obtained with a simpler slice, is a view.

There is an especially simple slice of an array that returns a view of the whole array:

```
N = M[:] # this is a view of the whole array M
```

Transpose and reshape as views

Some other important operations return views. For instance, transpose returns a view:

```
M = random.random_sample((3,3))
N = M.T
N.base is M # True
```

The same applies for all reshaping operations:

```
v = arange(10)
C = v.reshape(-1,1) # column matrix
C.base is v # True
```

Array copy

Sometimes it is necessary to explicitly request that the data be copied. This is simply achieved with the NumPy function called `array`:

```
M = array([[1.,2.],[3.,4.]])
N = array(M.T) # copy of M.T
```

We may verify that the data has indeed been copied:

```
N.base is None # True
```

Comparing arrays

Comparing two arrays is not as simple as it may seem. Consider the following code, which is intended to check whether two matrices are close to each other:

```
A = array([0.,0.])
B = array([0.,0.])
if abs(B-A) < 1e-10: # an exception is raised here
    print("The two arrays are close enough")
```

This code raises the exception when the `if` statement is executed:

```
ValueError: The truth value of an array with more than one element is
ambiguous. Use a.any() or a.all()
```

In this section, we explain why this is so and how to remedy this state of affairs.

Boolean arrays

Boolean arrays are useful for advanced array indexing (refer to section *Indexing with Boolean arrays*). A Boolean array is simply an array for which the entries have the type `bool`:

```
A = array([True,False]) # Boolean array
A.dtype # dtype('bool')
```

Any comparison operator acting on arrays will create a Boolean array instead of a simple Boolean:

```
M = array([[2, 3],
           [1, 4]])
M > 2 # array([[False, True],
      #         [False, True]])
M == 0 # array([[False, False],
       #         [False, False]])
N = array([[2, 3],
           [0, 0]])
M == N # array([[True, True],
       #         [False, False]])
...
```

Note that because array comparison creates Boolean arrays, one cannot use array comparison directly in conditional statements, for example, `if` statements. the solution is to use the methods `all` and `any`:

```
A = array([[1,2],[3,4]])
B = array([[1,2],[3,3]])
A == B # creates array([[True, True], [True, False]])
(A == B).all() # False
(A != B).any() # True
if (abs(B-A) < 1e-10).all():
    print("The two arrays are close enough")
```

Checking for equality

Checking for equality of two float arrays is not straight forward, because two floats may be very close without being equal. In NumPy, it is possible to check for equality with `allclose`. This function checks for equality of two arrays up to a given precision:

```
data = random.rand(2)*1e-3
small_error = random.rand(2)*1e-16
data == data + small_error # False
allclose(data, data + small_error, rtol=1.e-5, atol=1.e-8)    # True
```

The tolerance is given in terms of a relative tolerance bound, `rtol`, and an absolute error bound, `atol`. The command `allclose` is a short form of: `(abs(A-B) < atol+rtol*abs(B)).all()`.

Note that `allclose` can be also applied to scalars:

```
data = 1e-3
error = 1e-16
data == data + error # False
allclose(data, data + error, rtol=1.e-5, atol=1.e-8)   #True
```

Boolean operations on arrays

You cannot use `and`, `or`, and `not` on Boolean arrays. Indeed, those operators force the casting from array to Boolean, which is not permitted. Instead, we can use the operators given in the following table (*Table 5.1*) for componentwise logical operations on Boolean arrays:

Logic operator	Replacement for Boolean arrays
A and B	A & B
A or B	A | B
not A	~ A

Table 5.1 Logical operators and, or and not do not work with arrays.

```
A = array([True, True, False, False])
B = array([True, False, True, False])
A and B # error!
A & B # array([True, False, False, False])
A | B # array([True, True, True, False])
~A # array([False, False, True, True])
```

Here is an example usage of logical operators with Boolean arrays:

Suppose that we have a sequence of data that is marred with some measurement error. Suppose further that we run a regression and it gives us a deviation for each value. We wish to obtain all the exceptional values and all the values with little deviation that are lower than a given threshold:

```
data = linspace(1,100,100) # data
deviation = random.normal(size=100) # the deviations
          #don't forget the parentheses in next statement!
exceptional = data[(deviation<-0.5)|(deviation>0.5)]
exceptional = data[abs(deviation)>0.5] # same result
small = data[(abs(deviation)<0.1)&(data<5.)] # small deviation and data
```

Array indexing

We have already seen that one may index arrays by combinations of slices and integers, this is the basic slicing technique. There are, however, many more possibilities, which allow for a variety of ways to access and modify array elements.

Indexing with Boolean arrays

It is often useful to access and modify only parts of an array, depending on its value. For instance, one might want to access all the positive elements of an array. This turns out to be possible using Boolean arrays, which act like masks to select only some elements of an array. The result of such an indexing is *always* a vector. For instance, consider the following example:

```
B = array([[True, False],
           [False, True]])
M = array([[2, 3],
           [1, 4]])
M[B] # array([2,4]), a vector
```

In fact, the `M[B]` call is equivalent to `M.flatten()[B]`. One may then replace the resulting vector by another vector. For instance, one may replace all the elements by zero (refer to section *Broadcasting* for more information):

```
M[B] = 0
M # [[0, 3], [1, 0]]
```

Or one may replace all the selected values by others:

```
M[B] = 10, 20
M # [[10, 3], [1, 20]]
```

By combining the creation of Boolean arrays (`M > 2`), smart indexing (indexing with Boolean array), and broadcasting, one may use the following elegant syntax:

```
M[M>2] = 0    # all the elements > 2 are replaced by 0
```

The expression broadcasting here refers to the tacit conversion of the scalar 0 to a vector of an appropriate shape.

Using where

The command `where` gives a useful construct that can take a Boolean array as a condition and either return the indexes of the array elements satisfying the condition or return different values depending on the values in the Boolean array.

The basic structure is:

```
where(condition, a, b)
```

This will return values from `a` when the condition is `True` and values from `b` when it is `False`.

For instances consider, a *Heaviside* function:

$$H(x) = \begin{cases} 0 & x < 0 \\ 1 & x \geq 0 \end{cases}$$

The following code implements a Heaviside function:

```
def H(x):
    return where(x < 0, 0, 1)
x = linspace(-1,1,11)   # [-1. -0.8 -0.6 -0.4 -0.2 0. 0.2 0.4 0.6 0.8 1. ]
print(H(x))             # [0 0 0 0 0 1 1 1 1 1 1]
```

The second and third arguments can be either arrays of the same size as the condition (the Boolean array) or scalars. We give two more example to demonstrated how to manipulate elements from an array or a scalar depending on a condition:

```
x = linspace(-4,4,5)
# [-4. -2.  0.  2.  4.]

print(where(x > 0, sqrt(x), 0))
# [ 0.+0.j 0.+0.j 0.+0.j 1.41421356+0.j  2.+0.j ]
print(where(x > 0, 1, -1)) # [-1 -1 -1  1  1]
```

If the second and third arguments are omitted, then a tuple containing the indexes of the elements satisfying the condition is returned.

For example consider the use of `where` with only one argument in the following code:

```
a = arange(9)
b = a.reshape((3,3))

print(where(a > 5))    # (array([6, 7, 8]),)

print(where(b > 5))    # (array([2, 2, 2]), array([0, 1, 2]))
```

Performance and Vectorization

When it comes to performance of your Python code, it often boils down to the difference between interpreted code and compiled code. Python is an interpreted programming language and basic Python code is executed directly without any intermediate compilation to machine code. With a compiled language, the code needs to be translated to machine instructions before execution.

The benefits of an interpreted language are many but interpreted code cannot compete with compiled code for speed. To make your code faster, you can write some parts in a compiled language like FORTRAN, C, or C++. This is what NumPy and SciPy do.

For this reason, it is best to use functions in NumPy and SciPy over interpreted versions whenever possible. NumPy array operations such as matrix multiplication, matrix-vector multiplication, matrix factorization, scalar products, and so on are much faster than any pure Python equivalent. Consider the simple case of scalar products. The scalar product is much slower than the compiled NumPy function, `dot(a,b)` (more than 100 times slower for arrays with about 100 elements):

```
def my_prod(a,b):
    val = 0
    for aa,bb in zip(a,b):
        val += aa*bb
    return val
```

Measuring the speed of your functions is an important aspect of scientific computing. Refer to section *Measuring execution time* in `Chapter 13`, *Testing,* for details on measuring execution times.

Vectorization

To improve performance, one has to vectorize the code often. Replacing `for` loops and other slower parts of the code with NumPy slicing, operations, and functions can give significant improvements. For example, the simple addition of a scalar to a vector by iterating over the elements is very slow:

```
for i in range(len(v)):
    w[i] = v[i] + 5
```

where using NumPy's addition is much faster:

```
w = v + 5
```

Using NumPy slicing can also give significant speed improvements over iterating with `for` loops. To demonstrate this let us consider forming the average of neighbors in a two-dimensional array:

```
def my_avg(A):
    m,n = A.shape
    B = A.copy()
    for i in range(1,m-1):
        for j in range(1,n-1):
            B[i,j] = (A[i-1,j] + A[i+1,j] + A[i,j-1] + A[i,j+1])/4
    return B

def slicing_avg(A):
    A[1:-1,1:-1] = (A[:-2,1:-1] + A[2:,1:-1] +
    A[1:-1,:-2] + A[1:-1,2:])/4
    return A
```

These functions both assign each element the average of its four neighbors. The second version, using slicing, is much faster.

Besides replacing `for` loops and other slower constructions with NumPy functions, there is a useful function called `vectorize`, refer to section *Functions acting on arrays* in `Chapter 4, Linear Algebra – Arrays`. This will take a function and create a vectorized version that applies the function on all elements of an array using functions wherever possible.

Consider the following example for vectorizing a function:

```
def my_func(x):
    y = x**3 - 2*x + 5
    if y>0.5:
        return y-0.5
    else:
        return 0
```

Applying this by iterating over an array is very slow:

```
for i in range(len(v)):
    v[i] = my_func(v[i])
```

Instead, use `vectorize` to create a new function, like this:

```
my_vecfunc = vectorize(my_func)
```

This function can then be applied to the array directly:

```
v = my_vecfunc(v)
```

The vectorized option is much faster (around 10 times faster with arrays of length 100).

Broadcasting

Broadcasting in NumPy denotes the ability to guess a common, compatible shape between two arrays. For instance, when adding a vector (one-dimensional array) and a scalar (zero-dimensional array), the scalar is extended to a vector, in order to allow for the addition. The general mechanism is called broadcasting. We will first review that mechanism from a mathematical point of view, and then proceed to give the precise rules for broadcasting in NumPy.

Mathematical view

Broadcasting is often performed in mathematics, mainly implicitly. Examples are expressions such as $f(x) + C$ or $f(x) + g(y)$. We'll give an explicit description of that technique in this section.

We have in mind the very close relationship between functions and NumPy arrays, as described in section *Mathematical preliminaries* of `Chapter 4`, *Linear Algebra – Arrays*.

Constant functions

One of the most common examples of broadcasting is the addition of a function and a constant; if C is a scalar, one often writes:

$$f := \sin + C$$

This is an abuse of notation since one should not be able to add functions and constants. Constants are however implicitly broadcast to functions. The broadcast version of the constant C is the function $\bar{C}$ defined by:

$$\overline{C}(x) := C \quad \forall x$$

Now it makes sense to add two functions together:

$$f = \sin + \overline{C}$$

We are not being pedantic for the sake of it, but because a similar situation may arise for arrays, as in the following code:

```
vector = arange(4)  # array([0.,1.,2.,3.])
vector + 1.         # array([1.,2.,3.,4.])
```

In this example, everything happens as if the scalar `1.` had been converted to an array of the same length as `vector`, that is, `array([1.,1.,1.,1.])`, and then added to `vector`.

This example is exceedingly simple, so we proceed to show less obvious situations.

Functions of several variables

A more intricate example of broadcasting arises when building functions of several variables. Suppose, for instance, that we were given two functions of one variable, f and g, and that we want to construct a new function F according to the formula:

$$F(x, y) = f(x) + g(y)$$

This is clearly a valid mathematical definition. We would like to express this definition as the sum of two functions in two variables defined as

$$\overline{f}(x, y) := f(x) \quad \forall y$$
$$\overline{g}(x, y) := g(y) \quad \forall x$$

and now we may simply write:

$$F := \overline{f} + \overline{g}.$$

The situation is similar to that arising when adding a column matrix and a row matrix:

```
C = arange(2).reshape(-1,1)  # column
R = arange(2).reshape(1,-1)  # row
C + R                        # valid addition: array([[0.,1.],[1.,2.]])
```

This is especially useful when sampling functions of two variables, as shown in section *Typical examples*.

General mechanism

We have seen how to add a function and a scalar and how to build a function of two variables from two functions of one variable. Let us now focus on the general mechanism that makes this possible. The general mechanism consists of two steps: reshaping and extending.

First, the function g is reshaped to a function $\widetilde{g}$ that takes two arguments. One of these arguments is a dummy argument, which we take to be zero, as a convention:

$$\widetilde{g}(0, y) := g(y).$$

Mathematically, the domain of definition of $\widetilde{g}$ is now $\{0\} \times \mathbb{R}$. Then the function f is reshaped in a way similar to:

$$\widetilde{f}(x, 0) := f(x)$$

Now both $\widetilde{f}$ and $\widetilde{g}$ take two arguments, although one of them is always zero. We proceed to the next step, extending. It is the same step that converted a constant into a constant function (refer to the constant function example).

The function $\widetilde{f}$ is extended to:

$$\overline{f}(x, y) := \widetilde{f}(x, 0) \qquad \forall y$$

The function $\widetilde{g}$ is extended to:

$$\overline{g}(x, y) := \widetilde{g}(0, y) \qquad \forall y$$

Now the function of two variables F, which was sloppily defined by $F(x,y) = f(x) + g(y)$, may be defined without reference to its arguments:

$$F := \overline{f} + \overline{g}.$$

For example, let us describe the preceding mechanism for constants. A constant is a scalar, that is, a function of zero arguments. The reshaping step is thus to define the function of one (empty) variable:

$$\widetilde{C}(0) := C.$$

Now the extension step proceeds simply by:

$$\overline{C}(x) := \widetilde{C}(0).$$

Conventions

The last ingredient is the convention on how to add the extra arguments to a function, that is, how the reshaping is automatically performed. By convention, a function is automatically reshaped by adding zeros on the left.

For example, if a function g of two arguments has to be reshaped to three arguments, the new function would be defined by:

$$\widetilde{g}(0, x, y) := g(x, y).$$

Broadcasting arrays

We now repeat the observation that arrays are merely functions of several variables (refer to section *Mathematical preliminaries* in Chapter 4, *Linear Algebra – Arrays*). Array broadcasting thus follows exactly the same procedure as explained above for mathematical functions. Broadcasting is done automatically in NumPy.

In the following figure (*Figure 5.1*), we show what happens when adding a matrix of shape (4, 3) to a matrix of size (1, 3). The second matrix is of the shape (4, 3):

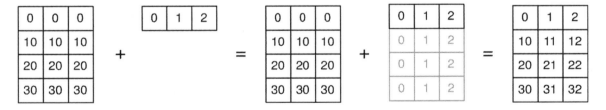

Figure 5.1: Broadcasting between a matrix and a vector.

The broadcasting problem

When NumPy is given two arrays with different shapes, and is asked to perform an operation that would require the two shapes to be the same, both arrays are broadcast to a common shape.

Suppose the two arrays have shapes s_1 and s_2. This broadcasting is performed in two steps:

1. If the shape s_1 is shorter than the shape s_2 then ones are added on the left of the shape s_1. This is a reshaping.
2. When the shapes have the same length, the array is extended to match the shape s_2 (if possible).

Suppose we want to add a vector of shape (3,) to a matrix of shape (4, 3). The vector needs be broadcast. The first operation is a reshaping; the shape of the vector is converted from (3,) to (1, 3). The second operation is an extension; the shape is converted from (1, 3) to (4, 3).

For instance, suppose a vector of size n is to be broadcast to the shape (m, n):

1. v is automatically reshaped to $(1, n)$.
2. v is extended to (m, n).

To demonstrate this we consider a matrix defined by:

```
M = array([[11, 12, 13, 14],
           [21, 22, 23, 24],
           [31, 32, 33, 34]])
```

and vector given by:

```
v = array([100, 200, 300, 400])
```

Now we may add M and v directly:

```
M + v # works directly
```

The result is this matrix:

$$\begin{bmatrix} 111 & 212 & 313 & 414 \\ 121 & 222 & 323 & 424 \\ 131 & 232 & 333 & 434 \end{bmatrix}$$

Shape mismatch

It is not possible to automatically broadcast a vector v of length n to the shape (n, m). This is illustrated in the following figure:

The broadcasting will fail, because the shape (n,) may not be automatically broadcast to the shape (m, n). The solution is to manually reshape v to the shape (n, 1). The broadcasting will now work as usual (by extension only):

```
M + v.reshape(-1,1)
```

Here is another example, define a matrix by:

```
M = array([[11, 12, 13, 14],
           [21, 22, 23, 24],
           [31, 32, 33, 34]])
```

and a vector by:

```
v = array([100, 200, 300])
```

Now automatic broadcasting will fail, because automatic reshaping does not work:

```
M + v # shape mismatch error
```

The solution is thus to take care of the reshaping manually. What we want in that case is to add 1 on the right, that is, transform the vector into a column matrix. The broadcasting then works directly:

```
M + v.reshape(-1,1)
```

For the shape parameter -1, refer to section *Accessing and changing the shape* of `Chapter 4`, *Linear Algebra - Arrays.* The result is this matrix:

$$\begin{bmatrix} 111 & 112 & 113 & 114 \\ 221 & 222 & 223 & 224 \\ 331 & 332 & 333 & 334 \end{bmatrix}$$

Typical examples

Let us examine some typical examples where broadcasting may come in handy.

Rescale rows

Suppose `M` is an $n \times m$ matrix, and we want to multiply each row by a coefficient. The coefficients are stored in a vector `coeff` with n components. In that case, automatic reshaping will not work, and we have to execute:

```
rescaled = M*coeff.reshape(-1,1)
```

Rescale columns

The setup is the same here, but we would like to rescale each column with a coefficient stored in a vector `coeff` of length m. In this case, automatic reshaping will work:

```
rescaled = M*coeff
```

Obviously, we may also do the reshaping manually and achieve the same result with:

```
rescaled = M*coeff.reshape(1,-1)
```

Functions of two variables

Suppose u and v are vectors and we want to form the matrix W with elements $w_{ij} = u_i + v_j$. This would correspond to the function $F(x, y) = x + y$. The matrix W is merely defined by:

```
W=u.reshape(-1,1) + v
```

If the vectors u and v are [0, 1] and [0, 1, 2] respectively, the result is:

$$W = \begin{bmatrix} 0 & 1 & 2 \\ 1 & 2 & 3 \end{bmatrix}$$

More generally, suppose that we want to sample the function $w(x, y) := \cos(x) + \sin(2y)$. Supposing that the vectors x and y are defined, the matrix w of sampled values is obtained by:

```
w = cos(x).reshape(-1,1) + sin(2*y)
```

Note that this is very frequently used in combination with ogrid. The vectors obtained from ogrid are already conveniently shaped for broadcasting. This allows for the following elegant sampling of the function $\cos(x) + \sin(2y)$:

```
x,y = ogrid[0:1:3j,0:1:3j]
# x,y are vectors with the contents of linspace(0,1,3)
w = cos(x) + sin(2*y)
```

The syntax of ogrid needs some explanation. First, ogrid is no function. It is an instance of a class with a __getitem__ method (refer to section *Attributes* in Chapter 8, *Classes*). That is why it is used with brackets instead of parentheses.

The two commands are equivalent:

```
x,y = ogrid[0:1:3j, 0:1:3j]
x,y = ogrid.__getitem__((slice(0, 1, 3j),slice(0, 1, 3j)))
```

The stride parameter in the preceding example is a complex number. This is to indicate that it is the number of steps instead of the step size. The rules for the stride parameter might be confusing at first glance:

- If the stride is a real number, then it defines the size of the steps between start and stop and stop is not included in the list.
- If the stride is a complex number s, then the integer part of s.imag defines the number of steps between start and stop and stop is included in the list.

Another example for the output of `ogrid` is a tuple with two arrays, which can be used for broadcasting:

```
x,y = ogrid[0:1:3j, 0:1:3j]
```

gives:

```
array([[ 0. ],
       [ 0.5],
       [ 1. ]])
array([[ 0. ,  0.5,  1. ]])
```

which is equivalent to:

```
x,y = ogrid[0:1.5:.5, 0:1.5:.5]
```

Sparse matrices

Matrices with a small number of nonzero entries are called **sparse matrices**. Sparse matrices occur, for example, in scientific computing when describing discrete differential operators in the context of numerically solving partial differential equations.

Sparse matrices often have large dimensions, sometimes so large that the entire matrix (with zero entries) would not even fit in the available memory. This is one motivation for a special type for sparse matrices. Another motivation is better performance of operations where zero matrix entries can be avoided.

There are only a very limited number of algorithms for general, unstructured sparse matrices in linear algebra. Most of them are iterative in nature and based on efficient implementations of matrix-vector multiplication for sparse matrices.

Examples for sparse matrices are diagonal or banded matrices. The simple pattern of these matrices allows straightforward storing strategies; the principal diagonal and the sub- and super-diagonals are stored in 1D arrays. Conversion from a sparse representation to the classical array type and vice-versa can be done by the command `diag`.

In general, there is not such a simple structure and the description of sparse matrices requires special techniques and standards. Here we present a row and a column oriented type for sparse matrices, both available through the module `scipy.sparse`.

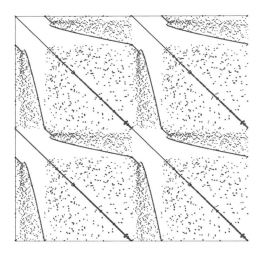

Figure 5.2: A stiffness matrix from a finite element model of an elastic plate. The pixels denote nonzero entries in the 1250 × 1250 matrix

Sparse matrix formats

The `scipy.sparse` module provides many different storing formats from sparse matrices. We describe here only the most important ones: CSR, CSC, and LIL. The LIL format should be used for generating and altering sparse matrices; CSR and CSC are efficient formats for matrix-matrix and matrix-vector operations.

Compressed sparse row

The compressed sparse row format (CSR) uses three arrays: `data`, `indptr`, and `indices`:

- The 1D array `data` stores all the nonzero values in order. It has as many elements as there are nonzero elements, often denoted by the variable `nnz`.

- The 1D array `indptr` contains integers such that `indptr[i]` is the index of the element in `data`, which is the first nonzero element of row *i*. If the entire row *i* is zero, then `indptr[i]==indptr[i+1]`. If the original matrix has *m* rows, then `len(indptr)==m+1`.
- The 1D array `indices` contains the column index information in such a way that `indices[indptr[i]:indptr[i+1]]` is an integer array with the column indexes of the nonzero elements in row *i*. Obviously, `len(indices)==len(data)==nnz`.

Let's see an example:
The CSR format of the matrix:

$$A = \begin{pmatrix} 1. & 0. & 2. & 0. \\ 0. & 0. & 0. & 0. \\ 3. & 0. & 0. & 0. \\ 1. & 0. & 0. & 4. \end{pmatrix}$$

is given by the three arrays:

```
data = (1. 2. 3. 4.)
indptr = (0 2 2 3 5)
indices = (0 2 0 0 3)
```

The module `scipy.sparse` provides a type, `csr_matrix`, with a constructor, which can be used in the following ways:

- With a 2D array as argument
- With a matrix in one of the other sparse formats in `scipy.sparse`
- With a shape argument, `(m,n)`, to generate a zero matrix in CSR format
- By a 1D array for the `data` and an integer array `ij` with the shape `(2,len(data))` such that `ij[0,k]` is the row index and `ij[1,k]` is the column index of `data[k]` of the matrix
- The three arguments, `data`, `indptr`, and `indices`, can be given to the constructor directly

The first two options are there for conversion purposes while the last two directly define the sparse matrix.

Consider the above example in python look like:

```
import scipy.sparse as sp
A = array([[1,0,2,0],[0,0,0,0],[3.,0.,0.,0.],[1.,0.,0.,4.]])
AS = sp.csr_matrix(A)
```

Among others, the following attributes are provided:

```
AS.data       # returns array([ 1., 2., 3., 1., 4.])
AS.indptr     # returns array([0, 2, 2, 3, 5])
AS.indices    # returns array([0, 2, 0, 0, 3])
AS.nnz        # returns 5
```

Compressed Sparse Column

The CSR format has a column oriented twin – the compressed sparse column (CSC) format. The only difference in it compared to the CSR format is the definition of the indptr and indices arrays, which are now column-related. The type for the CSC format is csc_matrix and its use corresponds to csr_matrix, explained previously in this section.

Continuing the same example in CSC format:

```
import scipy.sparse as sp
A = array([[1,0,2,0],[0,0,0,0],[3.,0.,0.,0.],[1.,0.,0.,4.]])
AS = sp.csc_matrix(A)
AS.data       # returns array([ 1., 3., 1., 2., 4.])
AS.indptr     # returns array([0, 3, 3, 4, 5])
AS.indices    # returns array([0, 2, 3, 0, 3])
AS.nnz        # returns 5
```

Row-based linked list format

The linked list sparse format stores the nonzero matrix entries rowwise in a list data such that data[k] is a list of the nonzero entries in row *k*. If all entries in that row are 0, it contains an empty list.

A second list, rows, contains at position *k* a list of column indexes of the nonzero elements in row *k*. Here is an example in **Row-Based linked List Format (LIL)** format:

```
import scipy.sparse as sp
A = array([[1,0,2,0],[0,0,0,0], [3.,0.,0.,0.], [1.,0.,0.,4.]])
AS = sp.lil_matrix(A)
AS.data      # returns array([[1.0, 2.0], [], [3.0], [1.0, 4.0]],
dtype=object)
```

```
AS.rows      # returns array([[0, 2], [], [0], [0, 3]], dtype=object)
AS.nnz       # returns 5
```

Altering and slicing matrices in LIL format

The LIL format is the one best suited for slicing, that is, extracting submatrices in LIL format, and for changing the sparsity pattern by inserting nonzero elements. Slicing is demonstrated by the next example:

```
BS = AS[1:3,0:2]
BS.data      # returns array([[], [3.0]], dtype=object)
BS.rows      # returns array([[], [0]], dtype=object)
```

Insertion of a new nonzero element automatically updates the attributes:

```
AS[0,1] = 17
AS.data # returns array([[1.0, 17.0, 2.0], [], [3.0], [1.0, 4.0]])
AS.rows              # returns array([[0, 1, 2], [], [0], [0, 3]])
AS.nnz               # returns 6
```

These operations are discouraged in the other sparse matrix formats as they are extremely inefficient.

Generating sparse matrices

The NumPy commands eye, identity, diag, and rand have their sparse counterparts. They take an additional argument; it specifies the sparse matrix format of the resulting matrix.

The following commands generate the identity matrix but in different sparse matrix formats:

```
import scipy.sparse as sp
sp.eye(20,20,format = 'lil')
sp.spdiags(ones((20,)),0,20,20, format = 'csr')
sp.identity(20,format ='csc')
```

The sp.rand command takes an additional argument describing the density of the generated random matrix. A dense matrix has density 1 while a zero matrix has density 0:

```
import scipy.sparse as sp
AS=sp.rand(20,200,density=0.1,format='csr')
AS.nnz # returns 400
```

There is no direct correspondence to the NumPy command `zeroes`. Matrices completely filled with zeros are generated by instantiating the corresponding type with the shape parameters as constructor parameters:

```
import scipy.sparse as sp
Z=sp.csr_matrix((20,200))
Z.nnz    # returns 0
```

Sparse matrix methods

There are methods to convert one sparse type into another or into an array:

```
AS.toarray # converts sparse formats to a numpy array
AS.tocsr
AS.tocsc
AS.tolil
```

The type of a sparse matrix can be inspected by the methods `issparse`, `isspmatrix_lil`, `isspmatrix_csr`, and `isspmatrix_csc`.

Elementwise operations +, *, /, and ** on sparse matrices are defined as for NumPy arrays. Regardless of the sparse matrix format of the operands, the result is always a `csr_matrix`. Applying elementwise operating functions to sparse matrices requires first transforming them to either CSR or CSC format and applying the functions to their `data` attribute, as demonstrated by the next example.

The elementwise sine of a sparse matrix can be defined by an operation on its `data` attribute:

```
import scipy.sparse as sp
def sparse_sin(A):
    if not (sp.isspmatrix_csr(A) or sp.isspmatrix_csc(A)):
        A = A.tocsr()
    A.data = sin(A.data)
    return A
```

For matrix-matrix or matrix-vector multiplications, there is a sparse matrix method, `dot`. It returns either a `csr_matrix` or a 1D NumPy `array`:

```
import scipy.sparse as sp
A = array([[1,0,2,0],[0,0,0,0],[3.,0.,0.,0.],[1.,0.,0.,4.]])
AS = sp.csr_matrix(A)
b = array([1,2,3,4])
c = AS.dot(b)        # returns array([ 7., 0., 3., 17.])
C = AS.dot(AS)       # returns  csr_matrix
d = dot(AS,b)        # does not return the expected result!
```

Avoid using NumPy's command `dot` on sparse matrices, as this might lead to unexpected results. Use the command `dot` from `scipy.sparse` instead.

Other linear algebra operations such as system solving, least squares, eigenvalues, and singular values are provided by the `scipy.sparse.linalg` module.

Summary

The concept of views is one of the important topics you should have learned from this chapter. Missing this topic will give you a hard time when debugging your code. Boolean arrays occur at various places throughout this book. They are handy and compact tools for avoiding lengthy `if` constructions and loops when working with arrays. In nearly all large computational projects, sparse matrices become an issue. You saw how these are handled and which related methods are available.

6
Plotting

Plotting in Python can be done with the `pyplot` part of the matplotlib module. With matplotlib you can create high-quality figures and graphics and also plot and visualize your results. Matplotlib is open source and freely available software, [21]. The matplotlib website also contains excellent documentation with examples, [35]. In this section, we will show you how to use the most common features. The examples in the upcoming sections assume that you have imported the module as:

```
from matplotlib.pyplot import *
```

In case you want to use the plotting commands in IPython, it is recommended that you run the magic command `%matplotlib` directly after starting the IPython shell. This prepares IPython for interactive plotting.

Basic plotting

The standard plotting function is `plot`. Calling `plot(x,y)` creates a figure window with a plot of y as a function of x. The input arguments are arrays (or lists) of equal length. It is also possible to use `plot(y)`, in which case the values in y will be plotted against their index, that is, `plot(y)` is a short form of `plot(range(len(y)),y)`.

Here is an example that shows how to plot $\sin(x)$ for $x \in [-2\pi, 2\pi]$ using 200 sample points and sets markers at every fourth point:

```
# plot sin(x) for some interval
x = linspace(-2*pi,2*pi,200)
plot(x,sin(x))

# plot marker for every 4th point
samples = x[::4]
```

```
plot(samples,sin(samples),'r*')

# add title and grid lines
title('Function sin(x) and some points plotted')
grid()
```

The result is shown in the following figure (*Figure 6.1*):

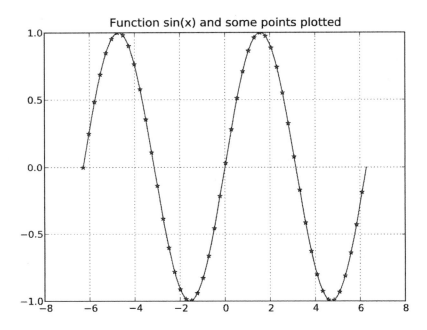

Figure 6.1: A plot of the function sin(x) with grid lines shown.

As you can see, the standard plot is a solid blue curve. Each axis gets automatically scaled to fit the values but can also be set manually. Color and plot options can be given after the first two input arguments. Here, r* indicates red star-shaped markers. Formatting is covered in more detail in the next section. The `title` command puts a title text string above the plot area.

Calling `plot` multiple times will overlay the plots in the same window. To get a new clean figure window, use `figure()`. The `figure` command might contain an integer, for example, `figure(2)`, which can be used to switch between figure windows. If there is no figure window with that number, a new one is created, otherwise, the window is activated for plotting and all subsequent plotting commands apply to that window.

Multiple plots can be explained using the `legend` function, along with adding labels to each plot call. The following example fits polynomials to a set of points using the commands `polyfit` and `polyval`, and plots the result with a legend:

```
# —Polyfit example—
x = range(5)
y = [1,2,1,3,5]
p2 = polyfit(x,y,2)
p4 = polyfit(x,y,4)

# plot the polynomials and points
xx = linspace(-1,5,200)
plot(xx, polyval(p2, xx), label='fitting polynomial of degree 2')
plot(xx, polyval(p4, xx),
            label='interpolating polynomial of degree 4')
plot(x,y,'*')

# set the axis and legend
axis([-1,5,0,6])
legend(loc='upper left', fontsize='small')
```

Here you can also see how to manually set the range of the axis using `axis([xmin,xmax,ymin,ymax])`. The `legend` command takes optional arguments on placement and formatting; in this case the legend is put in the upper-left corner and typeset with a small font size, as shown in the following figure (*Figure 6.2*).

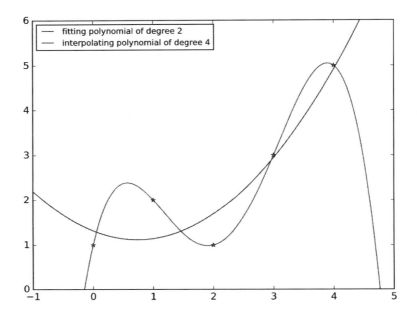

Figure 6.2: Two polynomials fitted to the same points.

As final examples for basic plotting, we demonstrate how to do scatter plots and logarithmic plots in two dimensions.

Example of 2D point scatter plot:

```
# create random 2D points
import numpy
x1 = 2*numpy.random.standard_normal((2,100))
x2 = 0.8*numpy.random.standard_normal((2,100)) + array([[6],[2]])
plot(x1[0],x1[1],'*')
plot(x2[0],x2[1],'r*')
title('2D scatter plot')
```

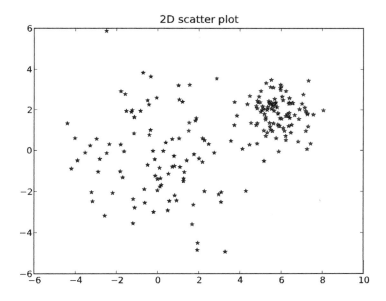

Figure 6.3(a): An example of a scatter plot

The following code is an example of a logarithmic plot using `loglog`:

```
# log both x and y axis
x = linspace(0,10,200)
loglog(x,2*x**2, label = 'quadratic polynomial',
                        linestyle = '-', linewidth = 3)
loglog(x,4*x**4, label = '4th degree polynomial',
                        linestyle = '-.', linewidth = 3)
loglog(x,5*exp(x), label = 'exponential function', linewidth = 3)
title('Logarithmic plots')
legend(loc = 'best')
```

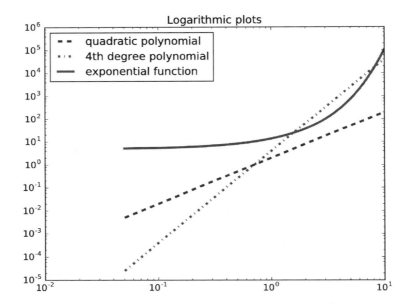

Figure 6.3(b): An example of a plot with logarithmic x and y axis

The examples shown in the preceding figure (*Figure 6.3(a)* and *Figure 6.3(b)*) used some parameters of `plot` and `loglog` which allow special formatting. In the next section, we will explain the parameters in more detail.

Formatting

The appearance of figures and plots can be styled and customized to look how you want them to look. Some important variables are `linewidth`, which controls the thickness of plot lines; `xlabel`, `ylabel`, which set the axis labels, `color` for plot colors, and `transparent` for transparency. This section will tell you how to use some of them. The following is an example with more keywords:

```
k = 0.2
x = [sin(2*n*k) for n in range(20)]
plot(x, color='green', linestyle='dashed', marker='o',
              markerfacecolor='blue', markersize=12, linewidth=6)
```

There are short commands that can be used if you only need basic style changes, for example, setting the color and line style. The following table (*Table 6.1*) shows some examples of these formatting commands. You may use either the short string syntax `plot(..., 'ro-')`, or the more explicit syntax `plot(..., marker='o', color='r', linestyle='-')`.

Line Style linestyle		Marker marker		Color color	
String Argument	Description	String Argument	Description	String Argument	Description
-	solid	.	point	b	blue
--	dashed	,	pixel	g	green
-.	dashed dotted	o	circle	r	red
:	dotted	v , ^	triangle down up	c	cyan
		<, >	triangle left, right	m	magenta
		s, p	square, pentagon	y	yellow
		*, + , x	star, plus, x	k	black
		d, D	thin diamond, diamond	w	white

Table 6.1: Some common plot formatting arguments

To set the color to green with the `'o'` marker we write:

```
plot(x,'go')
```

To plot histograms instead of regular plots, the `hist` command is used:

```
# random vector with normal distribution
sigma, mu = 2, 10
x = sigma*numpy.random.standard_normal(10000)+mu
hist(x,50,normed=1)
z = linspace(0,20,200)
plot(z, (1/sqrt(2*pi*sigma**2))*exp(-(z-mu)**2/(2*sigma**2)),'g')
# title with LaTeX formatting
title('Histogram with '.format(mu,sigma))
```

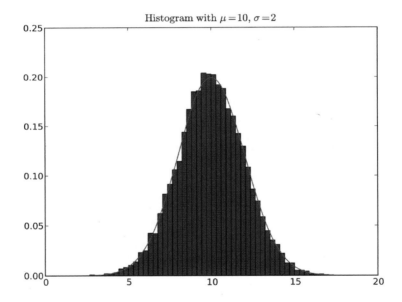

Figure 6.4 normal distribution with 50 bins and a green curve indicating the true distribution

The resulting plot looks similar to the preceding figure (*Figure 6.4*). The title, and any other text, can be formatted using LaTeX to show mathematical formulas. LaTeX formatting is enclosed within a pair of $ signs. Also, note the string formatting done using the `format` method, refer to section *Strings* in `Chapter 2`, *Variables and Basic Types*.

Sometimes the brackets for the string formatting interfere with LaTeX bracket environments. If this occurs, replace the LaTeX bracket with a double bracket, for example, x_{1} should be replaced with x_{{1}}. The text might contain sequences that overlap with string escape sequences, for example, \tau will be interpreted as the tab character \t. An easy workaround is to add r before the string, for example r'\tau'; this makes it a raw string.

Placing several plots in one figure window can be done using the subplot command. Consider the following example, which iteratively averages out the noise on a sine curve.

```
def avg(x):
    """ simple running average """
    return (roll(x,1) + x + roll(x,-1)) / 3
# sine function with noise
x = linspace(-2*pi, 2*pi,200)
y = sin(x) + 0.4*rand(200)

# make successive subplots
for iteration in range(3):
    subplot(3, 1, iteration + 1)
    plot(x,y, label = '{:d} average{}'.format(iteration, 's' if iteration >
1 else ''))
    yticks([])
    legend(loc = 'lower left', frameon = False)
    y = avg(y) #apply running average
subplots_adjust(hspace = 0.7)
```

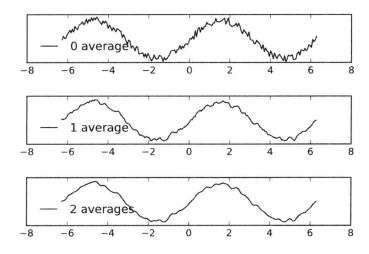

Figure 6.5: An example of plotting several times in the same figure window.

The function `avg` uses a `roll` call to shift all values of the array. `subplot` takes three arguments: the number of vertical plots, the number of horizontal plots, and an index indicating which location to plot in (counted row-wise). Note that we used the `subplots_adjust` command to add extra space to adjust the distance between both the subplots.

A useful command is `savefig` which lets you save a figure as an image (this can also be done from the figure window). Many image and file formats are supported by this command, they are specified by the filename's extension as:

```
savefig('test.pdf')   # save to pdf
```

or

```
savefig('test.svg')   # save to svg (editable format)
```

You can place the image against a non-white background, for example, a webpage. For this, the `transparent` parameter can be set to make the figure's background transparent:

```
savefig('test.pdf', transparent=True)
```

If you intend to embed a figure into a LaTeX document, it is recommended that you reduce the surrounding white space by setting the figure's bounding box tight around the drawing, as shown here:

```
savefig('test.pdf', bbox_inches='tight')
```

Meshgrid and contours

A common task is a graphical representation of a scalar function over a rectangle:

$$f : [a, b] \times [c, d] \to \mathbb{R}$$

For this, first we have to generate a grid on the rectangle [a,b] x [c,d]. This is done using the `meshgrid` command:

```
n = ... # number of discretization points along the x-axis
m = ... # number of discretization points along the x-axis
X, Y = meshgrid(linspace(a,b,n), linspace(c,d,m))
```

X and Y are arrays with (n,m) shape such that $X[i,j], Y[i,j]$ contains the coordinates of the grid point $P_{i,j}$ as shown in the next figure *(Figure 6.6)*:

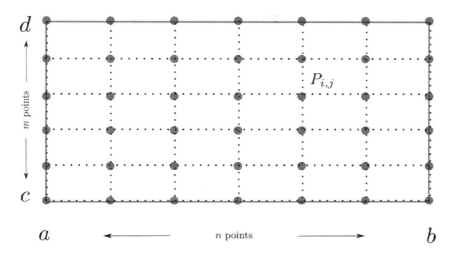

Figure 6.6: A rectangle discretized by meshgrid

A rectangle discretized by `meshgrid` will be used to visualize the behavior of an iteration. Bur first we will use it to plot level curves of a function. This is done by the command `contour`.

As an example we choose Rosenbrock's banana function:

$$f(x,y) = (1-x)^2 + 100(y-x^2)^2$$

It is used to challenge optimization methods. The function values descend towards a banana-shaped valley, which itself decreases slowly towards the function's global minimum at (1, 1).

First we display the level curves using `contour`.

```
rosenbrockfunction = lambda x,y: (1-x)**2+100*(y-x**2)**2
X,Y = meshgrid(linspace(-.5,2.,100), linspace(-1.5,4.,100))
Z = rosenbrockfunction(X,Y)
contour(X,Y,Z,logspace(-0.5,3.5,20,base=10),cmap='gray')
title('Rosenbrock Function: ')
xlabel('x')
ylabel('y')
```

This plots the level curve at the levels given by the fourth parameter and uses the colormap `gray`. Furthermore, we used logarithmically spaced steps from $10^{0.5}$ to 10^3 using the function `logscale` to define the levels, as shown in the next figure.

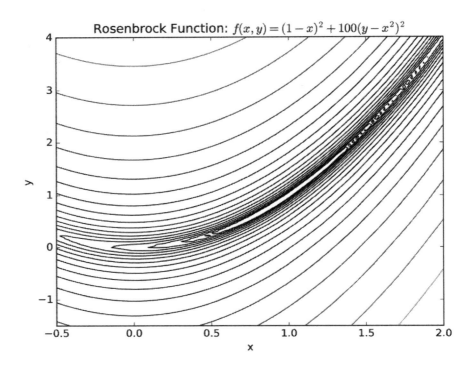

Figure 6.7: A contour plot of Rosenbrock function

In the preceding example, an anonymous function indicated by the keyword `lambda` is used to keep the code compact. Anonymous functions are explained in section *Anonymous functions – the lambda keyword* in `Chapter 7`, *Functions, Anonymous functions*. If levels are not given as arguments to `contour`, the function chooses appropriate levels by itself .

The `contourf` function performs the same function as `contour` but fills the plot with colors according to different levels. Contour plots are ideal for visualizing the behavior of a numerical method. We illustrate this here by showing the iterations of an optimization method.

We continue the preceding example and depict the steps towards the minimum of the Rosenbrock function generated by Powell's method, [27], which we will apply to find the minimum of the Rosenbrock function:

```
import scipy.optimize as so
rosenbrockfunction = lambda x,y: (1-x)**2+100*(y-x**2)**2
X,Y=meshgrid(linspace(-.5,2.,100),linspace(-1.5,4.,100))
Z=rosenbrockfunction(X,Y)
cs=contour(X,Y,Z,logspace(0,3.5,7,base=10),cmap='gray')
rosen=lambda x: rosenbrockfunction(x[0],x[1])
solution, iterates = so.fmin_powell(rosen,x0=array([0,-0.7]),retall=True)
x,y=zip(*iterates)
plot(x,y,'ko') # plot black bullets
plot(x,y,'k:',linewidth=1) # plot black dotted lines
title("Steps of Powell's method to compute a  minimum")
clabel(cs)
```

The iterative method `fmin_powell` applies Powell's method to find a minimum. It is started by a given start value of x_0 and reports all iterates when the option `retall=True` is given. After sixteen iterations, the solution $x=0$, $y=0$ was found. The iterations are depicted as bullets in the following contour plot (*Figure 6.8*).

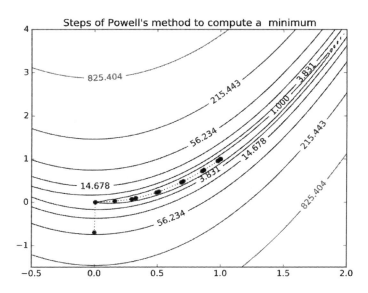

Figure 6.8: A contour plot of Rosenbrock function with a search path of an optimization method

`contour` also creates a contour set object that we assigned to the variable `cs`. This is then used by `clabel` to annotate the levels of the corresponding function values, as shown in the preceding figure (*Figure 6.8*).

Images and contours

Let us take a look at some examples of visualizing arrays as images. The following function will create a matrix of color values for the Mandelbrot fractal. Here we consider a fixed point iteration, that depends on a complex parameter c:

$$z_{n+1} = z_n^2 + c \quad \text{with} \quad z_0 = c \in \mathbb{C}$$

Depending on the choice of this parameter it may or may not create a bounded sequence of complex values z_n.

For every value of c, we check if z_n exceeds a prescribed bound. If it remains below the bound within `maxit` iterations, we assume the sequence to be bounded.

Note how, in the following piece of code,`meshgrid` is used to generate a matrix of complex parameter values c:

```
def mandelbrot(h,w, maxit=20):
    X,Y = meshgrid(linspace(-2, 0.8, w), linspace(-1.4, 1.4, h))
    c = X + Y*1j
    z = c
    exceeds = zeros(z.shape, dtype=bool)

    for iteration in range(maxit):
        z   = z**2 + c
        exceeded = abs(z) > 4
        exceeds_now = exceeded & (logical_not(exceeds))
        exceeds[exceeds_now] = True
        z[exceeded] = 2  # limit the values to avoid overflow
    return exceeds

imshow(mandelbrot(400,400),cmap='gray')
axis('off')
```

The command `imshow` displays the matrix as an image. The selected color map shows the regions where the sequence appeared unbounded in white and others in black. Here we used `axis('off')` to turn off the axis as this might be not so useful for images.

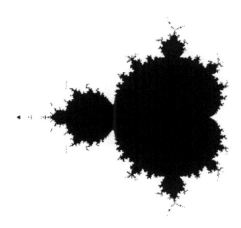

Figure 6.9: An example of using imshow to visualize a matrix as an image.

By default, `imshow` uses interpolation to make the images look nicer. This is clearly seen when the matrices are small. The next figure shows the difference between using:

```
imshow(mandelbrot(40,40),cmap='gray')
```

and

```
imshow(mandelbrot(40,40), interpolation='nearest', cmap='gray')
```

In the second example, pixel values are just replicated.

Figure 6.10: The difference between using the linear interpolation of imshow compared to using nearest neighbor interpolation

For more details on working and plotting with images using Python refer to [30].

Matplotlib objects

Till now, we have used the `pyplot` module of matplotlib. This module makes it easy for us to use the most important plot commands directly. Mostly, we are interested in creating a figure and display it immediately. Sometimes, though, we want to generate a figure that should be modified later by changing some of its attributes. This requires us to work with graphical objects in an object-oriented way. In this section, we will present some basic steps to modify figures. For a more sophisticated object oriented approach to plotting in Python, you have to leave `pyplot` and have to dive directly into `matplotlib` with its extensive documentation.

The axes object

When creating a plot that should be modified later, we need references to a figure and an axes object. For this we have to create a figure first and then define some axes and their location in the figure. And we should not forget to assign these objects to a variable:

```
fig = figure()
ax = subplot(111)
```

A figure can have several axes objects depending on the use of `subplot`. In a second step plots are associated with a given axes object:

```
fig = figure(1)
ax = subplot(111)
x = linspace(0,2*pi,100)
# We set up a function that modulates the amplitude of the sin function
amod_sin = lambda x: (1.-0.1*sin(25*x))*sin(x)
# and plot both...
ax.plot(x,sin(x),label = 'sin')
ax.plot(x, amod_sin(x), label = 'modsin')
```

Here we used an anonymous function indicated by the `lambda` keyword . We will explain this construct later in section *Anonymous functions – the lambda keyword* in Chapter 7, *Functions*. In fact, these two plot commands fill the list `ax.lines` with two `Lines2D` objects:

```
ax.lines #[<matplotlib.lines.Line2D at ...>, <matplotlib.lines.Line2D at
...>]
```

It is a good practice to use labels so that we can later identify objects in an easy way:

```
for il,line in enumerate(ax.lines):
    if line.get_label() == 'sin':
        break
```

We set up now things in a way that allows further modifications. The figure we got so far is shown in preceding figure (*Figure 6.11, left*).

Modifying line properties

We just identified a particular line object by its label. It is an element of the list `ax.lines` list with the index `il`. All its properties are collected in a dictionary

```
dict_keys(['marker', 'markeredgewidth', 'data', 'clip_box',
'solid_capstyle', 'clip_on', 'rasterized', 'dash_capstyle', 'path',
'ydata', 'markeredgecolor', 'xdata', 'label', 'alpha', 'linestyle',
'antialiased', 'snap', 'transform', 'url',
'transformed_clip_path_and_affine', 'clip_path', 'path_effects',
'animated', 'contains', 'fillstyle', 'sketch_params', 'xydata',
'drawstyle', 'markersize', 'linewidth', 'figure', 'markerfacecolor',
'pickradius', 'agg_filter', 'dash_joinstyle', 'color', 'solid_joinstyle',
'picker', 'markevery', 'axes', 'children', 'gid', 'zorder', 'visible',
'markerfacecoloralt'])
```

which can be obtained by the command:

```
ax.lines[il].properties()
```

They can be changed by corresponding setter methods. Let us change the line style of the sine – curve:

```
ax.lines[il].set_linestyle('-.')
ax.lines[il].set_linewidth(2)
```

We can even modify the data, as shown:

```
ydata=ax.lines[il].get_ydata()
ydata[-1]=-0.5
ax.lines[il].set_ydata(ydata)
```

The result is shown in the next figure(*Figure 6.11, right*):

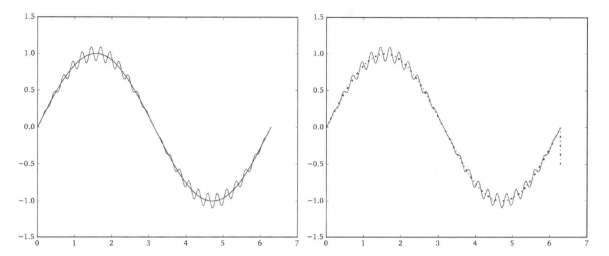

Figure 6.11: The amplitude modulated sine-function (left) and a curve with the last data point corrupted (right).

Annotations

One useful axes method is `annotate`. It sets an annotation at a given position and points, with an arrow, to another position in the drawing. The arrow can be given properties in a dictionary:

```
annot1=ax.annotate('amplitude modulated\n curve', (2.1,1.0),(3.2,0.5),
        arrowprops={'width':2,'color':'k',
 'connectionstyle':'arc3,rad=+0.5',
                    'shrink':0.05},
        verticalalignment='bottom', horizontalalignment='left',fontsize=15,
                bbox={'facecolor':'gray', 'alpha':0.1, 'pad':10})
annot2=ax.annotate('corrupted data', (6.3,-0.5),(6.1,-1.1),
        arrowprops={'width':0.5,'color':'k','shrink':0.1},
        horizontalalignment='center', fontsize=12)
```

In the first annotation example above, the arrow points to a point with the coordinates (*2.1, 1.0*) and the left bottom coordinate of the text is (*3.2, 0.5*). If not otherwise specified, the coordinates are given in the convenient data-coordinate system, which refers to the data used to generate the plots.

Furthermore, we demonstrated a couple of arrow properties specified by the `arrowprop` dictionary. You can scale the arrow by the `shrink` key. The setting `'shrink':0.05` reduces the arrow size by 5% to keep a distance to the curve it points to. You can let the arrow follow a spline arc or give it other shapes using the `connectionstyle` key.

Text properties or even a bounding box around the text can be made by extra keyword arguments to the annotate method, refer to the following figure (*Figure 6.12, left*):

Experimenting with annotations requires sometimes to remove attempts that we would like to reject. Therefore we assigned the annotate object to a variable, which allows us to remove the annotation by its `remove` method:

```
annot1.remove()
```

Filling areas between curves

Filling is an ideal tool to highlight differences between curves, such as noise on top of expected data, approximations versus exact functions, and so on.

Filling is done by the axis method

```
ax.fill_between(x,y1,y2)
```

For the next figure we used:

```
axf = ax.fill_between(x, sin(x), amod_sin(x), facecolor='gray')
```

`where` is a very convenient parameter that needs a Boolean array to specify the additional filling conditions.

```
axf = ax.fill_between(x, sin(x), amod_sin(x),where=amod_sin(x)-sin(x) > 0,
facecolor='gray')
```

The Boolean array which selects the regions to fill is `amod_sin(x)-sin(x) > 0`.

The next figure shows the curve with both variants of filling areas:

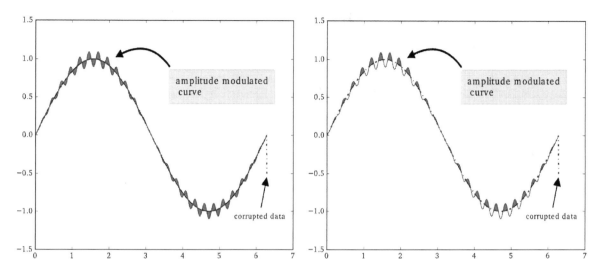

Figure 6.12: The amplitude modulated sin-function with annotations and filled areas(left) and a modified figure with only partially filled areas by using the where parameter (right).

If you test these commands yourself, do not forget to remove the complete filling before you try out the partial filling, otherwise you will not see any change:

```
axf.remove()
```

Related filling commands are `fill` and `fill_betweenx`.

Ticks and ticklabels

Figures in talks, posters, and publications look much nicer if they are not overloaded with unnecessary information. You want to direct the spectator to those parts that contain the message. In our example, we clean up the picture by removing ticks from the *x*-axis and *y*-axis and by introducing problem related tick labels:

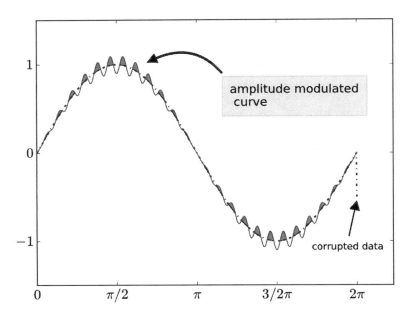

Figure 6.13: The completed example of the amplitude modulated sine – function with annotations and filled areas and modified ticks and tick labels.

```
ax.set_xticks(array([0,pi/2,pi,3/2*pi,2*pi]))
ax.set_xticklabels(('$0$','$\pi/2$','$\pi$','$3/2 \pi$','$2
\pi$'),fontsize=18)
ax.set_yticks(array([-1.,0.,1]))
ax.set_yticklabels(('$-1$','$0$','$1$'),fontsize=18)
```

Note that we used LaTeX formatting in the strings to represent Greek letters, to set formulas correctly, and to use a LaTeX font. It is also a good practice to increase the font size so that the resulting figure can be scaled down into a text document without affecting the readability of the axes. The final result of this guiding example is shown in the previous figure (*Figure 6.13*).

Making 3D plots

There are some useful `matplotlib` tool kits and modules that can be used for a variety of special purposes. In this section, we describe a method for producing 3D-plots.

The `mplot3d` toolkit provides 3D plotting of points, lines, contours, surfaces, and all other basic components as well as 3D rotation and scaling. Making a 3D plot is done by adding the keyword `projection='3d'` to the axes object as shown in the following example:

```
from mpl_toolkits.mplot3d import axes3d

fig = figure()
ax = fig.gca(projection='3d')
# plot points in 3D
class1 = 0.6 * random.standard_normal((200,3))
ax.plot(class1[:,0],class1[:,1],class1[:,2],'o')
class2 = 1.2 * random.standard_normal((200,3)) + array([5,4,0])
ax.plot(class2[:,0],class2[:,1],class2[:,2],'o')
class3 = 0.3 * random.standard_normal((200,3)) + array([0,3,2])
ax.plot(class3[:,0],class3[:,1],class3[:,2],'o')
```

As you can see, you need to import the `axes3D` type from `mplot3d`. The resulting plot displays the scattered 3D-data which can be seen in the following figure (*Figure 6.14*)

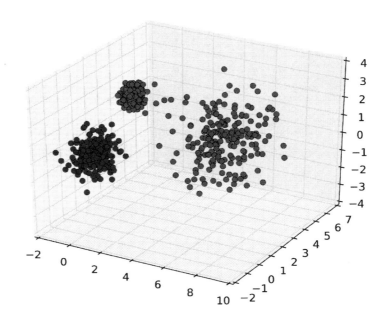

Figure 6.14: Plotting 3D data using mplot3d toolkit

Plotting surfaces is just as easy. The following example uses the built-in function `get_test_data` to create a sample data for plotting a surface. Consider the following example of a surface plot with transparency.

```
X,Y,Z = axes3d.get_test_data(0.05)

fig = figure()
ax = fig.gca(projection='3d')
# surface plot with transparency 0.5
ax.plot_surface(X,Y,Z,alpha=0.5)
```

The *alpha* value sets the transparency. The surface plot is shown in the following figure (*Figure 6.15*).

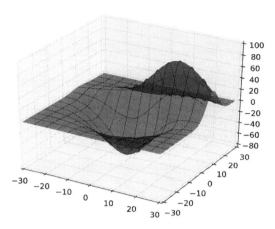

Figure 6.15: Example for plotting a surface mesh with three 2D projections.

You can also plot contours in any of the coordinate projections as in the next example.

```
fig = figure()
ax = fig.gca(projection = '3d')
ax.plot_wireframe(X,Y,Z,rstride = 5,cstride = 5)

# plot contour projection on each axis plane
ax.contour(X,Y,Z, zdir='z',offset = -100)
ax.contour(X,Y,Z, zdir='x',offset = -40)
ax.contour(X,Y,Z, zdir='y',offset = 40)

# set axis limits
ax.set_xlim3d(-40,40)
ax.set_ylim3d(-40,40)
ax.set_zlim3d(-100,100)

# set labels
ax.set_xlabel('X axis')
ax.set_ylabel('Y axis')
ax.set_zlabel('Z axis')
```

Note the commands for setting the axis limits. The standard `matplotlib` commands for setting the axis limits are `axis([-40, 40, -40, 40])`, this works fine for 2D plots. However, `axis([-40,40,-40,40,-40,40])` does not work. For 3D plots you need to use the object oriented version of the commands, `ax.set_xlim3d(-40,40)` and likewise. The same goes for labeling the axis; note the commands for setting the labels. For 2D plots you can do `xlabel('X axis')` and `ylabel('Y axis')` but there is no `zlabel` command. Instead, in 3D plots you need to use `ax.set_xlabel('X axis')` and likewise, as shown in the preceding example.

The resulting figure from this code is the following

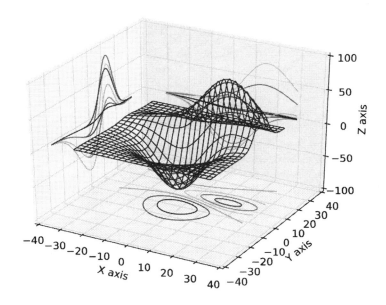

There are many options for formatting the appearance of the plots, including color and transparency of surfaces. The `mplot3d` documentation website, [23], has the details.

Making movies from plots

If you have data that evolves, you might want to save it as a movie besides showing it in a figure window, similar to the `savefig` command. One way to do this is with the `visvis` module available at visvis (refer to [37] for more information).

Here is a simple example of evolving a circle using an implicit representation. Let the circle be represented by the zero level, $\{x; f(x) = 0\}$, of a function $f : \mathbb{R}^2 \to \mathbb{R}$. Alternatively, consider the disk $\{x; f(x) \leq 0\}$ inside the zero set. If the value of f decreases at a rate v then the circle will move outward with rate $v/\|\nabla f\|$.

This can be implemented as:

```
import visvis.vvmovie as vv

# create initial function values
x = linspace(-255,255,511)
X,Y = meshgrid(x,x)
f = sqrt(X*X+Y*Y) - 40 #radius 40

# evolve and store in a list
imlist = []
for iteration in range(200):
    imlist.append((f>0)*255)
    f -= 1 # move outwards one pixel
vv.images2swf.writeSwf('circle_evolution.swf',imlist)
```

The result is a Flash movie (*.swf file) of a growing black circle, as shown in the next figure (*Figure 6.16*):

Figure 6.16: An example of evolving a circle

In this example, a list of arrays was used to create the movie. The `visvis` module can also save an GIF animation and on certain platforms an AVI animation (*.gif and *.avi files), and there is also the possibility to capturing movie frames directly from the figure window. These options, however, require some more packages to be installed on your system (for example, `PyOpenGL` and `PIL`, the Python Imaging Library). See the documentation on the `visvis` webpage for more details.

Another option is to use `savefig` to create images, one for each frame.

```
# create initial function values
x = linspace(-255,255,511)
X,Y = meshgrid(x,x)
f = sqrt(X*X+Y*Y) - 40 #radius 40
for iteration in range(200):
    imshow((f>0)*255)
    gray()
    axis('off')
    savefig('circle_evolution_{:d}.png'.format(iteration))
    f -= 1
```

These images can then be combined using a standard video editing software, for example, Mencoder or ImageMagick. This approach has the advantage that you can make high-resolution videos by saving high-resolution images.

Summary

A graphical representation is the most compact form in which to present mathematical results or the behavior of an algorithm. This chapter provided you with the basic tools for plotting and introduced you to a more sophisticated way to work with graphical objects, such as figures, axes, and lines in an object-oriented way.

In this chapter, you learned how to make plots, not only classical x/y-plots but also 3D-plots and histograms. We gave you an appetizer on making films. You also saw how to modify plots considering them to be graphical objects with related methods and attributes which can be set, deleted, or modified.

Exercises

Ex. 1 → Write a function that plots an ellipse given its center coordinates (x,y), the half axis a and b rotation angle θ.

Ex. 2 → Write a short program that takes a 2D array, e.g., the preceding Mandelbrot contour image, and iteratively replace each value by the average of its neighbors. Update a contour plot of the array in a figure window to animate the evolution of the contours. Explain the behavior.

Ex. 3 → Consider an $N \times N$ matrix or image with integer values. The mapping

$$I : (x, y) \mapsto (2x + y, x + y) \bmod N$$

is an example of a mapping of a toroidal square grid of points onto itself. This has the interesting property that it distorts the image by shearing and then moving the pieces outside the image back using the modulu function `mod`. Applied iteratively, this results in randomizing the image in a way that eventually returns the original. Implement the following sequence:

$$I^{(m+1)}(x, y) = I^{(m)}(2x + y \bmod N, x + y \bmod N)$$

and save out the first N steps to files or plot them in a figure window.

As an example image, you can use the classic 512 × 512 Lena test image from `scipy.misc`.

```
from scipy.misc import lena
I = lena()
```

The result should look like this:

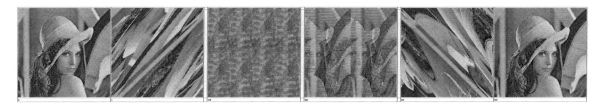

Compute the *x* and *y* mappings and use array indexing (refer to section *Array Indexing* in `Chapter 5`, *Advance Array Concepts*) to copy the pixel values.

Ex. 4 → Reading and plotting on images. SciPy comes with the `imread` function (in the `scipy.misc` module) for reading images, (refer to section *Reading and Writing Images* in `Chapter 12`, *Input and output*). Write a short program that reads an image from file and plots the image contour at a given gray level value overlaid on the original image.

You can get a gray level version of the image by averaging the color channels like this: `mean(im,axis=2)`

Ex. 5 → Image edges. The zero crossings of the 2D Laplacian are a good indication of image edges. Modify the program in the previous exercise to use the `gaussian_laplace` or `laplace` function from the `scipy.ndimage` module to compute the 2D Laplacian and overlay the edges on top of the image.

Ex. 6 → Reformulate the Mandelbrod fractal example (see section *Images and Contours*) by using `orgid` instead of `meshgrid`, see also the explanation `ogrid` in *Function of two variables* in Chapter 5, *Advanced Array Concepts*. What is the difference between `orgid`, `mgrid`, and `meshgrid`?

7
Functions

This chapter introduces functions, a fundamental building block in programming. We show how to define them, how to handle input and output, how to properly use them, and how to treat them as objects.

Basics

In mathematics, a function is written as a map that uniquely assigns an element y from the range R to every element x from the domain D.

This is expressed by $f : D \rightarrow R$

Alternatively, when considering particular elements x and y, one writes $f : x \rightarrow y$

Here, f is called the name of the function and $f(x)$ is its value when applied to x. Here, x is sometimes called the argument of f. Let's first look at an example before considering functions in Python.

For example, $D = \mathbb{R} \times \mathbb{R}$ and $y = f(x_1, x_2) = x_1 - x_2$. This function maps two real numbers to their difference.

In mathematics, functions can have numbers, vectors, matrices, and even other functions as arguments. Here is an example of a function with mixed arguments:

$$I(f, a, b) = \int_a^b f(x)x$$

.

In this case, a number is returned. When working with functions, we have to distinguish between two different steps:

- The definition of the function
- The evaluation of the function, that is, the computation of *f(x)* for a given value of *x*

The first step is done once, while the second can be performed many times for various arguments. Functions in programming languages follow the same concept and apply it to a wide range of types of input arguments, for example, strings, lists, or any object. We demonstrate a definition of the function by considering the given example again:

```
def subtract(x1, x2):
    return x1 - x2
```

The keyword `def` indicates that we are going to define a function. `subtract` is the function's name and x1 and *x2* are its parameters. The colon indicates that we are using a block command and the value that is returned by the function follows the `return` keyword. Now, we can evaluate this function. This function is called with its parameters replaced by input arguments:

```
r = subtract(5.0, 4.3)
```

The result 0.7 is computed and assigned to the r variable.

Parameters and arguments

When defining a function, its input variables are called the parameters of the function. The input used when executing the function is called its argument.

Passing arguments – by position and by keyword

We will consider the previous example again, where the function takes two parameters, namely x1 and x2.

Their names serve to distinguish the two numbers, which in this case cannot be interchanged without altering the result. The first parameter defines the number from which the second parameter is subtracted. When subtract is called, every parameter is replaced by an argument. Only the order of the arguments matters; the arguments can be any objects. For instance, we may call the following:

```
z = 3
e = subtract(5,z)
```

Besides this standard way of calling a function, which is by passing the arguments by position, it might sometimes be convenient to pass arguments using keywords. The names of the parameters are the keywords; consider the following instance:

```
z = 3
e = subtract(x2 = z, x1 = 5)
```

Here, the arguments are assigned to the parameters by name and not by position in the call. Both ways of calling a function can be combined so that the arguments given by position come first and the arguments given by keyword follow last. We show this by using the function plot, which was described in Chapter 6, *Plotting*:

```
plot(xp, yp, linewidth = 2, label = 'y-values')
```

Changing arguments

The purpose of parameters is to provide the function with the necessary input data. Changing the value of the parameter inside the function normally has no effect on its value outside the function:

```
def subtract(x1, x2):
    z = x1 - x2
    x2 = 50.
    return z
a = 20.
b = subtract(10, a)      # returns -10
a    # still has the value 20
```

This applies to all immutable arguments, such as strings, numbers, and tuples. The situation is different if mutable arguments, such as lists or dictionaries, are changed.

For example, passing mutable input arguments to a function and changing them inside the function can change them outside the function too:

```
def subtract(x):
    z = x[0] - x[1]
    x[1] = 50.
    return z
a = [10,20]
b = subtract(a)      # returns -10
a     # is now [10, 50.0]
```

Such a function misuses its arguments to return results. We strongly dissuade you from such constructions and recommend that you do not change input arguments inside the function (for more information refer to *Default Arguments* section).

Access to variables defined outside the local namespace

Python allows functions to access variables defined in any of its enclosing program units. These are called global variables, in contrast to local variables. The latter are only accessible within the function. For example, consider the following code:

```
import numpy as np # here the variable np is defined
def sqrt(x):
    return np.sqrt(x) # we use np inside the function
```

This feature should not be abused. The following code is an example of what not to do:

```
a = 3
def multiply(x):
    return a * x # bad style: access to the variable a defined outside
```

When changing the variable a the function, `multiply` tacitly changes its behavior:

```
a=3
multiply(4)   # returns 12
a=4
multiply(4)   # returns 16
```

It is much better in that case to provide the variable as a parameter through the argument list:

```
def multiply(x, a):
    return a * x
```

Global variables can be useful when working with closures. Namespaces and scopes are discussed more extensively in `Chapter 11`, *Namespaces, Scopes, and Modules*.

Default arguments

Some functions can have many parameters, and among them some might only be of interest in nonstandard situations. It would be practical if arguments could automatically be set to standard (default) values. We demonstrate the use of default arguments by looking at the command `norm` in the `scipy.linalg` module. It computes various norms of matrices and vectors.

The following snippet calls for computing the **Frobenius norm** of the 3 × 3 identity matrix are equivalent (more on matrix norms can be found in [10]):

```
import scipy.linalg as sl
sl.norm(identity(3))
sl.norm(identity(3), ord = 'fro')
sl.norm(identity(3), 'fro')
```

Note that in the first call, no information about the `ord` keyword is given. How does Python know that it should compute the Frobenius norm and not another norm, for example, the Euclidean 2-norm?

The answer to the previous question is the use of default values. A default value is a value already given by the function definition. If the function is called without providing this argument, Python uses the value that the programmer provided when the function was defined.

Suppose we call the function `subtract` only one argument; we get an error message:

```
TypeError: subtract() takes exactly 2 arguments (1 given)
```

To allow the omission of the argument x2, the definition of the function has to provide a default value, for example:

```
def subtract(x1, x2 = 0):
    return x1 - x2
```

To summarize, arguments can be given as positional arguments and keyword arguments. All positional arguments have to be given first. You do not need to provide all keyword arguments as long as those omitted arguments have default values in the function definition.

Beware of mutable default arguments

The default arguments are set upon function definition. Changing mutable arguments inside a function has a side effect when working with default values, for example:

```
def my_list(x1, x2 = []):
    x2.append(x1)
    return x2
my_list(1)   # returns [1]
my_list(2)   # returns [1,2]
```

Variable number of arguments

Lists and dictionaries may be used to define or call functions with a variable number of arguments. Let's define a list and a dictionary as follows:

```
data = [[1,2],[3,4]]
style = dict({'linewidth':3,'marker':'o','color':'green'})
```

Then we can call the `plot` function using starred (*) arguments:

```
plot(*data,**style)
```

A variable name prefixed by * , such as *data in the preceding example, means that a list that gets unpacked in the function call is provided. In this way, a list generates positional arguments. Similarly, a variable name prefixed by **, such as **style in the example, unpacks a dictionary to keyword arguments. Refer to the following figure (*Figure 7.1*):

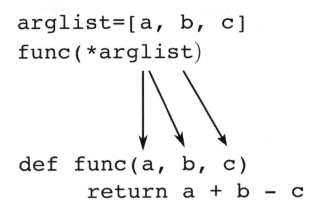

Figure 7.1: Starred arguments in function calls

You might also want to use the reverse process, where all given positional arguments are packed into a list and all keyword arguments are packed into a dictionary when passed to a function.

In the function definition, this is indicated by parameters prefixed by `*` and `**`, respectively. You will often find the `*args` and `**kwargs` parameters in code documentation, refer *Figure 7.2*.

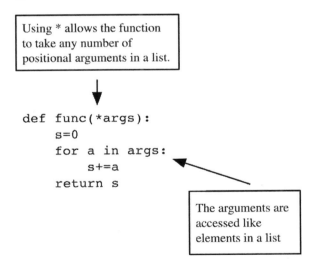

Figure 7.2: Starred arguments in function definitions

Return values

A function in Python always returns a single object. If a function has to return more than one object, these are packed and returned as a single tuple object.

For instance, the following function takes a complex number z and returns its polar coordinate representation as magnitude r and angle φ according to Euler's formula:

$$z = r^{i\varphi}.$$

And the Python counterpart would be this:

```
def complex_to_polar(z):
    r = sqrt(z.real ** 2 + z.imag ** 2)
    phi = arctan2(z.imag, z.real)
    return (r,phi)  # here the return object is formed
```

Here, we used the `sqrt(x)` NumPy function for the square root of a number x and `arctan2(x,y)` for the expression $\tan^{-1}(x/y)$.

Let us try our function:

```
z = 3 + 5j  # here we define a complex number
a = complex_to_polar(z)
r = a[0]
phi = a[1]
```

The last three statements can be written more elegantly in a single line:

```
r,phi = complex_to_polar(z)
```

We can test our function by calling `polar_to_comp`; refer to *Exercise 1*.

If a function has no `return` statement, it returns the value `None`. There are many cases where a function does not need to return any value. This could be because the variables passed to a function may be subject to modification. Consider, for instance, the following function:

```
def append_to_list(L, x):
    L.append(x)
```

The preceding function does not return anything because it modifies one of the objects that is given as an argument. We mentioned in *Parameters and Arguments* section why this is useful. There are many methods that behave in the same way. To mention the list methods only, the `append`, `extend`, `reverse`, and `sort` methods do not return anything (that is, they return `None`). When an object is modified by a method in this way, the modification is called in-place. It is difficult to know whether a method changes an object, except by looking at the code or the documentation.

Another reason for a function, or a method, not to return anything is when it prints out a message or writes to a file.

The execution stops at the first occurring `return` statement. Lines after that statement are dead code, which will never be executed:

```
def function_with_dead_code(x):
    return 2 * x
    y = x ** 2 # these two lines ...
    return y   # ... are never executed!
```

Recursive functions

In mathematics, many functions are defined recursively. In this section, we will show how this concept can be used even when programming a function. This makes the relation of the program to its mathematical counterpart very clear, which may ease the readability of the program.

Nevertheless, we recommend that you use this programming technique with care, especially within scientific computing. In most applications, the more straightforward iterative approach is more efficient. This will become immediately clear from the following example.

Chebyshev polynomials are defined by a three-term recursion:

$$T_n(x) = 2xT_{n-1}(x) - T_{n-2}(x)$$

Such a recursion needs to be initialized, that is, $T_0(x) = 1$, $T_1(x) = x$.

In Python, this three term recursion can be realized by the following function definition:

```
def chebyshev(n, x):
    if n == 0:
        return 1.
    elif n == 1:
        return x
    else:
        return 2. * x * chebyshev(n - 1, x) \
                    - chebyshev(n - 2 ,x)
```

The function is then called like this:

```
chebyshev(5, 0.52)  # returns 0.39616645119999994
```

This example also illustrates the risk of dramatically wasting computation time. The number of function evaluations increases exponentially with the recursion level and most of these evaluations are just duplicates of previous computations. While it might be tempting to use recursive programs for demonstrating the strong relation between code and mathematical definition, a production code will avoid this programming technique (refer to *Exercise* 6). We also refer to a technique called memoization (refer to [22] for more details) that combines recursive programming with a caching technique to save replicated function evaluations.

A recursive function usually has a level parameter. In the previous example, it is *n*. It is used to control the function's two main parts:

- The base case, here, the first two `if` branches
- The recursive body, in which the function itself is called once or several times with smaller level parameters.

The number of levels passed by an execution of a recursive function is called the recursion depth. This quantity should not be too large; otherwise the computation might no longer be effective and in the ultimate case, the following error will be raised:

```
RuntimeError: maximum recursion depth exceeded
```

The maximal recursion depth depends on the memory of the computer you use. This error also occurs when the initialization step is missing in the function definition. We encourage the use of recursive programs for very small recursion depths (for more information, refer to the section *Infinite Iteration* of `Chapter 9`, *Iterating*.

Function documentation

You should document your functions using a string at the beginning. This is called docstring:

```
def newton(f, x0):
    """
    Newton's method for computing a zero of a function
    on input:
    f   (function) given function f(x)
    x0  (float) initial guess
    on return:
    y   (float) the approximated zero of f
    """

    ...
```

When calling `help(newton)`, you get this docstring displayed together with the call of this function:

```
Help on function newton in module __main__:

newton(f, x0)
    Newton's method for computing a zero of a function
    on input:
    f   (function) given function f(x)
    x0  (float) initial guess
    on return:
    y   (float) the approximated zero of f
```

The docstring is internally saved as an attribute, __doc__, of the given function. In the example, it's `newton.__doc__`. The minimal information you should provide in a docstring is the purpose of the function and the description of the input and output objects. There are tools to automatically generate full code documentation by collecting all docstrings in your program (for more information refer to [32]).

Functions are objects

Functions are objects, like everything else in Python. One may pass functions as arguments, change their names, or delete them. For example:

```
def square(x):
    """
    Return the square of x
    """
    return x ** 2
square(4) # 16
sq = square # now sq is the same as square
sq(4) # 16
del square # square doesn't exist anymore
print(newton(sq, .2)) # passing as argument
```

Passing functions as arguments is very common when applying algorithms in scientific computing. The functions `fsolve` in `scipy.optimize` for computing a zero of a given function or `quad` in `scipy.integrate` for computing integrals are typical examples.

A function itself can have a different number of arguments with differing types. So, when passing your function `f` to another function `g` as argument, make sure that `f` has exactly the form described in the docstring of `g`.

The docstring of `fsolve` gives information about its `func` parameter:

```
func -- A Python function or method which takes at least one
              (possibly vector) argument.
```

Partial application

Let's start with an example of a function with two variables.

The function $(\omega, t) \mapsto f(\omega, t) = \sin(2\pi\omega t)$ can be viewed as a function in two variables. Often one considers ω not as a free variable but as a fixed parameter of a family of functions f_ω:

$$t \mapsto f_\omega(t) = \sin(2\pi\omega t)$$

This interpretation reduces a function in two variables to a function in one variable, t, given a fixed parameter value ω. The process of defining a new function by fixing (freezing) one or several parameters of a function is called partial application.

Partial applications are easily created using the Python module `functools`, which provides a function called `partial` for precisely this purpose. We illustrate this by constructing a function that returns a sine for a given frequency:

```
import functools
def sin_omega(t, freq):
    return sin(2 * pi * freq * t)

def make_sine(frequency):
    return functools.partial(sin_omega, freq = frequency)
```

Using Closures

Using the view that functions are objects, partial applications can be realized by writing a function, which itself returns a new function, with a reduced number of input arguments. For instance, the function could be defined as follows:

```
def make_sine(freq):
    "Make a sine function with frequency freq"
    def mysine(t):
        return sin_omega(t, freq)
    return mysine
```

In this example the inner function `mysine` has access to the variable `freq`; it is neither a local variable of this function nor is it passed to it via the argument list. Python allows such a construction (refer to *Namespaces* section in `Chapter 11`, *Namespaces, Scopes, and Modules*).

Anonymous functions – the lambda keyword

The keyword lambda is used in Python to define anonymous functions, that is; functions without a name and described by a single expression. You might just want to perform an operation on a function that can be expressed by a simple expression without naming this function and without defining this function by a lengthy `def` block.

 The name *lambda* originates from a special branch of calculus and mathematical logic, the λ-calculus.

For instance, to compute the following expression, we may use SciPy's function `quad`, which requires the function to be integrated as its first argument and the integration bounds as the next two arguments:

$$\int_0^1 x^2 + 5x$$

Here, the function to integrate is just a simple one-liner and we use the `lambda` keyword to define it:

```
import scipy.integrate as si
si.quad(lambda x: x ** 2 + 5, 0, 1)
```

The syntax is as follows:

```
lambda parameter_list: expression
```

The definition of the `lambda` function can only consist of a single expression and in particular, cannot contain loops. `lambda` functions are, just like other functions, objects and can be assigned to variables:

```
parabola = lambda x: x ** 2 + 5
parabola(3) # gives 14
```

The lambda construction is always replaceable

It is important to note that lambda construction is only syntactic sugar in Python. Any lambda construction may be replaced by an explicit function definition:

```
parabola = lambda x: x**2+5
# the following code is equivalent
def parabola(x):
    return x ** 2 + 5
```

The main reason to use a construction is for very simple functions, when a full function definition would be too cumbersome.

`lambda` functions provide a third way to make closures as we demonstrate by continuing with the previous example:

We use the `sin_omega` function to compute the integral of the sine function for various frequencies:

```
import scipy.integrate as si
for iteration in range(3):
    print(si.quad(lambda x: sin_omega(x, iteration*pi), 0, pi/2.) )
```

Functions as decorators

In the partial application section, we saw how a function can be used to modify another function. A decorator is a syntax element in Python that conveniently allows us to alter the behavior of a function without changing the definition of the function itself. Let us start with the following situation:

Assume that we have a function that determines the degree of sparsity of a matrix:

```
def how_sparse(A):
    return len(A.reshape(-1).nonzero()[0])
```

This function returns an error if it is not called with an array object as input. More precisely, it will not work with an object that does not implement the `reshape` method. For instance, the `how_sparse` function will not work with a list, because lists have no `reshape` method. The following helper function modifies any function with one input parameter so that it tries to make a type conversion to an array:

```
def cast2array(f):
    def new_function(obj):
        fA = f(array(obj))
        return fA
    return new_function
```

Thus, the modified function `how_sparse = cast2array(how_sparse)` can be applied to any object that can be cast to an array. The same functionality is achieved if the definition of `how_sparse` is decorated with the type conversion function. It is recommend also to consider the `functools.wraps` (refer to [8] for more details):

```
@cast2array
def how_sparse(A):
    return len(A.reshape(-1).nonzero()[0])
```

To define a decorator, you need a callable object such as a function that modifies the definition of the function to be decorated. The main purposes are:

- To increase code readability by separating parts from a function that do not directly serve its functionality (for example, memoizing)
- To put common preamble and epilogue parts of a family of similar functions in a common place (for example, type checking)
- To be able to easily switch off and on additional functionalities of a function (for example, test prints, tracing)

Summary

Functions are not only the ideal tools for making your program modular, but they also reflect mathematical thinking. You learned the syntax of function definitions and to distinguish between defining and calling a function.

We considered functions as objects that can be modified by other functions. When working with functions, it is important to be familiar with the notion of the scope of a variable and how information is passed into a function by parameters.

Sometimes, it is convenient to define functions on the fly with so-called anonymous functions. For this, we introduced the keyword lambda.

Exercises

Ex 1 → Write a function `polar_to_comp`, which takes two arguments r and φ and returns the complex number $z = r^{i\varphi}$. Use the NumPy function `exp` for the exponential function.

Ex 2 → In the description of the Python module `functools`, (refer to [8] for more detail on functools) you find the following Python function:

```
def partial(func, *args, **keywords):
    def newfunc(*fargs, **fkeywords):
        newkeywords = keywords.copy()
        newkeywords.update(fkeywords)
        return func(*(args + fargs), **newkeywords)
    newfunc.func = func
    newfunc.args = args
    newfunc.keywords = keywords
    return newfunc
```

Explain and test this function.

Ex 3 → Write a decorator for the function `how_sparse`, which cleans the input matrix A by setting the elements that are less than 1.e-16 to zero (consider example in section *Function as decorators*).

Ex 4 → A continuous function f with $f(a)f(b) < 0$ changes its sign in the interval $[a, b]$ and has at least one root (zero) in this interval. Such a root can be found with the bisection method. This method starts from the given interval. Then it investigates the sign changes in the subintervals,

$$\left[a, \frac{a+b}{2} \right] \quad \text{and} \quad \left[\frac{a+b}{2}, b \right].$$

If the sign changes in the first subinterval b is redefined to be:

$$b := \frac{a+b}{2}$$

Otherwise, it is redefined in the same manner to:

$$a := \frac{a+b}{2}$$

And the process is repeated until the *b-a* is less than a given tolerance.

- Implement this method as a function that takes as arguments:
  - – the function f
  - – the initial interval $[a, b]$
  - – the tolerance
- This function `bisec` should return the final interval and its midpoint.
- Test the method with the function `arctan` and also with the polynomial $f(x) = 3 x^2$ -5 in the interval [1.1, 1.4], and alternatively in [1.3, 1.4].

Ex. 5 → The greatest common divisor of two integers can be computed with Euclid's algorithm described by the following recursion:

$$\gcd(a, b) = \begin{cases} a & \text{if } b = 0 \\ \gcd(b, a \bmod b) & \text{otherwise} \end{cases}$$

Write a function that computes the greatest common divisor of two integers. Write another function that computes the least common multiple of these numbers using the relation:

$$\mathrm{lcm}(a, b) = \frac{|ab|}{\gcd(a, b)}$$

Ex. 6 → Study the recursive implementation of Chebyshev polynomials, consider the example in section *Recursive Function*. Rewrite the program in a non-recursive way and study computation time versus polynomial degree (see also the `timeit` module).

8
Classes

In mathematics, when we write sin, we refer to a mathematical object for which we know many methods from elementary calculus. For example:

- We might want to evaluate sin x at x=0.5, that is, compute sin(0.5), which returns a real number
- We might want to compute its derivative, which gives us another mathematical object, cos
- We might want to compute the first three coefficients of its Taylor polynomial

These methods may be applied not only to sin but also to other sufficiently smooth functions. There are, however, other mathematical objects (for example, the number 5) for which these methods make no sense. Objects that have the same methods are grouped together in abstract classes, for example, functions. Every statement and every method that can be applied to functions applies in particular to sin or cos. Other examples for such classes might be a rational number, for which a denominator and numerator method exist; an interval, which has a left and right boundary method; an infinite sequence, for which we can ask whether it has a limit, and so on.

In this case, sin is called an instance of the class. The mathematical phrase *Let g be a function* ... is, in this context, called instantiation. Here, g is the name of the function; one of many attributes that can be assigned to it. Another attribute might be its domain.

The mathematical object $p(x) = 2x^2 - 5$ is just like the sine function. Every function method applies to p, but we can also define special methods for p. We might, for instance, ask for p's coefficients. These methods can be used to define the class of polynomials. As polynomials are functions, they additionally inherit all methods of the function class.

In mathematics, we often use the same operator symbol for completely different operations. For instance, in 5+4 and sin + cos, the operator symbol + has different meanings. By using the same symbol, one tries to express the similarities of mathematical operations. We have introduced these terms from object-oriented programming by applying them to mathematical examples:

- Classes
- Instance and instantiation
- Inheritance
- Methods
- Attributes
- Operator overloading

In this chapter, we will show how these concepts are used in Python.

Introduction to classes

We will illustrate the concept of classes with an example of rational numbers, that is, numbers of the form $q = q_N/q_D$, where q_N and q_D are integers.

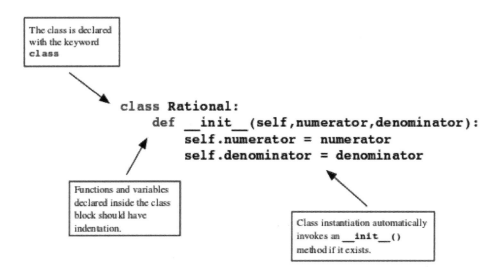

Figure 8.1: An example of a class declaration

We use rational numbers here only as an example for the class concept. For future work in Python with rational numbers use the *fractions* module (refer to [6]).

Class syntax

The definition of a class is made by a block command with the `class` keyword, the name of the class, and some statements in the block (refer to *Figure 8.1*):

```
class RationalNumber:
    pass
```

An instance of this class (or in other words, an object of the type `RationalNumber`) is created by

```
r = RationalNumber()
```

and a query `type(a)` returns the answer, `<class'__main__.RationalNumber'>`. If we want to investigate whether an object is an instance of this class, we can use this:

```
if isinstance(a, RationalNumber):
    print('Indeed it belongs to the class RationalNumber')
```

So far we've generated an object of the `RationalNumber` type, which has no data yet. Furthermore, there are no methods defined to perform operations with these objects. This will be the subject of the next sections.

The __init__ method

Now we provide our example class with some attributes; that is, we give it defining data. In our case, this data will be the values of the denominator and the numerator. To this end, we have to define a method, __init__, used to initialize the class with these values:

```
class RationalNumber:
    def __init__(self, numerator, denominator):
        self.numerator = numerator
        self.denominator = denominator
```

Before we explain the special __init__ function, which we added to the class, we demonstrate the instantiation of a RationalNumber object:

```
q = RationalNumber(10, 20)     # Defines a new object
q.numerator     # returns 10
q.denominator    # returns 20
```

A new object of type RationalNumber is created by using the class name as if it was a function. This statement does two things:

- It first creates an empty object, q.
- Then it applies the __init__ function to it; that is, q.__init__(10, 20) is executed.

The first parameter of __init__ refers to the new object itself. On function call, this first parameter is replaced by the object's instance. This applies to all methods of the class and not only to the special method __init__. The special role of this first parameter is reflected by the convention to name it self. In the previous example, the __init__ function defines two attributes of the new object, numerator and denominator.

Attributes and methods

One of the main reasons for working with classes is that objects can be grouped together and bound to a common object. We saw this already when looking at rational numbers; denominator and numerator are two objects which we bound to an instance of the RationalNumber class. They are called attributes of the instance. The fact that an object is an attribute of a class instance becomes apparent from the way they are referenced, which we have used tacitly before:

```
<object>.attribute
```

Here are some examples of instantiation and attribute reference:

```
q = RationalNumber(3, 5) # instantiation
q.numerator     # attribute access
q.denominator

a = array([1, 2])     # instantiation
a.shape

z = 5 + 4j     # instantiation
z.imag
```

Once an instance is defined we can set, change or delete attributes of that particular instance. The syntax is the same as for regular variables:

```
q = RationalNumber(3, 5)
r = RationalNumber(7, 3)
q.numerator = 17
del r.denominator
```

Changing or deleting an attribute may have undesired side effects, which might even render the object useless. We will be learning more on this in the section *Attributes that depend on each other*. As functions are objects too, we can also use functions as attributes; they are called methods of the instance:

```
<object>.method(<arguments...>)
```

For example, let us add a method to the class RationalNumber that converts the number to a float:

```
class RationalNumber:
...
    def convert2float(self):
        return float(self.numerator) / float(self.denominator)
```

Again, this method takes as its first (and only) argument, self, the reference to the object itself. We use this method with a regular function call:

```
q = RationalNumber(10, 20)    # Defines a new object
q.convert2float() # returns 0.5
```

This is equivalent to the following call:

```
RationalNumber.convert2float(q)
```

Note again that the object instance is inserted as the first argument of the function. This use of the first argument explains the error message that would occur if this particular method were used with additional arguments:

The q.convert2float(15) call provokes this error message:

```
TypeError: convert2float() takes exactly 1 argument (2 given)
```

The reason this does not work is that `q.convert2float(15)` is precisely equivalent to `RationalNumber.convert2float(q, 15)`, which fails because `RationalNumber.convert2float` takes only one argument.

Special methods

The special method `__repr__` gives us the ability to define the way the object is represented in a Python interpreter. For rational numbers, a possible definition of this method could be as follows:

```
class RationalNumber:
    ...
    def __repr__(self):
        return '{} / {}'.format(self.numerator, self.denominator)
```

With this method defined, just typing q returns 10 / 20.

We would like to have a method that performs addition of two rational numbers. A first attempt could result in a method like this:

```
class RationalNumber:
    ...
    def add(self, other):
        p1, q1 = self.numerator, self.denominator
        if isinstance(other, int):
            p2, q2 = other, 1
        else:
            p2, q2 = other.numerator, other.denominator
        return RationalNumber(p1 * q2 + p2 * q1, q1 * q2)
```

A call to this method takes the following form:

```
q = RationalNumber(1, 2)
p = RationalNumber(1, 3)
q.add(p)    # returns the RationalNumber for 5/6
```

It would be much nicer if we could write q + p instead. But so far, the plus sign is not defined for the RationalNumber type. This is done by using the __add__ special method. So, just renaming add to __add__ allows for using the plus sign for rational numbers:

```
q = RationalNumber(1, 2)
p = RationalNumber(1, 3)
q + p # RationalNumber(5, 6)
```

The expression q + p is in fact an alias for the expression q.__add__(p). In the table (*Table 8.1*), you will find the special methods for binary operators, such as +, −, or *.

Operator	Method	Operator	Method
+	__add__	+=	__iadd__
*	__mul__	*=	__imul__
−	__sub__	−=	__isub__
/	__truediv__	/=	__itruediv__
//	__floordiv__	//=	__ifloordiv__
**	__pow__		
==	__eq__	!=	__ne__
<=	__le__	<	__lt__
>=	__ge__	>	__gt__
()	__call__	[]	__getitem__

Table 8.1: Some Python operators & corresponding class methods, you can find the complete list [31]

The implementation of those operators for a new class is called operator overloading. Another example of operator overloading is a method for examining whether two rational numbers are the same:

```
class RationalNumber:
...
    def __eq__(self, other):
        return self.denominator * other.numerator ==
            self.numerator * other.denominator
```

It is used like this:

```
p = RationalNumber(1, 2) # instantiation
q = RationalNumber(2, 4) # instantiation
p == q # True
```

Operations between objects belonging to different classes need special care:

```
p = RationalNumber(1, 2) # instantiation
p + 5  # corresponds to p.__add__(5)
5 + p  # returns an error
```

By default, the + operator invokes the left operand's method, __add__. We programmed it so that it allows both, objects of type int and objects of type RationalNumber. In the statement 5 + p, the operands are commuted and the __add__ method of the build-in int type is invoked. This method returns an error as it does not know how to handle rational numbers. This case can be handled by the method __radd__, with which we will equip the RationalNumber class now. The method __radd__ is called reverse addition.

Reverse operations

If operations like + are applied to two operands of different types, the corresponding method (in this case, __add__) of the left operand is invoked first. If this raises an exception, the reverse method (here, __radd__) of the right operand is called. If this method does not exist, a TypeError exception is raised.

Consider an example of reverse operation. In order to enable the operation 5+p where p is an instance of RationalNumber, we define this:

```
class RationalNumber:
    ....
    def __radd__(self, other):
        return self + other
```

Note that __radd__ interchanges the order of the arguments; self is the object of type RationalNumber while other is the object that has to be converted.

Using a class instance together with brackets, (,) or [,] invokes a call to one of the special methods __call__ or __getitem__, giving the instance the behavior of a function or of an iterable (refer to the *Table 8.1* for these and other special methods):

```
class Polynomial:
    ...
    def __call__(self, x):
        return self.eval(x)
```

Which now may be used as follows:

```
p = Polynomial(...)
p(3.) # value of p at 3.
```

The __getitem__ special method makes sense if the class provides an iterator (It is recommended to refer section *Iterators* in `Chapter 9`, *Iterating* before you consider the following example).

The recursion $u_{i+1} = a_1 u_i + a_0 u_{i-1}$ is called a three–term recursion. It plays an important role in applied mathematics, in particular in the construction of orthogonal polynomials. We can set up a three-term recursion as a class in the following way:

```
import itertools

class  Recursion3Term:
    def __init__(self, a0, a1, u0, u1):
        self.coeff = [a1, a0]
        self.initial = [u1, u0]
    def __iter__(self):
        u1, u0 = self.initial
        yield u0   # (see also Iterators section in Chapter 9)
        yield u1
        a1, a0 = self.coeff
        while True :
            u1, u0 = a1 * u1 + a0 * u0, u1
            yield u1
    def __getitem__(self, k):
        return list(itertools.islice(self, k, k + 1))[0]
```

Here, the __iter__ method defines a generator object, which allows us to use an instance of the class as an iterator:

```
r3 = Recursion3Term(-0.35, 1.2, 1, 1)
for i, r in enumerate(r3):
    if i == 7:
        print(r)   # returns 0.194167
        break
```

The __getitem__ method enables us to directly access the iterates as if r3 were a list:

```
r3[7] # returns 0.194167
```

Note that we used `itertools.islice` when coding the __getitem__ method (refer to section *Iterators* of `Chapter 9`, *Iterating*, for more information). An example of the use of __getitem__ together with slices and the function `ogrid` is given in the section *Function with two variables* in `Chapter 5`, *Advance Array Concepts*.

Attributes that depend on each other

Attributes of an instance can be changed (or created) by simply assigning them a value. However, if other attributes depend on the one just changed, it is desirable to change these simultaneously:

Let us consider a class that defines an object for planar triangles from three given points. A first attempt to set up such a class could be as follows:

```
class Triangle:
    def __init__(self,  A, B, C):
        self.A = array(A)
        self.B = array(B)
        self.C = array(C)
        self.a = self.C - self.B
        self.b = self.C - self.A
        self.c = self.B - self.A
    def area(self):
        return abs(cross(self.b, self.c)) / 2
```

An instance of this triangle is created by this:

```
tr = Triangle([0., 0.], [1., 0.], [0., 1.])
```

And its area is computed by this:

```
tr.area() # returns 0.5
```

If we change an attribute, say point *B*, the corresponding edges *a* and *c* are not automatically updated and the computed area is wrong:

```
tr.B = [12., 0.]
tr.area() # still returns 0.5, should be 6 instead.
```

A remedy is to define a method that is executed when an attribute is changed; such a method is called a setter method. Correspondingly, one might ask for a method that is executed when a value of an attribute is requested; such a method is called a getter method.

The property function

The function `property` links an attribute to such a getter, setter, and deleter method. It might also be used to assign a documentation string to an attribute:

```
attribute = property(fget = get_attr, fset = set_attr,
                     fdel = del_attr, doc = string)
```

We continue with the previous example with a setter method and consider the `Trinagle` class again. If the following statement is included in `Triangle`

```
B = property(fget = get_B, fset = set_B, fdel = del_B, doc = 'The point B of
a triangle')
```

a command

```
tr.B = <something>
```

invokes the setter method, `set_B`.

Let us modify the Triangle class:

```
class Triangle:
    def __init__(self, A, B, C):
        self._A = array(A)
        self._B = array(B)
        self._C = array(C)
        self._a = self._C - self._B
        self._b = self._C - self._A
        self._c = self._B - self._A
    def area(self):
        return abs(cross(self._c, self._b)) / 2.
    def set_B(self, B):
        self._B = B
        self._a = self._C - self._B
        self._c = self._B - self._A
    def get_B(self):
        return self._B
    def del_Pt(self):
        raise Exception('A triangle point cannot be deleted')
    B = property(fget = get_B, fset = set_B, fdel = del_Pt)
```

If the attribute B is changed, then the method `set_B` stores the new value in the internal attribute _B and changes all depending attributes:

```
tr.B = [12., 0.]
tr.area() # returns 6.0
```

The way the `deleter` method is used here is to prevent deletion of attributes:

```
del tr.B # raises an exception
```

The use of an underscore as a prefix of attribute names is a convention used to indicate attributes that are not designed to be accessed directly. They are intended to hold data for attributes handled by setters and getters. These attributes are not private in the sense of other programming languages; they are just not intended to be accessed directly.

Bound and unbound methods

We will now take a closer look at attributes that are methods. Let us consider an example:

```
class A:
    def func(self,arg):
        pass
```

A little inspection shows us how the nature of `func` changes after creating an instance:

```
A.func  # <unbound method A.func>
instA = A()  # we create an instance
instA.func  #  <bound method A.func of ... >
```

Calling, for example, `A.func(3)` would result in an error message such as this:

```
TypeError: func() missing 1 required positional argument: 'arg'
```

`instA.func(3)` is executed as expected. Upon creation of an instance, the `func` method is bound to the instance. The `self` argument gets the instance assigned as its value. Binding a method to an instance makes the method usable as a function. Before that, it is of no use. Class methods, which we will consider later, are different in this aspect.

Class attributes

Attributes specified in the class declaration are called class attributes. Consider the following example:

```
class Newton:
    tol = 1e-8 # this is a class attribute
    def __init__(self,f):
        self.f = f # this is not a class attribute
    ....
```

Class attributes are useful for simulating default values and can be used if values have to be reset:

```
N1 = Newton(f)
N2 = Newton(g)
```

Both instances have an attribute, `tol`, with the value initialized in the class definition:

```
N1.tol # 1e-8
N2.tol # 1e-8
```

Altering the class attribute automatically affects all the corresponding attributes of all instances:

```
Newton.tol = 1e-10
N1.tol # 1e-10
N2.tol # 1e-10
```

Altering `tol` for one instance does not affect the other instance:

```
N2.tol = 1.e-4
N1.tol   # still 1.e-10
```

But now `N2.tol` is detached from the class attribute. Changing `Newton.tol` no longer has any effect on `N2.tol`:

```
Newton.tol = 1e-5 # now all instances of the Newton classes have 1e-5
N1.tol # 1.e-5
N2.tol # 1e-4 but not N2.
```

Class methods

We saw in the previous section on *Bound and unbound methods* how methods are either bound to an instance of a class or remain in a state as unbound methods. Class methods are different. They are always bound methods. They are bound to the class itself.

We will first describe the syntactic details and then give some examples to show what these methods can be used for. To indicate that a method is a class method the decorator line precedes the method definition:

```
@classmethod
```

While standard methods make a reference to an instance by the use of their first argument, the first argument of a class method refers to the class itself. By convention the first argument is called `self` for standard methods and `cls` for class methods.

- Standard case:

```
class A:
    def func(self,*args):
        <...>
```

- Class method case:

```
class B:
    @classmethod
    def func(cls,*args):
        <...>
```

In practice, class methods may be useful for executing commands before an instance is created, for instance, in a preprocessing step. See the following example:

In this example we show how class methods can be used to prepare data before creating an instance:

```
class Polynomial:
    def __init__(self, coeff):
        self.coeff = array(coeff)
    @classmethod
    def by_points(cls, x, y):
        degree = x.shape[0] - 1
        coeff = polyfit(x, y, degree)
        return cls(coeff)
    def __eq__(self, other):
        return allclose(self.coeff, other.coeff)
```

The class is designed so, that a polynomial object is created by specifying its coefficients. Alternatively, the `by_points` class method allows us to define a polynomial by interpolation points. We can transform the interpolation data to the polynomial coefficients even when no instance of Polynomial is available:

```
p1 = Polynomial.by_points(array([0., 1.]), array([0., 1.]))
p2 = Polynomial([1., 0.])

print(p1 == p2)   # prints True
```

Another example of a class method is presented in an example later in this chapter. In that example, a class method is used to access information related to several (or all) instances from this class.

Subclassing and inheritance

In this section, we will introduce some central concepts from object-oriented programming: abstract classes, subclasses, and inheritance. To guide you through these concepts, we consider another mathematical example: one-step methods for solving a differential equation. The generic form of an ordinary initial value problem is

$$x'(t) = f(x(t), t) \qquad x(0) = x_0 \qquad t \in [t_0, t_e]$$

The data is the right-hand side function f, the initial value x_0, and the interval of interest $[t_0, t_e]$. The solution of this problem is a function $x : [t_0, t_e] \to \mathbb{R}$. A numerical algorithm gives this solution as a vector u of discrete values u_i being approximations to $x(t_i)$. Here, $t_i \in [t_0, t_e]$ and $t_i = t_{i-1} + h$ are discretized values of the independent variable t, which in physical models often represents time.

A one-step method constructs the solution values u_i by the recursion steps:

$$u_{i+1} = u_i + h\Phi(f, u_i, t_i, h).$$

Here, Φ is a step function that characterizes the individual methods (refer to [28]):

- **Explicit Euler:** $\Phi(f, u_i, t_i, h) = f(u_i, t_i)$

- **Midpoint Rule:** $\Phi(f, u_i, t_i, h) = f(u_i + \frac{h}{2}f(u_i), t_i + \frac{h}{2})$

- **Runge–Kutta 4:** $\Phi(f, u_i, t_i, h) = \frac{1}{6}(s_1 + 2s_2 + 2s_3 + s_4)$
  with
  $s_1 = f(u_i, t_i) \qquad s_2 = f(u_i + \frac{h}{2}s_1, t_i + \frac{h}{2})s_3 = f(u_i + \frac{h}{2}s_2, t_i + \frac{h}{2}) \qquad s_4 = f(u_i + s_3, t_i + h)$

What we did here is the typical way of describing a mathematical algorithm. We first described a method by its idea, giving its steps in an abstract way. To actually use it, we have to fill in the parameters of a concrete method, in this example, the function Φ. This is also the way things are explained in object-oriented programming. First, we set up a class with the abstract description of the method:

```python
class OneStepMethod:
    def __init__(self, f, x0, interval, N):
        self.f = f
        self.x0 = x0
        self.interval = [t0, te] = interval
        self.grid = linspace(t0, te, N)
        self.h = (te - t0) / N

    def generate(self):
        ti, ui = self.grid[0], self.x0
        yield ti, ui
        for t in self.grid[1:]:
            ui = ui + self.h * self.step(self.f, ui, ti)
            ti = t
            yield ti, ui

    def solve(self):
        self.solution = array(list(self.generate()))

    def plot(self):
        plot(self.solution[:, 0], self.solution[:, 1])

    def step(self, f, u, t):
        raise NotImplementedError()
```

This abstract class, with its methods, is used as a template for the individual methods:

```python
class ExplicitEuler(OneStepMethod):
    def step(self, f, u, t):
        return f(u, t)

class MidPointRule(OneStepMethod):
    def step(self, f, u, t):
        return f(u + self.h / 2 * f(u, t), t + self.h / 2)
```

Note that in the class definitions, the name of the abstract class that we used as a template, `OneStepMethod`, is given as an extra argument:

```python
class ExplicitEuler(OneStepMethod)
```

That class is called the parent class. All methods and attributes of the parent class are inherited by the subclasses as long as they are not overridden. They are overridden if they are redefined in the subclass. The `step` method is redefined in the subclasses, while the method `generate` is generic for the entire family and therefore inherited from the parent. Before considering further details, we will demonstrate how these three classes can be used:

```
def f(x, t):
    return -0.5 * x

euler = ExplicitEuler(f, 15., [0., 10.], 20)
euler.solve()
euler.plot()
hold(True)
midpoint = MidPointRule(f, 15., [0., 10.], 20)

midpoint.solve()
midpoint.plot()
```

You can avoid the repetition of common parameter lists by using the star operator (refer to section *Variable Number of Argument* in `Chapter 7`, *Functions* for more details):

```
...
argument_list = [f, 15., [0., 10.], 20]
euler = ExplicitEuler(*argument_list)
...
midpoint = MidPointRule(*argument_list)
...
```

Note that the abstract class has never been used to create an instance. As the `step` method was not completely defined, calling it raises an exception of type `NotImplementedError`.

Sometimes one has to access the methods or attributes of a parent class. This is done using the command `super`. This is useful when the child class uses its own __init__ method in order to extend the parent's __init__:

For example let us assume that we want to give every solver class a string variable with the solver's name. To this end, we provide the solver with an __init__ method as it overrides the parent's __init__ method. In the case that both methods should be used, we have to refer to the parent's method by the command `super`:

```
class ExplicitEuler(OneStepMethod):
    def __init__(self,*args, **kwargs):
        self.name='Explicit Euler Method'
        super(ExplicitEuler, self).__init__(*args,**kwargs)
    def step(self, f, u, t):
        return f(u, t)
```

Note that one could use the name of the parent class explicitly. The use of super instead allows us to change the name of the parent class without having to change all the references to the parent class.

Encapsulation

Sometimes the use of inheritance is impractical or even impossible. This motivates the use of encapsulation. We will explain the concept of encapsulation by considering Python functions, that is, objects of the Python type function, which we encapsulate in a new class, Function, and provide with some relevant methods:

```
class Function:
    def __init__(self, f):
        self.f = f
    def __call__(self, x):
        return self.f(x)
    def __add__(self, g):
        def sum(x):
            return self(x) + g(x)
        return type(self)(sum)
    def __mul__(self, g):
        def prod(x):
            return self.f(x) * g(x)
        return type(self)(prod)
    def __radd__(self, g):
        return self + g
    def __rmul__(self, g):
        return self * g
```

Note that the __add__ and __mul__ operations should return an instance of the same class. This is achieved by the return type(self)(sum) statement, which in this case is a more general form of writing return Function(sum). We can now derive subclasses by inheritance:

Consider as an example Chebyshev polynomials which can be computed in the interval [1,-1] by:

$$T_i(x) = \cos(i \arccos(x))$$

We construct a Chebyshev polynomial as an instance of the `Function` class:

```
T5 = Function(lambda x: cos(5 * arccos(x)))
T6 = Function(lambda x: cos(6 * arccos(x)))
```

Chebyshev polynomials are orthogonal in the sense:

$$\int_{-1}^{1} \frac{1}{\sqrt{1-x^2}} T_i(x) T_j(x) \, dx = 0 \text{ for } i \neq j \ .$$

This can easily be checked using this construction:

```
import scipy.integrate as sci

weight = Function(lambda x: 1 / sqrt((1 - x ** 2)))
[integral, errorestimate] =
        sci.quad(weight * T5 * T6, -1, 1) # (6.510878470473995e-17,
1.3237018925525037e-14)
```

Without encapsulation multiplying functions as simply as writing `weight * T5 * T6` would not have been possible.

Classes as decorators

In section *Function as decorators* in `Chapter 7`, *Functions* , we saw how functions can be modified by applying another function as a decorator. In previous examples, we saw how classes can be made to behave as functions as long as they are provided with the `__call__` method. We will use this here to show how classes can be used as decorators.

Let us assume that we want to change the behavior of some functions in such a way that before the function is invoked, all input parameters are printed. This could be useful for debugging purposes. We take this situation as an example to explain the use of a decorator class:

```
class echo:
    text = 'Input parameters of {name}n'+
        'Positional parameters {args}n'+
        'Keyword parameters {kwargs}n'
    def __init__(self, f):
        self.f = f
    def __call__(self, *args, **kwargs):
        print(self.text.format(name = self.f.__name__,
            args = args, kwargs = kwargs))
        return self.f(*args, **kwargs)
```

We use this class to decorate function definitions,

```
@echo
def line(m, b, x):
    return m * x + b
```

and call the function as usual,

```
line(2., 5., 3.)
line(2., 5., x=3.)
```

On the second call, we obtain the following output:

```
Input parameters of line
Positional parameters (2.0, 5.0)
Keyword parameters {'x': 3.0}

11.0
```

This example shows that both classes and functions can be used as decorators. Classes allow for more possibilities, as they can be used to collect data as well.

Indeed, we observe that:

- Every decorated function creates a new instance of the decorator class.
- Data collected by one instance can be saved and made accessible to another instance by class attributes (refer section *Attributes* in Chapter 8, *Classes*).

The last point emphasizes the difference with function decorators. We show this now by a decorator that counts function calls and stores the result in a dictionary with the function as key.

In order to analyze the performance of algorithms, it might be useful to count the calls of particular functions. We can get counter information without changing the function definition. The code is a slight modification of an example given in [4].

```python
class CountCalls:
    """
    Decorator that keeps track of the number of times
    a function is called.
    """
    instances = {}
    def __init__(self, f):
        self.f = f
        self.numcalls = 0
        self.instances[f] = self
    def __call__(self, *args, **kwargs):
        self.numcalls += 1
        return self.f(*args, **kwargs)
    @classmethod
    def counts(cls):
        """
        Return a dict of {function: # of calls} for all
        registered functions.
        """
        return dict([(f.__name__, cls.instances[f].numcalls)
                                for f in cls.instances])
```

Here, we use the class attribute`CountCalls.instances` to store the counters for each individual instance. Let us see how this decorator works:

```python
@CountCalls
def line(m, b, x):
    return m * x + b
@CountCalls
def parabola(a, b, c, x):
    return a * x ** 2 + b * x + c
line(3., -1., 1.)
parabola(4., 5., -1., 2.)

CountCalls.counts() # returns {'line': 1, 'parabola': 1}
parabola.numcalls # returns 1
```

Summary

One of the most important programming concepts in modern computer science is object-oriented programming. We learned in this chapter how to define objects as instances of classes, which we provide with methods and attributes. The first parameter of methods, usually denoted by `self`, plays an important and special role. You saw methods that can be used to define basic operations such as + and * for your own classes.

While in other programming languages attributes and methods can be protected against unintended use, Python allows a technique to hide attributes and access these hidden attributes through special getter and setter methods. To this end, you met an important function, `property`.

Exercises

Ex. 1 → Write a method `simplify` to the class `RationalNumber`. This method should return the simplified version of the fraction as a tuple.

Ex. 2 → To provide results with confidence intervals a special calculus, so-called interval arithmetic is introduced in numerical mathematics; (refer to [3, 14]). Define a class called `Interval` and provide it with methods for addition, subtraction, division, multiplication, and power (with positive integers only). These operations obey the following rules:

$$[a, b] + [c, d] = [a + c, b + d]$$
$$[a, b] \cdot [c, d] = [\min(a \cdot c, a \cdot d, b \cdot c, b \cdot d), \max(a \cdot c, a \cdot d, b \cdot c, b \cdot d)]$$
$$[a, b]/[c, d] = [\min(\tfrac{a}{c}, \tfrac{a}{d}, \tfrac{b}{c}, \tfrac{b}{d}), \max(\tfrac{a}{c}, \tfrac{a}{d}, \tfrac{b}{c}, \tfrac{b}{d})] \quad 0 \notin [c, d]$$
$$[a, b]^n = [a^n, b^n]$$

Provide this class with methods that allow operations of the type *a* + *I*, *a I*, *I* + *a*, *I a*, where *I* is an interval and *a* an integer or float. Convert an integer or float to an interval [a, a] first. (Hint: you may want to use function decorators for this; (refer to section *Function as decorators* in Chapter 7, *Functions*). Furthermore, implement the __contains__ method, which enables you to check if a given number belongs to the interval using the syntax x in I for an object I of type Interval. Test your class by applying a polynomial f=lambda x: 25*x**2-4*x+1 to an interval.

Ex. 3 → Consider the example under section *Classes as decorators*. Extend this example to obtain a *function decorator* that counts how often a certain function is called.

Ex. 4 → Compare the two ways to implement a method for reverse addition __radd__ in the class `RationalNumber`: the one given in the example in section *Special methods* and the one given here:

```
class RationalNumber:
    ....
    def __radd__(self, other):
        return other + self
```

Do you expect an error in this version? What is the error and how do you explain it? Test your answer by executing:

```
q = RationalNumber(10, 15)
5 + q
```

Ex. 4 → Consider the decorator class `CountCalls` as in example in section *Classes as decorators*. Provide this class with a method, `reset`, which sets the counters of all functions in the dictionary, `CountCalls.instances`, to zero. What would happen if the dictionary were replaced by an empty dictionary instead?

9
Iterating

In this chapter, we will present iteration using loops and iterators. We will show examples of how this can be used with lists and generators. Iteration is one of the fundamental operations a computer is useful for. Traditionally, iteration is achieved by a `for` loop. A `for` loop is a repetition of a block of instructions a certain number of times. Inside the loop, one has access to a loop variable, in which the iteration number is stored.

The Python idiom is slightly different. A `for` loop in Python is primarily designed to exhaust a list, that is, to enumerate the elements of a list. The effect is similar to the repetition effect just described if one uses a list containing the first n integers.

A `for` loop only needs one element of the list at a time. It is therefore desirable to use a `for` loop with objects that are able to create those elements on demand, one at a time. This is what iterators achieve in Python.

The for statement

The primary aim of the `for` statement is to traverse a list:

```
for s in ['a', 'b', 'c']:
    print(s), # a b c
```

In this example, the loop variable s is successively assigned to one element of the list. Notice that the loop variable is available after the loop has terminated. This may sometimes be useful; refer, for instance, the example in section *Controlling the flow inside the loop*.

One of the most frequent uses of a `for` loop is to repeat a given task a defined number of times, using the function `range` (refer to section *Lists* of `Chapter 1`, *Getting Started*).

```
for iteration in range(n): # repeat the following code n times
    ...
```

If the purpose of a loop is to go through a list, many languages (including Python) offer the following pattern:

```
for k in range(...):
    ...
    element = my_list[k]
```

If the purpose of that code were to go through the list `my_list`, the preceding code would not make it very clear. For this reason, a better way to express this is as follows:

```
for element in my_list:
    ...
```

It is now clear at first glance that the preceding piece of code goes through the `my_list` list. Note that if you really need the index variable *k*, you may replace the preceding code by this:

```
for k, element in enumerate(my_list):
    ...
```

The intent of this piece of code is to go through `my_list` while keeping the index variable *k* available. A similar construction for arrays is the command `ndenumerate`.

Controlling the flow inside the loop

Sometimes it is necessary to jump out of the loop, or to go directly to the next loop iteration. These two operations are performed by the `break` and `continue` commands. The `break` keyword, as the name indicates, breaks the loop. Two situations can occur where the loop breaks:

- The loop is completely executed.
- The loop is left before it was completely executed (`break`).

For the first case, special actions can be defined in an `else` block, which is executed if the whole list is traversed. This is useful in general if the purpose of the `for` loop is to find something and stop. Examples might be searching for one element satisfying a certain property inside a list. If such an element is not found, the `else` block is executed.

Here is a common usage in scientific computing. Quite often, we use an iterating algorithm that is not guaranteed to succeed. In that case, it is preferable to use a (big) finite loop so that the program does not get caught in an infinite loop. The `for/else` construct allows such an implementation:

```
maxIteration = 10000
for iteration in range(maxIteration):
    residual = compute() # some computation
    if residual < tolerance:
        break
else: # only executed if the for loop is not broken
    raise Exception("The algorithm did not converge")
print("The algorithm converged in {} steps".format(iteration+1))
```

Iterators

A `for` loop is primarily used to traverse a list, but it picks the elements of the list one at a time. In particular, there is no need to store the whole list in memory for the loop to work properly. The mechanism that allows `for` loops to work without lists is that of iterators.

An iterable object produces objects (to be passed to a `for` loop). Such an object, `obj`, may be used inside a `for` loop, as follows:

```
for element in obj:
    ...
```

The notion of iterator thus generalizes the idea of lists. The simplest example of an iterable object is given by lists. The produced objects are simply the objects stored in the list:

```
L = ['A', 'B', 'C']
for element in L:
    print(element)
```

An iterable object need not produce existing objects. The objects may, instead, be produced on the fly.

A typical iterable is the object returned by the function `range`. This function works as if it would generate a list of integers, but instead, the successive integers are produced on the fly when they are needed:

```
for iteration in range(100000000):
    # Note: the 100000000 integers are not created at once
    if iteration > 10:
        break
```

If one really needs a list with all integers between 0 and 100,000,000, then it has to be formed explicitly:

```
l=list(range(100000000))
```

Generators

You can create your own iterators using the `yield` keyword. For example, a generator for odd numbers smaller than *n* can be defined:

```
def odd_numbers(n):
    "generator for odd numbers less than n"
    for k in range(n):
        if k % 2 == 1:
            yield k
```

Then you can use it as follows:

```
g = odd_numbers(10)
for k in g:
    ...     # do something with k
```

Or even like this:

```
for k in odd_numbers(10):
    ... # do something with k
```

Iterators are disposable

One salient feature of iterators is that they may be used only once. In order to use the iterator again, you will have to create a new iterator object. Note that an iterable object is able to create new iterators as many times as necessary. Let us examine the case of a list:

```
L = ['a', 'b', 'c']
iterator = iter(L)
list(iterator) # ['a', 'b', 'c']
list(iterator) # [] empty list, because the iterator is exhausted

new_iterator = iter(L) # new iterator, ready to be used
list(new_iterator) # ['a', 'b', 'c']
```

Each time a generator object is called, it creates a new iterator. Hence, when that iterator is exhausted, one has to call the generator again to obtain a new iterator:

```
g = odd_numbers(10)
for k in g:
    ... # do something with k

# now the iterator is exhausted:
for k in g: # nothing will happen!!
    ...

# to loop through it again, create a new one:
g = odd_numbers(10)
for k in g:.
    ...
```

Iterator tools

Here are a couple of iterator tools that often come in very handy:

- enumerate is used to enumerate another iterator. It produces a new iterator that yields pairs (iteration, element), where iteration stores the index of the iteration:

```
A = ['a', 'b', 'c']
for iteration, x in enumerate(A):
    print(iteration, x)
# result: (0, 'a') (1, 'b') (2, 'c')
```

- `reversed` creates an iterator from a list by going through that list backwards. Notice that this is different from creating a reversed list:

```
A = [0, 1, 2]
for elt in reversed(A):,
    print(elt)
    # result: 2 1 0
```

- `itertools.count` is a possibly infinite iterator of integers:

```
for iteration in itertools.count():
    if iteration > 100:
        break # without this, the loop goes on forever
    print("integer {}".format(iteration))
    # prints the 100 first integer
```

- `intertools.islice` truncates an iterator using the familiar `slicing` syntax; refer to Chapter 3, *Container Types*. One application is creating a finite iterator from an infinite one:

```
from itertools import count, islice
for iteration in islice(count(), 10):
    # same effect as range(10)
    ...
```

For example, let's find some odd numbers by combining `islice` with an infinite generator. First, we modify the generator for odd numbers so that it becomes an infinite generator:

```
def odd_numbers():
    k=-1
    while True:
        k+=1
        if k%2==1:
        yield k
```

Then, we use it with `islice` to get a list of some odd numbers:

```
list(itertools.islice(odd_numbers(),10,30,8)) # returns [21, 37, 53]
```

Generators of recursive sequences

Assume that a sequence is given by an induction formula. For instance, consider the Fibonacci sequence, defined by the recurrence formula: $u_n = u_{n-1} + u_{n-2}$.

This sequence depends on two initial values, namely u_0 and u_1, although for the standard Fibonacci sequence those numbers are taken as 0 and 1 respectively. A nifty way of programming the generation of such a sequence is by using generators, as follows:

```
def fibonacci(u0, u1):
    """
    Infinite generator of the Fibonacci sequence.
    """
    yield u0
    yield u1
    while True:
        u0, u1 = u1, u0+u1
        yield u1
```

This may then be used, for instance, like this:

```
# sequence of the 100 first Fibonacci numbers:
list(itertools.islice(fibonacci(0, 1), 100))
```

Arithmetic geometric mean

The iteration based on iteratively computing arithmetic and geometric means is called **AGM iteration** (refer to [1, p. 598] for more information):

$$a_{i+1} = \frac{a_i + b_i}{2},$$
$$b_{i+1} = \sqrt{a_i b_i}$$

It has the fascinating property that for $a_0 = 1$, $b_0 = \sqrt{1 - k^2}$:

$$\frac{\pi}{2} \lim_{i \to \infty} \frac{1}{a_i} = \int_0^{\frac{\pi}{2}} \frac{1}{\sqrt{1 - k^2 \sin^2(\theta)}} d\theta =: F(k, \pi/2)$$

The integral on the right-hand side is called a complete elliptic integral of the first kind. We now proceed to compute this elliptic integral. We use a generator to describe the iteration:

```python
def arithmetic_geometric_mean(a, b):
    """
    Generator for the arithmetic and geometric mean
    a, b initial values
    """
    while True:      # infinite loop
        a, b = (a+b)/2, sqrt(a*b)
        yield a, b
```

As the sequence $\{a_i\}$ is convergent, the sequence $\{c_i\}$ defined by $\{c_i\} = (a_i - b_i)/2$, converges to zero – a fact that will be used to terminate the iteration in the program to compute the elliptic integral:

```python
def elliptic_integral(k, tolerance=1e-5):
    """
    Compute an elliptic integral of the first kind.
    """
    a_0, b_0 = 1., sqrt(1-k**2)
    for a, b in arithmetic_geometric_mean(a_0, b_0):
        if abs(a-b) < tolerance:
            return pi/(2*a)
```

We have to make sure that the algorithm stops. Note that this code fully relies on the mathematical statement that the arithmetic geometric mean iteration converges (fast). In practical computing, we have to be careful while applying theoretical results, as they might no longer be valid in limited-precision arithmetic. The right way to make the preceding code safe is to use `itertools.islice`. The safe code is as follows (see the example under the section *Controlling the flow inside the loop* for another typical usage of the `for/else` statement):

```python
from itertools import islice
def elliptic_integral(k, tolerance=1e-5, maxiter=100):
    """
    Compute an elliptic integral of the first kind.
    """
    a_0, b_0 = 1., sqrt(1-k**2)
    for a, b in islice(arithmetic_geometric_mean(a_0, b_0),
                                              maxiter):
        if abs(a-b) < tolerance:
            return pi/(2*a)
    else:
        raise Exception("Algorithm did not converge")
```

As an application, elliptic integrals may be used to compute the period of a **pendulum** of length L starting at an angle θ (refer to [18, p.114] for more information) using:

$$T = 4\sqrt{\frac{L}{g}} F\left(\sin\frac{\theta}{2}, \frac{\pi}{2}\right)$$

Using this formula, the period of the pendulum is easily obtained:

```python
def pendulum_period(L, theta, g=9.81):
    return 4*sqrt(L/g)*elliptic_integral(sin(theta/2))
```

Convergence acceleration

We give an example of application of generators for convergence acceleration. This presentation follows closely the example given by *Pramode C.E* in *Python Generator Tricks* (refer [9] for more information).

Note that a generator may take an other generator as an input parameter. For instance, suppose that we have defined a generator that generates the elements of a converging sequence. It is then possible to improve the convergence by an acceleration technique due to *Euler* and *Aitken*, often called Aitken's Δ^2-method (Refer [33]). It transforms a sequence s_i into another by defining

$$s'_i := s_i - \frac{(s_{i+1} - s_i)^2}{s_{i+2} - 2s_{i+1} + s_i}.$$

Both sequences have the same limit, but the sequence s'_i converges significantly faster. One possible implementation is as follows:

```python
def Euler_accelerate(sequence):
    """
    Accelerate the iterator in the variable `sequence`.
    """
    s0 = next(sequence)  # Si
    s1 = next(sequence)  # Si+1
    s2 = next(sequence)  # Si+2
    while True:
        yield s0 - ((s1 - s0)**2)/(s2 - 2*s1 + s0)
        s0, s1, s2 = s1, s2, next(sequence)
```

As an example, we use the classical series:

$$S_N = \sum_{n=0}^{N} \frac{(-1)^n}{2n+1}$$

It converges towards $\pi/4$. We implement this series as a generator in the following code:

```
def pi_series():
    sum = 0.
    j = 1
    for i in itertools.cycle([1, -1]):
        yield sum
        sum += i/j
        j += 2
```

We may now use the accelerated version of that sequence using this:

```
Euler_accelerate(pi_series())
```

Accordingly, the first N elements of that accelerated sequence are obtained with:

```
itertools.islice(Euler_accelerate(pi_series()), N)
```

For instance, the following figure (*Figure 9.1*) shows the convergence rate of the log of the error for the standard version of the sequence defined by the above formula and its accelerated version:

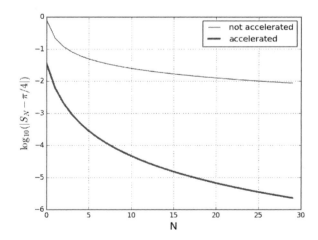

Figure 9.1: Comparison between the sequence defined and its accelerated version

List filling patterns

In this section we will compare different ways to fill lists. They are different in computational efficiency and also in code readability.

List filling with the append method

A ubiquitous programming pattern is to compute elements and store them in a list:

```
L = []
for k in range(n):
    # call various functions here
    # that compute "result"
    L.append(result)
```

This approach has a number of disadvantages:

- The number of iterations is decided in advance. If there is a break instruction, then the preceding code takes care of both generating values and deciding when to stop. This is not desirable and lacks flexibility.
- It makes the assumption that the user wants the whole history of the computation, for all the iterations. Suppose we are only interested in the sum of all the computed values. If there are many computed values, it does not make sense to store them, as it is much more efficient to add them one at a time.

List from iterators

Iterators provide us with an elegant solution to problems discussed previously:

```
def result_iterator():
    for k in itertools.count(): # infinite iterator
        # call various functions here
        # that compute "result"
        ...
        yield result
```

With iterators, we separate the task of generating the computed values without bothering about the stopping condition or about the storage. If the user of that code wants to store the n first values, it is easily done using the `list` constructor:

```
L = list(itertools.islice(result_iterator(), n)) # no append needed!
```

If the user wants the sum of the first n generated values, this construction is recommended:

```
# make sure that you do not use scipy.sum here
s = sum(itertools.islice(result_iterator(), n))
```

What we did here was separating the generation of elements on one hand, and storing those elements on the other.

If the purpose is really to build a list, and when the result at each step does not depend on previously computed elements, one may use the list comprehension syntax (refer to section *List* of Chapter 3, *Container Types*, for more information):

```
L = [some_function(k) for k in range(n)]
```

When iteratively computing values that depend on the previously computed values, list comprehensions cannot help.

Storing generated values

Using iterators to fill out lists will work nicely most of the time, but there are complications to this pattern when the algorithm computing the new values is liable to throw an exception; if the iterator raises an exception along the way, the list will not be available! The following example illustrates this problem.

Suppose we generate the sequence defined recursively by $u_{n+1} = u_n^2$. This sequence quickly diverges to infinity if the initial data u_0 is greater than one. Let us generate it with a generator:

```
import itertools
def power_sequence(u0):
    u = u0
    while True:
        yield u
        u = u**2
```

If you try to obtain the first *20* elements of the sequence (initialized by $u_0 = 2$) by executing,

```
list(itertools.islice(power_sequence(2.), 20))
```

an exception will be raised and no list will be available, not even the list of elements before the exception was raised. There is currently no way to obtain a partially filled list from a possibly faulty generator. The only way around is to use the append method wrapped in an exception-catching block (refer to section *Exceptions* in `Chapter 10`, *Error Handling*, for more details):

```
generator = power_sequence(2.)
L = []
for iteration in range(20):
    try:
        L.append(next(generator))
    except Exception:
        ...
```

When iterators behave as lists

Some list operations also work on iterators. We will now examine the equivalents of *list comprehensions* and *list zipping* (refer to section *List* of `Chapter 3`, *Container Types*, for more details).

Generator expression

There is an equivalent of list comprehension for generators. Such a construction is called a generator expression:

```
g = (n for n in range(1000) if not n % 100)
# generator for  100, 200, ... , 900
```

This is useful in particular for computing sums or products because those operations are incremental; they only need one element at a time:

```
sum(n for n in range(1000) if not n % 100) # returns 4500
```

In that code, you notice that the `sum` function is given one argument, which is a generator expression. Note that Python syntax allows us to omit the enclosing parentheses of generators when a generator is used as the *only* argument of a function.

Let us compute the Riemann zeta function ζ, whose expression is

$$\zeta(s) := \sum_{n=1}^{\infty} \frac{1}{n^s}$$

With a generator expression, we may compute a partial sum of this series in one line:

```
sum(1/n**s for n in itertools.islice(itertools.count(1), N))
```

Note that we could also have defined a generator of the sequence $1/n^s$ as follows:

```
def generate_zeta(s):
    for n in itertools.count(1):
        yield 1/n**s
```

Then we simply obtain the sum of the first *N* terms using:

```
def zeta(N, s):
    # make sure that you do not use the scipy.sum here
    return sum(itertools.islice(generate_zeta(s), N))
```

We point out that we used this way of computing the zeta (ζ) function as a demonstration of the use of generators in an elegant way. It is certainly not the most accurate and computationally efficient way to evaluate this function.

Zipping iterators

We saw in section *List*, `Chapter 3`, *Container Types*, that it is possible to create a list out of two by zipping them together. The same operation exists for iterators:

```
xg = x_iterator()  # some iterator
yg = y_iterator()  # another iterator

for x, y in zip(xg, yg):
    print(x, y)
```

The zipped iterator stops as soon as one of the iterators is exhausted. This is the same behavior as for a zip operation on lists.

Iterator objects

As we mentioned earlier, a `for` loop only needs an iterable object. Lists, in particular, are iterable. This means that a list is able to create an iterator from its contents. In fact, this is true for any object (not only lists): any object may be made iterable.

This is achieved via the __iter__ method, which should return an iterator. Here we give an example where the __iter__ method is a generator:

```
class OdeStore:
    """
    Class to store results of ode computations
    """
    def __init__(self, data):
        "data is a list of the form [[t0, u0], [t1, u1],...]"
        self.data = data

    def __iter__(self):
        "By default, we iterate on the values u0, u1,..."
        for t, u in self.data:
            yield u
store = OdeStore([[0, 1], [0.1, 1.1], [0.2, 1.3]])
for u in store:
    print(u)
# result: 1, 1.1, 1.3
list(store) # [1, 1.1, 1.3]
```

If you try to use the features of an iterator with an object that is not iterable, an exception will be raised:

```
>>> list(3)
TypeError: 'int' object is not iterable
```

In this example, the list function tries to iterate through the object 3 by calling the __iter__ method. But this method is not implemented for integers and thus the exception is raised. The same would happen if we tried to cycle through a non-iterable object:

```
>>> for iteration in 3: pass
TypeError: 'int' object is not iterable
```

Infinite iterations

Infinite iterations are obtained either with an infinite iterator, with a `while` loop, or by recursion. Obviously, in practical cases, some condition stops the iteration. The difference with finite iterations is that it is impossible to say by a cursory examination of the code, whether the iteration will stop or not.

The while loop

The `while` loop may be used to repeat a code block until a condition is fulfilled:

```
while condition:
    <code>
```

A `while` loop is equivalent to the following code:

```
for iteration in itertools.count():
    if not condition:
        break
    <code>
```

So a `while` loop is equivalent to an infinite iterator, which might be stopped if a condition is fulfilled. The danger of such a construction is obvious: the code may be trapped in an infinite loop if the condition is never fulfilled.

The problem in scientific computing is that one is not always sure that an algorithm will converge. Newton iteration, for instance, might not converge at all. If that algorithm were implemented inside a `while` loop, the corresponding code would be trapped in an infinite loop for some choices of initial conditions.

We therefore give an advice that finite iterators are often better suited for such a task. The following construction replaces, often advantageously, the use of a `while` loop:

```
maxit = 100
for nb_iterations in range(max_it):
    ...
else:
    raise Exception("No convergence in {} iterations".format(maxit))
```

The first advantage is that the code is guaranteed to execute in a finite time no matter what happens. The second advantage is that the variable `nb_iterations` contains the number of iterations that was necessary for the algorithm to converge.

Recursion

A recursion occurs when a function calls itself (refer to section *Recursive Function* in `Chapter 7`, *Functions*).

When doing recursions, it is the recursion depth, that is the number of iterations, which brings your computer to its limits. We demonstrate this here by considering a simple recursion, which actually contains no computations at all. It assigns to the iterates only the value zero:

```
def f(N):
    if N == 0:
        return 0
    return f(N-1)
```

Depending on your system, this program may choke for $N \geq 10000$ (too much memory is used). The result is that the Python interpreter crashes without further exception. Python provides a mechanism to raise an exception when a too high recursion depth is detected. This maximum recursion depth may be changed by executing:

```
import sys
sys.setrecursionlimit(1000)
```

The actual value of the recursion limit can be obtained by `sys.getrecursionlimit()`.

Be aware though, that choosing too high a number may imperil the stability of your code, since Python might crash before that maximum depth is reached. It is therefore often wise to leave the recursion limit as it is.

By comparison, the following, non recursive, program runs ten of millions of iterations without any problem:

```
for iteration in range(10000000):
    pass
```

We advocate that, if possible, recursion should be avoided in Python. This applies obviously only if there is an appropriate alternative iterative algorithm available. The first reason is that a recursion of depth N involves N function calls at the same time, which might result in a significant overhead. The second reason is that it is an infinite iteration, that is, it is difficult to give an upper bound to the number of steps necessary before the recursion is over.

Note that in some very special cases (tree traversal) recursion is unavoidable. Besides, in some cases (with small recursion depths) recursive programs might be preferred due to readability.

Summary

In this chapter, we studied iterators, a programming construct very near to a mathematical description of iterative methods. You saw the `yield` keyword and met finite and infinite iterators.

We showed that an iterator can be exhausted. More special aspects such as iterator comprehension and recursive iterators were introduced and demonstrated with the help of examples.

Exercises

Ex. 1 → Compute the value of the sum:

$$\sum_{i=1}^{200} \frac{1}{\sqrt{i}}$$

Ex. 2 → Create a generator that computes the sequence defined by the relation:

$$u_n = 2u_{n-1}$$

Ex. 3 → Generate all the even numbers.

Ex. 4 → Let $s_n := (1 + \frac{1}{n})^{2n}$. In calculus, it is shown that $\lim_{n \to \infty} s_n = e^2$. Determine experimentally the smallest number n such that $|s_n - e^2| < 10^{-5}$. Use a generator for this task.

Ex. 5 → Generate all prime numbers less than a given integer. Use the algorithm called Sieve of Eratosthenes.

Ex. 6 → Solving the differential equation $u' = -\sin u$ by applying the explicit Euler method results in the recursion:

$$u_{n+1} = u_n - h \sin u_n.$$

Write a generator that computes the solution values u_n for a given initial value u_0 and for a given value of the time step h.

Ex. 7 $\to$ Compute π using the formula:

$$\pi = \int_0^1 \frac{4}{1+x^2} x$$

The integral can be approximated using the composite trapezoidal rule, that is, by this formula:

$$\int_a^b f(x)x \approx \frac{h}{2}\left(f(a) + f(b)\right) + h\sum_{i=1}^{n-1} f(x_i)$$

where $x_i = a + ih$; $h = \frac{b-a}{n}$.

Program a *generator* for the values $y_i = f(x_i)$ and evaluate the formula by summing one term after the other. Compare your results with the `quad` function of SciPy.

Ex. 8 $\to$ Let $x = [1, 2, 3]$ and $y = [-1, -2, -3]$. What is the effect of the code `zip(*zip(x, y))`? Explain how it works.

Ex. 9 $\to$ Complete elliptic integrals can be computed by the function `scipy.special.ellipk`. Write a function, which counts the number of iterations needed with the AGM iteration until the result coincides up to a given tolerance (note that the input parameter m in `ellipk` corresponds to k^2 in the definition in the section *Arithmetic geometric mean*).

Ex. 10 $\to$ Consider the sequence defined by:

$$E_n := \int_0^1 x^n e^{x-1} \mathrm{d}x \; ; \; n = 1, 2, \ldots$$

It converges monotonically to zero: $E_1 > E_2 > \ldots > 0$. By integration by parts, one can show that the sequence E_n fulfills the following recursion:

$$E_n = 1 - nE_{n-1} \quad \text{with} \quad E_1 = 1 - \int_0^1 e^{x-1} \mathrm{d}x = e^{-1}.$$

Compute the first 20 terms of the recursion by using an appropriate generator and compare the results with those obtained by numerical integration with `scipy.integrate.quad`. Do the same by reversing the recursion:

$$E_{n-1} := \frac{1}{n}(1 - E_n) \quad \text{with} \quad E_{20} = 0$$

Use the `exp` function to evaluate the exponential function. What do you observe? Do you have an explanation? (refer to [29])

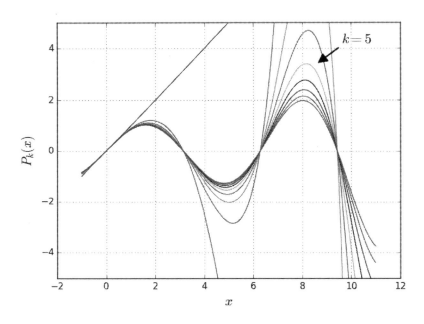

Figure 9.2: A convergence study of functions approximating to sin(x)

Ex. 11 → The sine-function can be expressed due to Euler as

$$\sin x = x \prod_{k=1}^{\infty} \left(1 - \frac{x^2}{k^2\pi^2}\right) = x \underbrace{\left(1 - \frac{x^2}{\pi^2}\right)\left(1 - \frac{x^2}{4\pi^2}\right)\left(1 - \frac{x^2}{9\pi^2}\right)}_{=:P_3(x)} \cdots$$

Write a generator that generates the function values $P_k(x)$. Set
`x=linspace(-1,3.5*pi,200)` and demonstrate graphically how good
$P_k(x)$ approximates sin for increasing k. In previous figure (*Figure 9.2*), the possible result is shown (refer to [11, Th. 5.2, p. 65]).

10
Error Handling

In this chapter, we will cover errors, exceptions, and how to find and fix them. Handling exceptions is an important part of writing reliable and usable code. We will introduce the basic built-in exceptions and show how to use and treat exceptions. We'll introduce debugging and show you how to use the built-in Python debugger.

What are exceptions?

One error programmers (even experienced ones) find is when code has incorrect syntax, meaning that the code instructions are not correctly formatted.

Consider an example of Syntax error:

```
>>> for i in range(10)
   File "<stdin>", line 1
      for i in range(10)
                         ^
SyntaxError: invalid syntax
```

The error occurs because of a missing colon at the end of the `for` declaration. This is an example of an exception being raised. In the case of `SyntaxError`, it tells the programmer that the code has incorrect syntax and also prints the line where the error occurred, with an arrow pointing to where in that line the problem is.

Exceptions in Python are derived (inherited) from a base class called `Exception`. Python comes with a number of built-in exceptions. Some common exception types are listed in *Table 10.1*, (for full list of built-in exceptions refer to [38]).

Here are two common examples of exceptions. As you might expect, `ZeroDivisionError` is raised when you try to divide by zero.

```
def f(x):
    return 1/x

>>> f(2.5)
0.4
>>> f(0)

Traceback (most recent call last):
  File "<stdin>", line 1, in <module>
  File "exception_tests.py", line 3, in f
    return 1/x
ZeroDivisionError: integer division or modulo by zero
```

Exception	Description
IndexError	Index is out of bounds, for example, `v[10]` when v only has 5 elements
KeyError	A reference to an undefined dictionary key
NameError	A name not found, for example, an undefined variable
LinAlgError	Errors in the `linalg` module, for example, when solving a system with a singular matrix
ValueError	Incompatible data value, for example, when using `dot` with incompatible arrays
IOError	I/O operation fails, for example, "file not found"
ImportError	A module or name is not found on import

Table10.1: Some frequently used built-in exceptions and their meaning

A division with zero raises `ZeroDivisionError` and prints out the file, line, and function name where the error occurred.

As we have seen before, arrays can only contain elements of the same data type. If you try to assign a value of an incompatible type, a `ValueError` is raised. An example, of a value error:

```
>>> a = arange(8.0)
>>> a
array([ 0., 1., 2., 3., 4., 5., 6., 7.])
>>> a[3] = 'string'
Traceback (most recent call last):
  File "<stdin>", line 1, in <module>
ValueError: could not convert string to float: string
```

Here, `ValueError` is raised because the array contains floats and an element cannot be assigned a string value.

Basic principles

Let's look at the basic principles on how to use exceptions by raising them with `raise` and catching them with `try` statements.

Raising exceptions

Creating an error is referred to as raising an exception. You saw some examples of exceptions in the previous section. You can also define your own exceptions, of a predefined type or type-less. Raising an exception is done with the command like this:

```
raise Exception("Something went wrong")
```

It might be tempting to print out error messages when something goes wrong, for example, like this:

```
print("The algorithm did not converge.")
```

This is not recommended for a number of reasons. Firstly, printouts are easy to miss, especially if the message is buried in many other messages being printed to your console. Secondly, and more importantly, it renders your code unusable by other code. The calling code will have no way of knowing that an error occurred and therefore have no way of taking care of it.

For these reasons, it is always better to raise an exception instead. Exceptions should always contain a descriptive message, for example:

```
raise Exception("The algorithm did not converge.")
```

This message will stand out clearly for the user. It also gives the opportunity for the calling code to know that an error occurred, and to possibly find a remedy.

Here is a typical example of checking the input inside a function to make sure it is usable before continuing. For an example, a simple check for negative values and the correct data type ensures the intended input of a function to compute factorials:

```
def factorial(n):
   if not (n >=0 and isinstance(n, (int,int32,int64))):
      raise ValueError("A positive integer is expected")
      ...
```

The user of the function will immediately know what the error is, if an incorrect input is given, and it is the user's responsibility to handle the exception. Note the use of the exception name when raising a predefined exception type, in this case `ValueError` followed by the message. By specifying the type of the exception, the calling code can decide to handle errors differently depending on what type of error is raised.

Summing up, it is always better to raise exceptions than to print error messages.

Catching exceptions

Dealing with an exception is referred to as catching an exception. Checking for exceptions is done with the `try` and `except` commands.

An exception stops the program execution flow and looks for the closest `try` enclosing block. If the exception is not caught, the program unit is left and it continues searching for the next enclosing `try` block in a program unit higher up in the calling stack. If no block is found and the exception is not handled, execution stops entirely; the standard traceback information is displayed.

Let's look at an example for the `try` statement:

```
try:
    <some code that might raise an exception>
except ValueError:
    print("Oops, a ValueError occurred")
```

In this case, if the code inside the `try` block raises an error of type `ValueError`, the exception will be caught and the message in the `except` block printed. If no exception occurs inside the `try` block, the `except` block is skipped entirely and execution continues.

The `except` statement can catch multiple exceptions. This is done by simply grouping them in a tuple, like this:

```
except (RuntimeError, ValueError, IOError):
```

The `try` block can also have multiple `except` statements. This makes it possible to handle exceptions differently depending on the type. Let's see an example of multiple exception types:

```
try:
    f = open('data.txt', 'r')
    data = f.readline()
    value = float(data)
except OSError as oe:
    print("{}:  {}".format(oe.strerror, oe.filename))
except ValueError:
    print("Could not convert data to float.")
```

Here an `OSError` will be caught if, for example, the file does not exist; and a `ValueError` will be caught if, for example, the data in the first line of the file is not compatible with the float data type.

In this example we assigned the `OSError` to a variable `oe` by the keyword `as`. This allows to access more details when handling this exception. Here we printed the error string `oe.strerror` and the name of the related file `oe.filename`. Each error type can have its own set of variables depending on the type. If the file does not exist, in the preceding example, the message will be:

```
I/O error(2): No such file or directory
```

On the other hand, if the file exists but you don't have permission to open it, the message will be:

```
I/O error(13): Permission denied
```

This is a useful way to format the output when catching exceptions.

The `try - except` combination can be extended with optional `else` and `finally` blocks. An example of using `else` can be seen in section *Testing the bisection algorithm* of Chapter 13, *Testing*. Combining `try` with `finally` gives a useful construction when cleanup work needs to happen at the end:

An example for making sure a file is closed properly:

```
try:
    f = open('data.txt', 'r')
    # some function that does something with the file
    process_file_data(f)
except:
    ...
finally:
    f.close()
```

This will make sure that the file is closed at the end no matter what exceptions are thrown while processing the file data. Exceptions that are not handled inside the `try` statement are saved and raised after the `finally` block. This combination is used in the `with` statement; see section *Context Managers — the with statement*.

User-defined exceptions

Besides the built-in Python exceptions, it is also possible to define your own exceptions. Such user-defined exceptions should inherit from the `Exception` base class. This can be useful when you define your own classes like the polynomial class in section *Polynomials* of Chapter 14, *Comprehensive Examples*.

Take a look at this small example of a simple user-defined exception:

```
class MyError(Exception):
    def __init__(self, expr):
        self.expr = expr
    def __str__(self):
        return str(self.expr)

try:
```

```
    x = random.rand()
    if x < 0.5:
        raise MyError(x)
except MyError as e:
    print("Random number too small", e.expr)
else:
    print(x)
```

A random number is generated. If the number is below 0.5, an exception is thrown and a message that the value is too small is printed. If no exception is raised, the number is printed.

In this example, you also saw a case of using `else` in a `try` statement. The block under `else` will be executed if no exception occurs.

It is recommended that you define your exceptions with names that end in `Error`, like the naming of the standard built-in exceptions.

Context managers — the with statement

There is a very useful construction in Python for simplifying exception handling when working with contexts, such as files or databases. The statement encapsulates the `try` ... `finally` structure in one simple command. Here is an example of using `with` to read a file:

```
with open('data.txt', 'r') as f:
    process_file_data(f)
```

This will try to open the file, run the specified operations on the file (for example, reading), and close the file. If anything goes wrong during the execution of `process_file_data`, the file is closed properly and then the exception is raised. This is equivalent to:

```
f = open('data.txt', 'r')
try:
    # some function that does something with the file
    process_file_data(f)
except:
    ...
finally:
    f.close()
```

We will use this option in section *File handling* of `Chapter 12`, *Input and Output*, when reading and writing files.

The preceding file reading example is an example of using context managers. Context managers are Python objects with two special methods, _ _enter_ _ and _ _exit_ _. Any object of a class that implements these two methods can be used as a context manager. In this example, the file object f is a context manager as there are f._ _enter_ _ and f._ _exit_ _ methods.

The _ _enter_ _ method should implement the initialization instructions, for example, opening a file or a database connection. If this method has a return statement, the returned object is accessed using the as construct. Otherwise, the as keyword is omitted. The _ _exit_ _ method contains the cleanup instructions, for example, closing a file or committing transactions and closing a database connection. For more explanations and an example of a self-written context manager, see the section *Timing with a context manager* of Chapter 13, *Testing*.

There are NumPy functions that can be used as context managers. For example, the load function supports context manager for some file formats. NumPy's function errstate can be used as a context manager to specify floating-point error handling behavior within a block of code.

Here is an example of working with errstate and a context manager:

```
import numpy as np       # note, sqrt in NumPy and SciPy
                         # behave differently in that example
with errstate(invalid='ignore'):
    print(np.sqrt(-1)) # prints 'nan'

with errstate(invalid='warn'):
    print(np.sqrt(-1)) # prints 'nan' and
                 # 'RuntimeWarning: invalid value encountered in sqrt'

with errstate(invalid='raise'):
    print(np.sqrt(-1)) # prints nothing and raises FloatingPointError
```

Refer section *Infinite and Not a Number* of Chapter 2, *Variables and Basic Types*, for more details on this example and section *Timing with a context manager* of Chapter 13, *Testing* for another example.

Finding Errors: Debugging

Errors in software code are sometimes referred to as *bugs*. Debugging is the process of finding and fixing bugs in code. This process can be performed at varying degrees of sophistication. The most efficient way is to use a tool called debugger. Having unittests in place is a good way to identify errors early, refer section *Using unittest* of `Chapter 13`, *Testing*. When it is not obvious where or what the problem is, a debugger is very useful.

Bugs

There are typically two kinds of bugs:

- An exception is raised and not caught.
- The code does not function properly.

The first case is usually easier to fix. The second can be more difficult as the problem can be a faulty idea or solution, a faulty implementation, or a combination of the two.

We are only concerned with the first case in what follows, but the same tools can be used to help find why the code does not do what it is supposed to.

The stack

When an exception is raised, you see the call stack. The call stack contains the trace of all the functions that called the code where the exception was raised.

A simple stack example:

```
def f():
    g()
def g():
    h()
def h():
    1//0

f()
```

The stack in this case is f, g, and h. The output generated by running this piece of code looks like this:

```
Traceback (most recent call last):
  File "stack_example.py", line 11, in <module>
    f()
  File "stack_example.py", line 3, in f
    g()
  File "stack_example.py", line 6, in g
    h() File "stack_example.py", line 9, in h
    1//0
ZeroDivisionError: integer division or modulo by zero
```

The error is printed. The sequence of functions leading up to the error is shown. The function f on line 11 was called, which in turn called g and then h. This caused the ZeroDivisionError.

A stack trace reports on the active stack certain point in the execution of a program. A stack trace lets you track the sequence of functions called up to a given point. Often this is after an uncaught exception has been raised. This is sometimes called post-mortem analysis, and the stack trace point is then the place where the exception occurred. Another option is to invoke a stack trace manually to analyze a piece of code where you suspect there is an error, perhaps before the exception occurs.

The Python debugger

Python comes with its own built-in debugger called pdb. Some development environments come with the debugger integrated. The following process still holds in most of these cases.

The easiest way to use the debugger is to enable stack tracing at the point in your code that you want to investigate. Here is a simple example of triggering the debugger based on the example mentioned in section *Return values* of Chapter 7, *Functions*:

```
import pdb

def complex_to_polar(z):
    pdb.set_trace()
    r = sqrt(z.real ** 2 + z.imag ** 2)
    phi = arctan2(z.imag, z.real)
    return (r,phi)
z = 3 + 5j
r,phi = complex_to_polar(z)

print(r,phi)
```

The `pdb.set_trace()` command starts the debugger and enables tracing of subsequent commands. The preceding code will show this:

```
> debugging_example.py(7)complex_to_polar()
-> r = sqrt(z.real ** 2 + z.imag ** 2)
(Pdb)
```

The debugger prompt is indicated with (Pdb). The debugger stops the program execution and gives you a prompt that lets you inspect variables, modify variables, step through commands, and so on.

The current line is printed at each step, so you can follow where you are and what will happen next. Stepping through commands is done with the command n (next), like this:

```
> debugging_example.py(7)complex_to_polar()
-> r = sqrt(z.real ** 2 + z.imag ** 2)
(Pdb) n
> debugging_example.py(8)complex_to_polar()
-> phi = arctan2(z.imag, z.real)
(Pdb) n
> debugging_example.py(9)complex_to_polar()
-> return (r,phi)
(Pdb)
...
```

The command n (next) will continue to the next line and print the line. If you need to see more than one line at the time, the list command l (list) shows the current line with surrounding code:

Listing surrounding code in the debugger:

```
> debugging_example.py(7)complex_to_polar()
-> r = sqrt(z.real ** 2 + z.imag ** 2)
(Pdb) l
  2
  3 import pdb
  4
  5 def complex_to_polar(z):
  6 pdb.set_trace()
  7 -> r = sqrt(z.real ** 2 + z.imag ** 2)
  8 phi = arctan2(z.imag, z.real)
  9 return (r,phi)
 10
 11 z = 3 + 5j
 12 r,phi = complex_to_polar(z)
(Pdb)
```

Inspection of variables can be done by printing their values to the console using the command p (print) followed by the variable name. An example of printing variables:

```
> debugging_example.py(7)complex_to_polar()
-> r = sqrt(z.real ** 2 + z.imag ** 2)
(Pdb) p z
(3+5j) (Pdb) n
> debugging_example.py(8)complex_to_polar()
-> phi = arctan2(z.imag, z.real)
(Pdb) p r
5.8309518948453007
(Pdb) c
(5.8309518948453007, 1.0303768265243125)
```

The p (print) command will print the variable; command c (continue) continues execution.

Changing a variable in mid-execution is useful. Simply assign the new value at the debugger prompt and step or continue the execution.

An example of changing variables:

```
> debugging_example.py(7)complex_to_polar()
-> r = sqrt(z.real ** 2 + z.imag ** 2)
(Pdb) z = 2j
(Pdb) z
2j
(Pdb) c
(2.0, 1.5707963267948966)
```

Here the variable z is assigned a new value to be used throughout the remaining code. Note that the final printout has changed.

Overview – debug commands

In *Table 10.2*, the most common debug commands are shown. For a full listing and description of commands, (see the documentation [25] for more information). Note that any Python command also works, for example, assigning values to variables.

Short variable names

If you want to inspect a variable with a name that coincides with any of the debugger's short commands, for example, h, you must use !h to display the variable.

Command	Action
h	Help (without arguments, it prints available commands)
l	List the code around the current line
q	Quit (exits the debugger and the execution stops)
c	Continue execution
r	Continue execution until the current function returns
n	Continue execution until the next line
p <expression>	Evaluate and print the expression in the current context

Table10.2: The most common debug commands for the debugger.

Debugging in IPython

IPython comes with a version of the debugger called ipdb. At the time of writing this book, the differences are very minor but this may change.

There is a command in IPython that automatically turns on the debugger in case of an exception. This is very useful when experimenting with new ideas or code. An example of how to automatically turn on the debugger in IPython:

```
In [1]: %pdb # this is a so - called IPython magic command
Automatic pdb calling has been turned ON

In [2]: a = 10

In [3]: b = 0

In [4]: c = a/b
```

```
ZeroDivisionError                       Traceback (most recent call last)
<ipython-input-4-72278c42f391> in <module>()
----> 1 c = a/b

ZeroDivisionError: integer division or modulo by zero
> <ipython-input-4-72278c42f391>(1)<module>()
      -1 c = a/b
ipdb>
```

The IPython magic command `%pdb` at the IPython prompt automatically enables the debugger when exceptions are raised. Here the debugger prompt shows `ipdb` instead to indicate that the debugger is running.

Summary

The key concepts in this chapter were exceptions and errors. We showed how an exception is raised to be later in another program unit caught. You can define your own exceptions and equip them with messages and current values of given variables.

Code may return unexpected results without throwing an exception. The technique to localize the source of the erroneous result is called debugging. We introduced debugging methods and hopefully encouraged you to train them so that you have them readily available when needed. The need for serious debugging comes sooner than you might expect.

11
Namespaces, Scopes, and Modules

In this chapter, we will cover Python modules. Modules are files containing functions and class definitions. The concept of a namespace and the scope of variables across functions and modules is also explained in this chapter.

Namespace

Names of Python objects, such as names of variables, classes, functions, and modules, are collected in namespaces. Modules and classes have their own named namespaces with the same name as these objects. These namespaces are created when a module is imported or a class is instantiated. The lifetime of a namespace of a module is as long as the current Python session. The lifetime of a namespace of a class instance is until the instance is deleted.

Functions create a local namespace when they are executed (invoked). It is deleted when the function stops the execution by a regular return or an exception. Local namespaces are unnamed.

The concept of namespaces puts a variable name in its context. For example, there are several functions with the name `sin` and they are distinguished by the namespace they belong to, as shown in the following code:

```
import math
import scipy
math.sin
scipy.sin
```

They are indeed different, as `scipy.sin` is a universal function accepting lists or arrays as input, where `math.sin` takes only floats. A list with all the names in a particular namespace can be obtained by the command `dir(<name of the namespace>)`. It contains two special names `__name__` and `__doc__`. The former refers to the name of the module and the latter to its docstring:

```
math.__name__ # returns math
math.__doc__ # returns 'This module is always ...'
```

There is a special namespace, `__builtin__`, which contains names that are available in Python without any `import`. It is a named namespace but its name need not be given when referring to a built-in object:

```
'float' in dir(__builtin__) # returns True
float is __builtin__.float # returns True
```

Scope of a variable

A variable defined in one part of a program needs not to be known in other parts. All program units to which it a certain variable is known are called the scope of that variable. We first give an example; let's consider the two nested functions:

```
e = 3
def my_function(in1):
    a = 2 * e
    b = 3
    in1 = 5
    def other_function():
      c = a
      d = e
      return dir()
    print("""
        my_function's namespace: {}
        other_function's namespace: {}
        """.format(dir(),other_function()))
    return a
```

Execution of `my_function(3)` results in:

```
my_function's namespace: ['a', 'b', 'in1', 'other_function']
other_function's namespace: ['a', 'c', 'd']
```

The variable e is in the namespace of the program unit that encloses the function my_function . The variable a is in the namespace of this function, which itself encloses the innermost function other_function. For the two functions, e is a global variable.

It is a good practice to pass information to a function only by its parameter list and not use the construction from the preceding example. An exception can be found in section *Anonymous functions* in Chapter 7, *Functions*, where global variables are used for closures. By assigning it a value, a variable automatically becomes a local variable:

```
e = 3
def my_function():
    e = 4
    a = 2
    print("my_function's namespace: {}".format(dir()))
```

Execution of

```
e = 3
my_function()
e # has the value 3
```

gives:

```
my_function's namespace: ['a', 'e']
```

Where e became a local variable. In fact, this piece of code now has two variables e belonging to different namespaces.

By using the global declaration statement, a variable defined in a function can be made global, that is, its value will be accessible even outside this function. The use of a global declaration is demonstrated as follows:

```
def fun():
    def fun1():
        global a
        a = 3
    def fun2():
        global b
        b = 2
        print(a)
    fun1()
    fun2() # prints a
    print(b)
```

Avoid using global

It would be advisable to avoid using this construct and the use of `global`. These kinds of code are hard to debug and maintain. The use of classes (refer to `Chapter 8`, *Classes*, for more information) makes `global` mainly obsolete.

Modules

In Python, a module is simply a file containing classes and functions. By importing the file in your session or script, the functions and classes become usable.

Introduction

Python comes with many different libraries by default. You may also want to install more of those for specific purposes, such as optimization, plotting, reading/writing file formats, image handling, and so on. NumPy and SciPy are two important examples of such libraries, matplotlib for plotting is another one. At the end of this chapter, we will list some useful libraries.

To use a library, you may either:

- Load only certain objects from a library, for example from NumPy:

    ```
    from numpy import array, vander
    ```

- Or load the entire library:

    ```
    from numpy import *
    ```

- Or give access to an entire library by creating a namespace with the library name:

    ```
    import numpy
    ...
    numpy.array(...)
    ```

    Prefixing a function from the library with the namespace gives access to this function and distinguishes this function from other objects with the same name.

Furthermore, the name of a namespace can be specified together with the `import` command:

```
import numpy as np
...
np.array(...)
```

Which option you use affects the readability of your code as well as the possibilities for mistakes. A common mistake is shadowing:

```
from scipy.linalg import eig
A = array([[1,2],[3,4]])
(eig, eigvec) = eig(A)
...
(c, d) = eig(B) # raises an error
```

A way to avoid this unintended effect is to use `import`:

```
import scipy.linalg as sl
A = array([[1,2],[3,4]])
(eig, eigvec) = sl.eig(A) # eig and sl.eig are different objects
...
(c, d) = sl.eig(B)
```

Throughout this book, we have used many commands, objects, and functions. These were imported into the local namespace by statements such as:

```
from scipy import *
```

Importing objects in this manner does not make the module from which they are imported evident. Some examples are given in the following table (*Table 11.1*):

Libraries	Methods
numpy	array, arange, linspace, vstack, hstack, dot, eye, identity, and zeros.
numpy.linalg	solve, lstsq, eig, and det.
matplotlib.pyplot	plot, legend, and cla.
scipy.integrate	quad.
copy	copy and deepcopy.

Table 11.1: Examples of importing objects

Modules in IPython

IPython is used under code development. A typical scenario is that you work on a file with some function or class definitions which you change within a development cycle. For loading the contents of such a file into the shell, you may use import but the file is loaded only once. Changing the file has no effect on later imports. That's where IPyhthon's magic command run enters the stage.

The IPython magic command

IPython has a special magic command named run that executes a file as if you ran it directly in Python. This means that the file is executed independently of what is already defined in IPython. This is the recommended method to execute files from within IPython when you want to test a script intended as a standalone program. You must import all you need in the executed file in the same way as if you were executing it from the command line. A typical example of running code in myfile.py is:

```
from numpy import array
...
a = array(...)
```

This script file is executed in Python by exec(open('myfile.py').read()). Alternatively, in IPython the magic command run myfile can be used if you want to make sure that the script runs independent of the previous imports. Everything that is defined in the file is imported into the IPython workspace.

The variable __name__

In any module, the special variable __name__ is defined as the name of the current module. In the command line (in IPython), this variable is set to __main__, which allows the following trick:

```
# module
import ...

class ...

if __name__ == "__main__":
    # perform some tests here
```

The tests will be run only when the file is directly run, not when it is imported.

Some useful modules

The list of useful Python modules is vast. In the following table, we have given a very short segment of such a list, focused on modules related to mathematical and engineering applications (*Table 11.2*):

Module	Description
scipy	Functions used in scientific computing
numpy	Support arrays and related methods
matplotlib	Plotting and visualization with the import submodule pyplot
functools	Partial application of functions
itertools	Iterator tools to provide special capabilities, like slicing to generators
re	Regular expressions for advanced string handling
sys	System specific functions
os	Operating system interfaces like directory listing and file handling
datetime	Representing dates and date increments
time	Returning wall clock time
timeit	Measures execution time
sympy	Computer arithmetic package (symbolic computations)
pickle	Pickling, special file in- and output format
shelves	Shelves, special file in- and output format
contextlib	Tools for context managers

Table 11.2: A non-exhaustive list of useful Python packages for engineering applications

Summary

We started the book by telling you that you had to import SciPy and other useful modules. Now you fully understand what importing means. We introduced namespaces and discussed the difference between import and from ... import *. The scope of a variable was already introduced in an earlier Chapter 7, *Functions*, but now you have a more complete picture of the importance of that concept.

12
Input and Output

In this chapter, we will cover some options for handling data files. Depending on the data and the desired format, there are several options for reading and writing. We will show some of the most useful alternatives.

File handling

File I/O (input and output) is essential in a number of scenarios. For example:

- Working with measured or scanned data. Measurements are stored in files that need to be read to be analyzed.
- Interacting with other programs. Save results to files so that they can be imported in other applications, and vice-versa.
- Storing information for future reference or comparisons.
- Sharing data and results with others, possibly on other platforms using other software.

In this section, we will cover how to handle file I/O in Python.

Interacting with files

In Python, an object of type `file` represents the contents of a physical file stored on disk. A new `file` object may be created using the following syntax:

```
myfile = open('measurement.dat','r') # creating a new file object from an
existing file
```

The contents of the file may be accessed, for instance, with this:

```
print(myfile.read())
```

Usage of file objects requires some care. The problem is that a file has to be closed before it can be reread or used by other applications, which is done using the following syntax:

```
myfile.close() # closes the file object
```

It is, however, not that simple because an exception might be triggered before the call to `close` is executed, which will skip the closing code (consider the following example). A simple way to make sure that a file will be properly closed is to use context managers. This construction, using the `with` keyword, is explained in more detail in section *Exception* in `Chapter 10`, *Error Handling*. Here is how it is used with files:

```
with open('measurement.dat','r') as myfile:
     ... # use myfile here
```

This ensures that the file is closed when one exits the `with` block, even if an exception is raised inside the block. The command works with context manager objects. We recommend that you read more on context managers in section *Exception* in `Chapter 10`, *Error Handling*. Here is an example showing why the `with` construct is desirable:

```
myfile = open(name,'w')
myfile.write('some data')
a = 1/0
myfile.write('other data')
myfile.close()
```

An exception is raised before the file is closed. The file remains open, and there is no guarantee of what data is written in the file or when it is written. Hence, the proper way to achieve the same result is this:

```
with open(name,'w') as myfile:
    myfile.write('some data')
    a = 1/0
    myfile.write('other data')
```

In that case, the file is cleanly closed just after the exception (here, `ZeroDivisionError`) is raised. Notice also that there is no need to close the file explicitly.

Files are iterable

A file is, in particular, iterable (refer to section *Iterators* of `Chapter 9`, *Iterating*). Files iterate their lines:

```
with open(name,'r') as myfile:
    for line in myfile:
        data = line.split(';')
        print('time {} sec temperature {} C'.format(data[0],data[1]))
```

The lines of the file are returned as strings. The string method `split` is a possible tool to convert the string to a list of strings. For example:

```
data = 'aa;bb;cc;dd;ee;ff;gg'
data.split(';') # ['aa', 'bb', 'cc', 'dd', 'ee', 'ff', 'gg']

data = 'aa bb cc dd ee ff gg'
data.split(' ') # ['aa', 'bb', 'cc', 'dd', 'ee', 'ff', 'gg']
```

Since the `myfile` object is iterable, we can also do a direct extraction into a list, as follows:

```
data = list(myfile)
```

File modes

As you can see in these examples of file handling, the `open` function takes at least two arguments. The first is obviously the filename, and the second is a string describing the way in which the file will be used. There are several such modes for opening files; the basic ones are:

```
with open('file1.dat','r') as ...    # read only
with open('file2.dat','r+') as ...   # read/write
with open('file3.dat','rb') as ...   # read in byte mode
with open('file4.dat','a') as ...    # append (write to the end of the file)
with open('file5.dat','w') as ... # (over-)write the file
with open('file6.dat','wb') as ... # (over-)write the file in byte mode
```

The `'r'`, `'r+'`, and `'a'` modes require that the file exists, whereas `'w'` will create a new file if no file with that name exists. Reading and writing with `'r'` and `'w'` is most common, as you saw in previous examples.

Consider an example of opening a file and adding data at the end of the file without modifying what is already there using the append `'a'` mode. Note the line break,`\n` :

```
with open('file3.dat','a') as myfile:
    myfile.write('something new\n')
```

NumPy methods

NumPy has built-in methods for reading and writing NumPy array data to text files. These are `numpy.loadtxt` and `numpy.savetxt`.

savetxt

Writing an array to a text file is simple:

```
savetxt(filename,data)
```

There are two useful parameters given as strings, `fmt` and `delimiter`, which control the format and the delimiter between columns. The defaults are space for the delimiter and `%.18e` for the format, which corresponds to the exponential format with all digits. The formatting parameters are used as follows:

```
x = range(100) # 100 integers
savetxt('test.txt',x,delimiter=',')    # use comma instead of space
savetxt('test.txt',x,fmt='%d') # integer format instead of float with e
```

loadtxt

Reading to an array from a text file is done with the help of the following syntax:

```
filename = 'test.txt'
data = loadtxt(filename)
```

Due to the fact that each row in an array must have the same length, each row in the text file must have the same number of elements. Similar to savetxt, the default values are float and the delimiter is space. These can be set using the dtype and delimiter parameters. Another useful parameter is comments, which can be used to mark what symbol is used for comments in the data file. An example for using the formatting parameters is as follows:

```
data = loadtxt('test.txt',delimiter=';')     # data separated by semicolons
data = loadtxt('test.txt',dtype=int,comments='#') # read to integer type,
                                              #comments in file begin with
a hash character
```

Pickling

The read and write methods you just saw convert data to strings before writing. Complex types (such as objects and classes) cannot be written this way. With Python's pickle module, you can save any object and also multiple objects to file.

Data can be saved in plaintext (ASCII) format or using a slightly more efficient binary format. There are two main methods: dump, which saves a pickled representation of a Python object to a file, and load, which retrieves a pickled object from the file. The basic usage is like this:

```
import pickle
with open('file.dat','wb') as myfile:
    a = random.rand(20,20)
    b = 'hello world'
    pickle.dump(a,myfile)     # first call: first object
    pickle.dump(b,myfile)     # second call: second object


import pickle
with open('file.dat','rb') as myfile:
    numbers = pickle.load(myfile) # restores the array
    text = pickle.load(myfile)    # restores the string
```

Note the order in which the two objects are returned. Besides the two main methods, it is sometimes useful to serialize a Python object to a string instead of a file. This is done with dumps and load. Consider an example for serializing an array and a dictionary:

```
a = [1,2,3,4]
pickle.dumps(a) # returns a bytes object
b = {'a':1,'b':2}
pickle.dumps(b) # returns a bytes object
```

A good example of using `dumps` is when you need to write Python objects or NumPy arrays to a database. These usually have support for storing strings, which makes it easy to write and read complex data and objects without any special modules. Besides the pickle module, there is also an optimized version called `cPickle`. It is written in C and is an option if you need fast reading and writing. The data produced by pickle and *cPickle* is identical and can be interchanged.

Shelves

Objects in dictionaries can be accessed by keys. There is a similar way to access particular data in a file by first assigning it a key. This is possible by using the module shelve:

```
from contextlib import closing
import shelve as sv
# opens a data file (creates it before if necessary)
with closing(sv.open('datafile')) as data:
    A = array([[1,2,3],[4,5,6]])
    data['my_matrix'] = A  # here we created a key
```

In the section *File handling*, we saw that the built-in `open` command generates a context manager, and we saw why this is important for handling external resources, such as files. In contrast to this command, `sv.open` does not create a context manager by itself. The `closing` command from the `contextlib` module is needed to transform it into an appropriate context manager. Consider the following example of restoring the file:

```
from contextlib import closing
import shelve as sv
with closing(sv.open('datafile')) as data: # opens a data file
    A = data['my_matrix']  # here we used the key
    ...
```

A shelve object has all dictionary methods, for example, keys and values, and can be used in the same way as a dictionary. Note that changes are only written in the file after the `close` or `sync` method has been called.

Reading and writing Matlab data files

SciPy has the ability to read and write data in Matlab's `.mat` file format using the module. The commands are `loadmat` and `savemat`. To load data, use the following syntax:

```
import scipy.io
data = scipy.io.loadmat('datafile.mat')
```

The variable data now contains a dictionary, with keys corresponding to the variable names saved in the `.mat` file. The variables are in NumPy array format. Saving to `.mat` files involves creating a dictionary with all the variables you want to save (variable name and value). The command is then `savemat`:

```
data = {}
data['x'] = x
data['y'] = y
scipy.io.savemat('datafile.mat',data)
```

This saves the NumPy arrays x and y with the same names when read into Matlab.

Reading and writing images

SciPy comes with some basic functions for handling images. The module function will read images to NumPy arrays. The function will save an array as an image. The following will read a *JPEG* image to an array, print the shape and type, then create a new array with a resized image, and write the new image to file:

```
import scipy.misc as sm

# read image to array
im = sm.imread("test.jpg")
print(im.shape)    # (128, 128, 3)
print(im.dtype)    # uint8

# resize image
im_small = sm.imresize(im, (64,64))
print(im_small.shape)    # (64, 64, 3)

# write result to new image file
sm.imsave("test_small.jpg", im_small)
```

Note the data type. Images are almost always stored with pixel values in the range *0...255* as 8-bit unsigned integers. The third shape value shows how many color channels the image has. In this case, *3* means it is a color image with values stored in this order: red `im[0]`, green `im[1]`, blue `im[2]`. A gray scale image would only have one channel.

For working with images, the SciPy module `scipy.misc` contains many useful basic image processing functions such as filtering, transforms, and measurements.

Summary

File handling is inevitable when dealing with measurements and other sources of a larger amount of data. Also communication with other programs and tools is done via file handling.

You learned to see a file as a Python object like others with important methods such as `readlines` and `write`. We showed how files can be protected by special attributes, which may allow only read or only write access.

The way you write to a file often influences the speed of the process. We saw how data is stored by pickling or by using the `shelve` method.

13
Testing

In this chapter, we will focus on two aspects of testing for scientific programming. The first aspect is the often difficult topic of what to test in scientific computing. The second aspect covers the question of how to test. We will distinguish between manual and automated testing. Manual testing is what is done by every programmer to quickly check that an implementation is working or not. Automated testing is the refined, automated variant of that idea. We will introduce some tools available for automatic testing in general, with a view on the particular case of scientific computing.

Manual testing

During the development of code, you do a lot of small tests in order to test its functionality. This could be called manual testing. Typically, you would test if a given function does what it is supposed to do, by manually testing the function in an interactive environment. For instance, suppose that you implement the bisection algorithm. It is an algorithm that finds a zero (root) of a scalar non-linear function. To start the algorithm, an interval has to be given with the property that the function takes different signs on the interval boundaries, see *Exercise 4*, `Chapter 7`, *Functions*, for more information.

You will then test an implementation of that algorithm, typically by checking that:

- A solution is found when the function has opposite signs at the interval boundaries
- An exception is raised when the function has the same sign at the interval boundaries

Manual testing, as necessary as it may seem to be, is unsatisfactory. Once you have convinced yourself that the code does what it is supposed to do, you formulate a relatively small number of demonstration examples to convince others of the quality of the code. At that stage, one often looses interest in the tests made during development and they are forgotten or even deleted. As soon as you change a detail and things no longer work correctly, you might regret that your earlier tests are no longer available.

Automatic testing

The correct way to develop any piece of code is to use automatic testing. The advantages are:

- The automated repetition of a large number of tests after every code refactoring and before any new versions are launched.
- A silent documentation of the use of the code.
- A documentation of the test coverage of your code: Did things work before a change or was a certain aspect never tested?

 Changes in the program and in particular in its structure which do not affect its functionality are called code refactoring.

We suggest developing tests in parallel to the code. Good design of tests is an art of its own and there is rarely an investment which guarantees such a good pay-off in development time savings as the investment in good tests.

Now we will go through the implementation of a simple algorithm with the automated testing methods in mind.

Testing the bisection algorithm

Let us examine automated testing for the bisection algorithm. With this algorithm, a zero of a real valued function is found. It is described section *Exercise 4* in `Chapter 7`, *Functions*. An implementation of the algorithm can have the following form:

```python
def bisect(f, a, b, tol=1.e-8):
    """
    Implementation of the bisection algorithm
    f real valued function
    a,b interval boundaries (float) with the property
    f(a) * f(b) <= 0
    tol tolerance (float)
    """
    if f(a) * f(b)> 0:
        raise ValueError("Incorrect initial interval [a, b]")
    for i in range(100):
        c = (a + b) / 2.
        if f(a) * f(c) <= 0:
            b = c
        else:
            a = c
        if abs(a - b) < tol:
            return (a + b) / 2
    raise Exception(
            'No root found within the given tolerance {}'.format(tol))
```

We assume this to be stored in the `bisection.py` file. As the first test case, we test that the zero of the function $f(x) = x$ is found:

```python
def test_identity():
    result = bisect(lambda x: x, -1., 1.)
    expected = 0.
    assert allclose(result, expected),'expected zero not found'

test_identity()
```

In this code, you meet the Python keyword `assert` for the first time. It raises `AssertionError` exception if its first argument returns the `False` value. Its optional second argument is a string with additional information. We use the function `allclose` in order to test for equality of floats.

Let us comment on some of the features of the test function. We use an assertion to make sure that an exception will be raised if the code does not behave as expected. We have to manually run the test in the `test_identity()` line.

There are many tools to automate this kind of call.

Let us now set up a test that checks if `bisect` raises an exception when the function has the same sign on both ends of the interval. For now, we will suppose that the exception raised is a `ValueError` exception. In the following example, we will check the initial interval [*a*,*b*]. For the bisection algorithm it should fulfill a sign condition:

```
def test_badinput():
    try:
        bisect(lambda x: x,0.5,1)
    except ValueError:
        pass
    else:
        raise AssertionError()

test_badinput()
```

In this case, an `AssertionError` is raised if the exception is not of the `ValueError` type . There are tools to simplify the preceding construction to check that an exception is raised.

Another useful test is the edge case test. Here we test arguments or user input, which is likely to create mathematically undefined situations or states of the program not foreseen by the programmer. For instance, what happens if both bounds are equal? What happens if $a > b$?

```
def test_equal_boundaries():
    result = bisect(lambda x: x, 0., 0.)
    expected = 0.
    assert allclose(result, expected), \
                    'test equal interval bounds failed'

def test_reverse_boundaries():
    result = bisect(lambda x: x, 1., -1.)
    expected = 0.
    assert allclose(result, expected),\
                    'test reverse interval bounds failed'

test_equal_boundaries()
test_reverse_boundaries()
```

Using unittest package

The standard `unittest` Python package greatly facilitates automated testing. This package requires that we rewrite our tests to be compatible. The first test would have to be rewritten in a `class`, as follows:

```python
from bisection import bisect
import unittest

class TestIdentity(unittest.TestCase):
    def test(self):
        result = bisect(lambda x: x,  -1.2,  1.,tol=1.e-8)
        expected = 0.
        self.assertAlmostEqual(result, expected)

if __name__=='__main__':
    unittest.main()
```

Let's examine the differences to the previous implementation. First, the test is now a method and a part of a class. The class must inherit from `unittest.TestCase`. The test method's name must start with `test`. Note that we may now use one of the assertion tools of the `unittest` package, namely `assertAlmostEqual`. Finally, the tests are run using `unittest.main`. We recommend to write the tests in a file separate from the code to be tested. That is why it starts with an `import`. The test passes and returns as follows:

```
Ran 1 test in 0.002s

OK
```

If we run it with a loose tolerance parameter, for example, `1.e-3`, a failure of the test would have been reported:

```
F
======================================================================
FAIL: test (__main__.TestIdentity)
----------------------------------------------------------------------
Traceback (most recent call last):
  File "<ipython-input-11-e44778304d6f>", line 5, in test
    self.assertAlmostEqual(result, expected)
AssertionError: 0.00017089843750002018 != 0.0 within 7 places
----------------------------------------------------------------------

Ran 1 test in 0.004s
FAILED (failures=1)
```

Tests can and should be grouped together as methods of a test class, as given in the following example:

```
import unittest
from bisection import bisect

class TestIdentity(unittest.TestCase):
    def identity_fcn(self,x):
        return x
    def test_functionality(self):
        result = bisect(self.identity_fcn, -1.2, 1.,tol=1.e-8)
        expected = 0.
        self.assertAlmostEqual(result, expected)
    def test_reverse_boundaries(self):
        result = bisect(self.identity_fcn, 1., -1.)
        expected = 0.
        self.assertAlmostEqual(result, expected)
    def test_exceeded_tolerance(self):
        tol=1.e-80
        self.assertRaises(Exception, bisect, self.identity_fcn,
                                            -1.2, 1.,tol)
if __name__=='__main__':
    unittest.main()
```

Here, in the last test we used the method `unittest.TestCase.assertRaises`. It tests whether an exception is correctly raised. Its first parameter is the exception type, for example, `ValueError`, `Exception`, and its second argument is the name of the function, which is expected to raise the exception. The remaining arguments are the arguments for this function. The command `unittest.main()` creates an instance of the `TestIdentity` class and executes those methods starting with `test`.

Test setUp and tearDown methods

The class `unittest.TestCase` provides two special methods, `setUp` and `tearDown`, which run before and after every call to a test method. This is needed when testing generators, which are exhausted after every test. We demonstrate this by testing a program which checks the line in a file in which a given string occurs for the first time:

```
class NotFoundError(Exception):
  pass

def find_string(file, string):
    for i,lines in enumerate(file.readlines()):
        if string in lines:
            return i
```

```
        raise NotFoundError(
            'String {} not found in File {}'.format(string,file.name))
```

We assume that this code is saved in the find_in_file.py file. A test has to prepare a file and open it and remove it after the test as given in the following example:

```
import unittest
import os # used for, for example, deleting files

from find_in_file import find_string, NotFoundError

class TestFindInFile(unittest.TestCase):
    def setUp(self):
        file = open('test_file.txt', 'w')
        file.write('aha')
        file.close()
        self.file = open('test_file.txt', 'r')
    def tearDown(self):
        self.file.close()
        os.remove(self.file.name)
    def test_exists(self):
        line_no=find_string(self.file, 'aha')
        self.assertEqual(line_no, 0)
    def test_not_exists(self):
        self.assertRaises(NotFoundError, find_string,
                                          self.file, 'bha')

if __name__=='__main__':
    unittest.main()
```

Before each test setUp is run and then tearDown is executed.

Parameterizing tests

One frequently wants to repeat the same test with different data sets. When using the functionalities of unittest this requires us to automatically generate test cases with the corresponding methods injected:

To this end, we first construct a test case with one or several methods that will be used, when we later set up test methods. Let's consider the bisection method again and let's check if the values it returns are really zeros of the given function.

We first build the test case and the method which we will use for the tests as follows:

```
class Tests(unittest.TestCase):
    def checkifzero(self,fcn_with_zero,interval):
        result = bisect(fcn_with_zero,*interval,tol=1.e-8)
        function_value=fcn_with_zero(result)
        expected=0.
        self.assertAlmostEqual(function_value, expected)
```

Then we dynamically create test functions as attributes of this class:

```
test_data=[
            {'name':'identity', 'function':lambda x: x,
                                    'interval' : [-1.2, 1.]},
            {'name':'parabola', 'function':lambda x: x**2-1,
                                    'interval' :[0, 10.]},
            {'name':'cubic', 'function':lambda x: x**3-2*x**2,
                                    'interval':[0.1, 5.]},
            ]
def make_test_function(dic):
        return lambda self :\
                    self.checkifzero(dic['function'],dic['interval'])
for data in test_data:
    setattr(Tests, "test_{name}".format(name=data['name']),
                                    make_test_function(data))
if __name__=='__main__':
  unittest.main()
```

In this example, the data is provided as a list of dictionaries. The make_test_function function dynamically generates a test function, which uses a particular data dictionary to perform the test with the previously defined method checkifzero. Finally, the command setattr is used to make these test functions methods of the class Tests.

Assertion tools

In this section, we collect the most important tools for raising an `AssertionError`. We saw the `assert` command and two tools from `unittest`, namely `assertAlmostEqual`. The following table (*Table 13.1*) summarizes the most important assertion tools and the related modules:

Assertion tool and application example	Module
`assert 5==5`	–
`assertEqual(5.27, 5.27)`	`unittest.TestCase`
`assertAlmostEqual(5.24, 5.2,places = 1)`	`unittest.TestCase`
`assertTrue(5 > 2)`	`unittest.TestCase`
`assertFalse(2 < 5)`	`unittest.TestCase`
`assertRaises(ZeroDivisionError,lambda x: 1/x,0.)`	`unittest.TestCase`
`assertIn(3,{3,4})`	`unittest.TestCase`
`assert_array_equal(A,B)`	`numpy.testing`
`assert_array_almost_equal(A, B, decimal=5)`	`numpy.testing`
`assert_allclose(A, B, rtol=1.e-3,atol=1.e-5)`	`numpy.testing`

Table 13.1: Assertion tools in Python, unittest and NumPy

Float comparisons

Two floating point numbers should not be compared with the == comparison, because the result of a computation is often slightly off due to rounding errors. There are numerous tools to test equality of floats for testing purposes. First, `allclose` checks that two arrays are almost equal. It can be used in a test function, as shown:

```
self.assertTrue(allclose(computed, expected))
```

Here, `self` refers to a `unittest.Testcase` instance. There are also testing tools in the `numpy` package `testing`. These are imported by using:

```
import numpy.testing
```

Testing that two scalars or two arrays are equal is done using
`numpy.testing.assert_array_allmost_equal` or
`numpy.testing.assert_allclose`. These methods differ in the way they describe the
required accuracy, as shown in the preceding table.

QR factorization decomposes a given matrix into a product of an orthogonal matrix *Q* and
an upper triangular matrix *R* as given in the following example:

```
import scipy.linalg as sl
A=rand(10,10)
[Q,R]=sl.qr(A)
```

Is the method applied correctly? We can check this by verifying that *Q* is indeed an
orthogonal matrix:

```
import numpy.testing as npt
npt.assert_allclose(
                dot(Q.T,self.Q),identity(Q.shape[0]),atol=1.e-12)
```

Furthermore, we might perform a sanity test by checking if *A* = *QR*:

```
import numpy.testing as npt
npt.assert_allclose(dot(Q,R),A))
```

All this can be collected into a `unittest` test case as follows:

```
import unittest
import numpy.testing as npt
from scipy.linalg import qr
from scipy import *

class TestQR(unittest.TestCase):
    def setUp(self):
        self.A=rand(10,10)
        [self.Q,self.R]=qr(self.A)
    def test_orthogonal(self):
        npt.assert_allclose(
            dot(self.Q.T,self.Q),identity(self.Q.shape[0]),
                                            atol=1.e-12)
    def test_sanity(self):
            npt.assert_allclose(dot(self.Q,self.R),self.A)

if __name__=='__main__':
    unittest.main()
```

Note in `assert_allclose` the parameter `atol` defaults to zero, which often causes problems, when working with matrices having small elements.

Unit and functional tests

Up to now, we have only used functional tests. A functional test checks whether the functionality is correct. For the bisection algorithm, this algorithm actually finds a zero when there is one. In that simple example, it is not really clear what a unit test is. Although, it might seem slightly contrived, it is still possible to make a unit test for the bisection algorithm. It will demonstrate how unit testing often leads to more compartmentalized implementation.

So, in the bisection method, we would like to check, for instance, that at each step the interval is chosen correctly. How to do that? Note that it is absolutely impossible with the current implementation, because the algorithm is hidden inside the function. One possible remedy is to run only one step of the bisection algorithm. Since all the steps are similar, we might argue that we have tested all the possible steps. We also need to be able to inspect the current bounds a and b at the current step of the algorithm. So we have to add the number of steps to be run as a parameter and change the return interface of the function. We will do that as shown:

```
def bisect(f,a,b,n=100):
    ...
    for iteration in range(n):
        ...
    return a,b
```

Note that we have to change the existing unit tests in order to accommodate for that change. We may now add a unit test as shown:

```
def test_midpoint(self):
    a,b = bisect(identity,-2.,1.,1)
    self.assertAlmostEqual(a,-0.5)
    self.assertAlmostEqual(b,1.)
```

Debugging

Debugging is sometimes necessary while testing, in particular if it is not immediately clear why a given test does not pass. In that case, it is useful to be able to debug a given test in an interactive session. This is however, made difficult by the design of the `unittest.TestCase` class, which prevents easy instantiation of test case objects. The solution is to create a special instance for debugging purpose only.

Suppose that, in the example of the `TestIdentity` class above, we want to test the `test_functionality` method. This would be achieved as follows:

```
test_case = TestIdentity(methodName='test_functionality')
```

Now this test can be run individually by:

```
test_case.debug()
```

This will run this individual test and it allows for debugging.

Test discovery

If you write a Python package, various tests might be spread out through the package. The `discover` module finds, imports, and runs these test cases. The basic call from the command line is:

```
python -m unittest discover
```

It starts looking for test cases in the current directory and recurses the directory tree downward to find Python objects with the `'test'` string contained in its name. The command takes optional arguments. Most important are `-s` to modify the start directory and `-p` to define the pattern to recognize the tests:

```
python -m unittest discover -s '.' -p 'Test*.py'
```

Measuring execution time

In order to take decisions on code optimization, one often has to compare several code alternatives and decide which code should be preferred based on the execution time. Furthermore, discussing execution time is an issue when comparing different algorithms. In this section, we present a simple and easy way to measure execution time.

Timing with a magic function

The easiest way to measure the execution time of a single statement is to use IPython's magic function %timeit.

The shell IPython adds additional functionality to standard Python. These extra functions are called magic functions.

As the execution time of a single statement can be extremely short, the statement is placed in a loop and executed several times. By taking the minimum measured time, one makes sure that other tasks running on the computer do not influence the measured result too much. Let's consider four alternative ways to extract nonzero elements from an array as follows:

```
A=zeros((1000,1000))
A[53,67]=10

def find_elements_1(A):
    b = []
    n, m = A.shape
    for i in range(n):
        for j in range(m):
            if abs(A[i, j]) > 1.e-10:
                b.append(A[i, j])
    return b

def find_elements_2(A):
    return [a for a in A.reshape((-1, )) if abs(a) > 1.e-10]

def find_elements_3(A):
    return [a for a in A.flatten() if abs(a) > 1.e-10]

def find_elements_4(A):
    return A[where(0.0 != A)]
```

Measuring time with IPython's magic function %timeit gives the following result:

```
In [50]: %timeit -n 50 -r 3 find_elements_1(A)
50 loops, best of 3: 585 ms per loop

In [51]: %timeit -n 50 -r 3 find_elements_2(A)
50 loops, best of 3: 514 ms per loop

In [52]: %timeit -n 50 -r 3 find_elements_3(A)
```

```
50 loops, best of 3: 519 ms per loop

In [53]: %timeit -n 50 -r 3 find_elements_4(A)
50 loops, best of 3: 7.29 ms per loop
```

The parameter -n controls how often the statement is executed before time is measured and the -r parameter controls the number of repetitions.

Timing with the Python module timeit

Python provides a timeit module, which can be used to measure execution time. It requires that first a time object is constructed. It is constructed from two strings, a string with setup commands and a string with the commands to be executed. We take the same four alternatives as in the preceding example. The array and function definitions are written now in a string called setup_statements and four-time objects are constructed as follows:

```python
import timeit
setup_statements="""
from scipy import zeros
from numpy import where
A=zeros((1000,1000))
A[57,63]=10.

def find_elements_1(A):
    b = []
    n, m = A.shape
    for i in range(n):
        for j in range(m):
            if abs(A[i, j]) > 1.e-10:
                b.append(A[i, j])
    return b

def find_elements_2(A):
    return [a for a in A.reshape((-1,)) if abs(a) > 1.e-10]

def find_elements_3(A):
    return [a for a in A.flatten() if abs(a) > 1.e-10]

def find_elements_4(A):
    return A[where( 0.0 != A)]
"""
experiment_1 = timeit.Timer(stmt = 'find_elements_1(A)',
                            setup = setup_statements)
experiment_2 = timeit.Timer(stmt = 'find_elements_2(A)',
                            setup = setup_statements)
```

```
experiment_3 = timeit.Timer(stmt = 'find_elements_3(A)',
                            setup = setup_statements)
experiment_4 = timeit.Timer(stmt = 'find_elements_4(A)',
                            setup = setup_statements)
```

The timer objects have a `repeat` method . It takes `repeat` and `number` parameters. It executes the statement of the timer object in a loop, measures the time, and repeats this experiment corresponding to the `repeat` parameter:

We continue the preceding example and measure execution times as shown:

```
t1 = experiment_1.repeat(3,5)
t2 = experiment_2.repeat(3,5)
t3 = experiment_3.repeat(3,5)
t4 = experiment_4.repeat(3,5)
# Results per loop in ms
min(t1)*1000/5 # 615 ms
min(t2)*1000/5 # 543 ms
min(t3)*1000/5 # 546 ms
min(t4)*1000/5 # 7.26 ms
```

In contrast to the method in the preceding example, we obtain lists of all the obtained measurements. As computing time may vary depending on the overall load of the computer, the minimal value in such a list can be considered a good approximation to the computation time necessary to execute the statement.

Timing with a context manager

Finally, we present the third method. It serves to show another application of a context manager. We first construct a context manager object for measuring the elapsed time as shown:

```
import time
class Timer:
    def __enter__(self):
        self.start = time.time()
        # return self
    def __exit__(self, ty, val, tb):
        end = time.time()
        self.elapsed=end-self.start
        print('Time elapsed {} seconds'.format(self.elapsed))
        return False
```

Recall that the _ _enter_ _ and _ _exit_ _ methods make this class a context manager. The _ _exit_ _ method's parameters `ty`, `val`, and `tb` are in the normal case `None`. If an exception is raised during execution, they take the exception type, its value, and traceback information. The `return False` indicates that the exception has not been caught so far.

We now show the use of the context manager to measure the execution time of the four alternatives in the previous example:

```
with Timer():
    find_elements_1(A)
```

This will then display a message like `Time elapsed 15.0129795074 ms.`

If the timing result should be accessible in a variable, the `enter` method must return the `Timer` instance (uncomment the `return` statement) and a `with ... as ...` construction has to be used:

```
with Timer() as t1:
    find_elements_1(A)
t1.elapsed # contains the result
```

Summary

No program development without testing! We showed the importance of well organized and documented tests. Some professionals even start development by first specifying tests. A useful tool for automatic testing is the module `unittest`, which we explained in detail. While testing improves the reliability of a code, profiling is needed to improve the performance. Alternative ways to code may result in large performance differences. We showed how to measure computation time and how to localize bottlenecks in your code.

Exercises

Ex. 1 → Two matrices A, B are called similar, if there exists a matrix S, such that $B = S^{-1} A S$. A and B have the same eigenvalues. Write a test checking that two matrices are similar, by comparing their eigenvalues. Is it a functional or a unit test?

Ex. 2 → Create two vectors of large dimension. Compare the execution time of various ways to compute their `dot` product:

- SciPy function: `dot(v,w)`
- Generator and sum: `sum((x*y for x,y in zip(v,w)))`
- Comprehensive list and sum: `sum([x*y for x,y in zip(v,w)])`

Ex. 3 → Let u be a vector. The vector v with components

$$v_i = \frac{u_i + u_{i+1} + u_{i+2}}{3}$$

is called a moving average of u. Determine which of the two alternatives to compute v is faster:

```
v = (u[:-2] + u[1:-1] + u[2:]) / 3
```

or

```
v = array([(u[i] + u[i + 1] + u[i + 2]) / 3
    for i in range(len(u)-3)])
```

14

Comprehensive Examples

In this chapter, we present some comprehensive and longer examples together with a brief introduction to the theoretical background and their complete implementation. By this, we want to show you how the concepts defined in this book are used in practice.

Polynomials

First, we will demonstrate the power of the Python constructs presented so far by designing a class for polynomials. We will give some theoretical background, which leads us to a list of requirements, and then we will give the code, with some comments.

Note, this class differs conceptually from the class `numpy.poly1d`.

Theoretical background

A polynomial: $p(x) = a_n x^n + a_{n-1} x^{n-1} + \ldots + a_1 x + a_0$ is defined by its degree, its representation, and its coefficients. The polynomial representation shown in the preceding equation is called a monomial representation. In this representation, the polynomial is written as a linear combination of monomials, x^i. Alternatively, the polynomial can be written in:

- Newton representation with the coefficients c_i and n points, $x_0, \ldots, x_{n-1}$:

$$p(x) = c_0 + c_1(x - x_0) + c_2(x - x_0)(x - x_1) + \ldots + c_n(x - x_0) \ldots (x - x_{n-1})$$

- Lagrange representation with the coefficients y_i and $n+1$ points, $x_0, \ldots, x_n$:

$$p(x) = y_0 l_0(x) + y_1 l_1(x) + \ldots + y_n l_n(x)$$

with the cardinal functions:

$$l_i(x) = \Pi_{j=0, j \neq i}^n \frac{x - x_i}{x_j - x_i}$$

There are infinitely many representations, but we restrict ourselves here to these three typical ones.

A polynomial can be determined from interpolation conditions:

$$p(x_i) = y_i \quad i = 0, \ldots, n$$

with the given distinct values x_i and arbitrary values y_i as input. In the Lagrange formulation, the interpolation polynomial is directly available, as its coefficients are the interpolation data. The coefficients for the interpolation polynomial in Newton representation can be obtained by a recursion formula, called the divided differences formula:

$$c_{i,0} = y_i, \quad \text{and}$$

$$c_{i,j} = \frac{c_{i+1,j-1} - c_{i,j-1}}{x_{i+j} - x_i} .$$

Finally, one sets $c_i := c_{0,i}$.

The coefficients of the interpolation polynomial in monomial representation are obtained by solving a linear system:

$$
\begin{bmatrix}
x_0^n & x_0^{n-1} & \cdots & x_0^1 & x_0^0 \\
x_1^n & x_1^{n-1} & \cdots & x_1^1 & x_1^0 \\
& & \vdots & & \\
x_n^n & x_n^{n-1} & \cdots & x_n^1 & x_n^0
\end{bmatrix}
\begin{bmatrix}
a_n \\
a_{n-1} \\
\vdots \\
a_0
\end{bmatrix}
=
\begin{bmatrix}
y_0 \\
y_1 \\
\vdots \\
y_n
\end{bmatrix}
$$

A matrix that has a given polynomial p (or a multiple of it) as its characteristic polynomial is called a companion matrix. The eigenvalues of the companion matrix are the zeros (roots) of the polynomial. An algorithm for computing the zeros of p can be constructed by first setting up its companion matrix and then computing the eigenvalues with `eig`. The companion matrix for a polynomial in Newton representation reads as follows:

$$\begin{bmatrix} x_0 & & & & & -c_{0,0} \\ 1 & x_1 & & & & -c_{0,1} \\ & 1 & x_2 & & & -c_{0,2} \\ & & \ddots & \ddots & & \vdots \\ & & & 1 & x_{n-2} & -c_{0,n-2} \\ & & & & 1 & x_{n-1} - c_{0,n-1} \end{bmatrix}$$

Tasks

We can now formulate some programming tasks:

1. Write a class called `PolyNomial` with the `points`, `degree`, `coeff`, and `basis` attributes, where:
   - `points` is a list of tuples (x_i, y_i)
   - `degree` is the degree of the corresponding interpolation polynomial
   - `coeff` contains the polynomial coefficients
   - `basis` is a string stating which representation is used

2. Provide the class with a method for evaluating the polynomial at a given point.

3. Provide the class with a method called `plot` that plots the polynomial over a given interval.

4. Write a method called `__add__` that returns a polynomial that is the sum of two polynomials. Be aware that only in the monomial case the sum can be computed by just summing up the coefficients.

5. Write a method that computes the coefficients of the polynomial represented in a monomial form.

6. Write a method that computes the polynomial's companion matrix.

7. Write a method that computes the zeros of the polynomial by computing the eigenvalues of the companion matrix.
8. Write a method that computes the polynomial that is the ith derivative of the given polynomial.
9. Write a method that checks whether two polynomials are equal. Equality can be checked by comparing all coefficients (zero leading coefficients should not matter).

The polynomial class

Let's now design a polynomial base class based on a monomial formulation of the polynomial. The polynomial can be initialized either by giving its coefficients with respect to the monomial basis or by giving a list of interpolation points, as follows:

```
import scipy.linalg as sl

class PolyNomial:
    base='monomial'
    def __init__(self,**args):
        if 'points' in args:
            self.points = array(args['points'])
            self.xi = self.points[:,0]
            self.coeff = self.point_2_coeff()
            self.degree = len(self.coeff)-1
        elif 'coeff' in args:
            self.coeff = array(args['coeff'])
            self.degree = len(self.coeff)-1
            self.points = self.coeff_2_point()
        else:
            self.points = array([[0,0]])
            self.xi = array([1.])
            self.coeff = self.point_2_coeff()
            self.degree = 0
```

The __init__ method of the new class uses the **args construction as discussed in section *Parameters and arguments* in Chapter 7, *Functions*. If no arguments are given, a zero polynomial is assumed. If the polynomial is given by interpolation points the method used to compute the coefficients by solving a Vandermonde system is given as follows:

```
def point_2_coeff(self):
    return sl.solve(vander(self.x),self.y)
```

If *k* coefficients are given also *k* interpolation points are constructed by:

```
def coeff_2_point(self):
    points = [[x,self(x)] for x in linspace(0,1,self.degree+1)]
    return array(points)
```

The `self(x)` command does a polynomial evaluation, which is done by providing a method, `__call__`:

```
def __call__(self,x):
    return polyval(self.coeff,x)
```

(Refer example in section *Special methods* in `Chapter 8`, *Classes*.) Here, this method uses the command `polyval`. As a next step, we just add for convenience two methods, which we decorate with the `property` decorator (refer section *Functions as decorators* in `Chapter 7`, *Functions)*:

```
@property
def x(self):
    return self.points[:,0]
@property
def y(self):
    return self.points[:,1]
```

Let's explain what is going on here. We define a method to extract the *x*-values of the data, which were used to define the polynomial. Similarly, a method to extract the *y*-values of the data is defined. With the `property` decorator, the result of calling the method is presented as if it were just an attribute of the polynomial. There are two coding alternatives:

1. We use a method call:

    ```
    def x(self):
        return self.interppoints[:,0]
    ```

    This gives access to the *x*-values by the call: `p.x()`.

2. We use the `property` decorator. It us to access the *x*-values simply by this statement: `p.x`

We choose the second variant. It is always a good practice to define a __repr__ method (refer section *Attributes* in `Chapter 8`, *Classes*). At least for a quick check of the results, this method is useful:

```
def __repr__(self):
    txt  = 'Polynomial of degree {degree} \n'
    txt += 'with coefficients {coeff} \n in {base} basis.'
    return txt.format(coeff=self.coeff, degree=self.degree,
                                        base=self.base)
```

We now provide a method for plotting the polynomial, as follows:

```
margin = .05
plotres = 500
def plot(self,ab=None,plotinterp=True):
    if ab is None: # guess a and b
        x = self.x
        a, b = x.min(), x.max()
        h = b-a
        a -= self.margin*h
        b += self.margin*h
    else:
        a,b = ab
    x = linspace(a,b,self.plotres)
    y = vectorize(self.__call__)(x)
    plot(x,y)
    xlabel('$x$')
    ylabel('$p(x)$')
    if plotinterp:
        plot(self.x, self.y, 'ro')
```

Note the use of the `vectorize` command (refer section *Functions acting on arrays* in `Chapter 4`, *Linear algebra – Arrays*. The __call__ method is specific to the monomial representation and has to be changed if a polynomial is represented in another basis. This is also the case for the computation of the polynomial's companion matrix:

```
def companion(self):
    companion = eye(self.degree, k=-1)
    companion[0,:] -= self.coeff[1:]/self.coeff[0]
    return companion
```

Once the companion matrix is available, the zeros of the polynomial are given by the eigenvalues:

```
def zeros(self):
    companion = self.companion()
    return sl.eigvals(companion)
```

For this end the function `eigvals` has to be imported from `scipy.linalg` first. Let's give some usage examples.

First, we create a polynomial instance from the given interpolation points:

```
p = PolyNomial(points=[(1,0),(2,3),(3,8)])
```

The polynomial's coefficients with respect to the monomial basis are available as an attribute of p:

```
p.coeff # returns array([ 1., 0., -1.])
```

This corresponds to the polynomial $p(x)=1\,x^2 + 0x - 1$. The default plot of the polynomial, obtained by `p.plot(-3.5,3.5)`, results in the following figure (*Figure 14.1*):

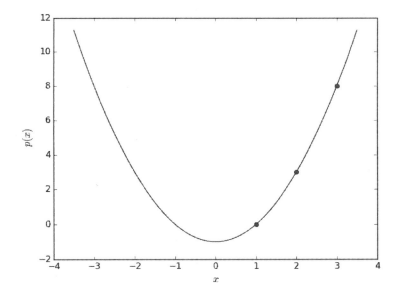

Figure 14.1: Result of the polynomial plot method

Finally, we compute the zeros of the polynomial, which in this case are two real numbers:

```
pz = p.zeros() # returns array([-1.+0.j, 1.+0.j])
```

The result can be verified by evaluating the polynomial at these points:

```
p(pz) # returns array([0.+0.j, 0.+0.j])
```

Newton polynomial

The NewtonPolyNomial class defines a polynomial described with respect to the Newton basis. We let it inherit some common methods from the polynomial base class, for example, polynomial.plot, polynomial.zeros, and even parts of the __init__ method, by using the super command (refer to section *Subclassing and Inheritance* in Chapter 8, *Classes*):

```
class NewtonPolynomial(PolyNomial):
    base = 'Newton'
    def __init__(self,**args):
        if 'coeff' in args:
            try:
                self.xi = array(args['xi'])
            except KeyError:
                raise ValueError('Coefficients need to be given'
                'together with abscissae values xi')
        super(NewtonPolynomial, self).__init__(**args)
```

Once the interpolation points are given, the computation of the coefficients is performed by:

```
def point_2_coeff(self):
    return array(list(self.divdiff()))
```

Here we used divided differences for computing the Newton representation of the polynomial, which is programmed as a generator here:

```
def divdiff(self):
    xi = self.xi
    row = self.y
    yield row[0]
    for level in range(1,len(xi)):
        row = (row[1:] - row[:-1])/(xi[level:] - xi[:-level])
        if allclose(row,0): # check: elements of row nearly zero
            self.degree = level-1
            break
        yield row[0]
```

Let us briefly check how this works:

```
pts = array([[0.,0],[.5,1],[1.,0],[2,0.]]) # here we define the
    interpolation data: (x,y) pairs
pN = NewtonPolynomial(points=pts) # this creates an instance of the
    polynomial class
pN.coeff # returns the coefficients array([ 0. , 2. , -4. ,
    2.66666667])
print(pN)
```

The print function executes the __repr__ method of the base class and returns the following text:

```
Polynomial of degree 3
  with coefficients [ 0.     2.    -4.      2.66666667]
  in Newton basis.
```

The polynomial evaluation is different from the corresponding method of the base class. The Newton.PolyNomial.__call__ method needs to override Polynomial.__call__:

```
def __call__(self,x):
    # first compute the sequence 1, (x-x_1), (x-x_1)(x-x_2),...
    nps = hstack([1., cumprod(x-self.xi[:self.degree])])
    return dot(self.coeff, nps)
```

Finally, we give the code for the companion matrix, which overrides the corresponding method of the parent class, as follows:

```
def companion(self):
    degree = self.degree
    companion = eye(degree, k=-1)
    diagonal = identity(degree,dtype=bool)
    companion[diagonal] = self.x[:degree]
    companion[:,-1] -= self.coeff[:degree]/self.coeff[degree]
    return companion
```

Note the use of Boolean arrays. The exercises will further build on this foundation.

Spectral clustering

An interesting application of eigenvectors is for clustering data. Using the eigenvectors of a matrix derived from a distance matrix, unlabelled data can be separated into groups. Spectral clustering methods get their name from the use of the spectrum of this matrix. A distance matrix for n elements (for example, the pairwise distance between data points) is an n × n symmetric matrix. Given such an n × n distance matrix M with distance values m_{ij}, we can create the Laplacian matrix of the data points as follows:

$$L = I - D^{-1/2}MD^{-1/2} \; ,$$

Here, I is the identity matrix and D is the diagonal matrix containing the row sums of M,

$$D = \mathrm{diag}(d_i), d_i = \sum_j m_{ij}$$

The data clusters are obtained from the eigenvectors of L. In the simplest case of data points with only two classes, the first eigenvector (that is, the one corresponding to the largest eigenvalue) is often enough to separate the data.

Here is an example for simple two-class clustering. The following code creates some 2D data points and clusters them based on the first eigenvector of the Laplacian matrix:

```
import scipy.linalg as sl

# create some data points
n = 100
x1 = 1.2 * random.randn(n, 2)
x2 = 0.8 * random.randn(n, 2) + tile([7, 0],(n, 1))
x = vstack((x1, x2))

# pairwise distance matrix
M = array([[ sqrt(sum((x[i] - x[j])**2))
                        for i in range(2*n)]
                        for j in range(2 * n)])

# create the Laplacian matrix
D = diag(1 / sqrt( M.sum(axis = 0) ))
L = identity(2 * n) - dot(D, dot(M, D))

# compute eigenvectors of L
S, V = sl.eig(L)
# As L is symmetric the imaginary parts
# in the eigenvalues are only due to negligible numerical errors S=S.real
V=V.real
```

The eigenvector corresponding to the largest eigenvalue gives the grouping (for example, by thresholding at *0*) and can be shown with:

```
largest=abs(S).argmax()
plot(V[:,largest])
```

The following figure (*Figure 14.2*) shows the result of spectral clustering of a simple two-class dataset:

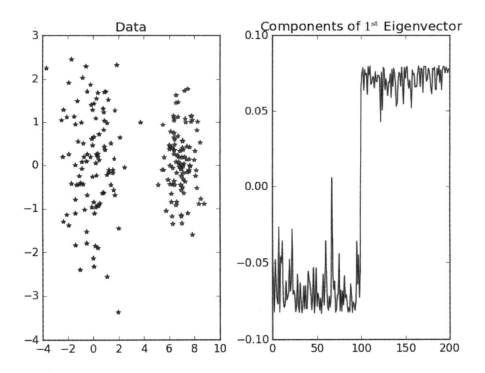

Figure 14.2: shows result of simple two-class clustering

For more difficult datasets and more classes, one usually takes the *k* eigenvectors corresponding to the *k* largest eigenvalues and then clusters the data with some other method, but using the eigenvectors instead of the original data points. A common choice is the *k*-means clustering algorithm, which is the topic of the next example:

The eigenvectors are used as input to *k*-means clustering, as follows:

```
import scipy.linalg as sl
import scipy.cluster.vq as sc
# simple 4 class data
x = random.rand(1000,2)
ndx = ((x[:,0] < 0.4) | (x[:,0] > 0.6)) &
                    ((x[:,1] < 0.4) | (x[:,1] > 0.6))
x = x[ndx]
n = x.shape[0]

# pairwise distance matrix
M = array([[ sqrt(sum((x[i]-x[j])**2)) for i in range(n) ]
                                    for j in range(n)])

# create the Laplacian matrix
D = diag(1 / sqrt( M.sum(axis=0) ))
L = identity(n) - dot(D, dot(M, D))

# compute eigenvectors of L
_,_,V = sl.svd(L)

k = 4
# take k first eigenvectors
eigv = V[:k,:].T

# k-means
centroids,dist = sc.kmeans(eigv,k)
clust_id = sc.vq(eigv,centroids)[0]
```

Note that we computed the eigenvectors here using the singular value decomposition, sl.svd. As *L* is symmetric, the result is the same as if we would have used sl.eig, but the eigenvectors come already ordered corresponding to the ordering of the eigenvalues. We also used throw-away variables. svd returns a list with three arrays, the left and right singular vectors U, V, and the singular values S, as follows:

```
U, S, V = sl.svd(L)
```

As we do not need U and S here, we can throw them away when unpacking the return value of svd:

```
_, _, V = sl.svd(L)
```

The result can be plotted using:

```
for i in range(k):
    ndx = where(clust_id == i)[0]
    plot(x[ndx, 0], x[ndx, 1],'o')
axis('equal')
```

The following figure shows the result of spectral clustering of a simple *multiclass dataset:*

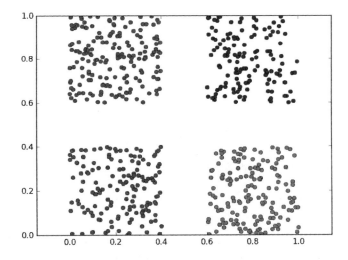

Figure 14.3: An example of spectral clustering of a simple four class dataset.

Solving initial value problems

In this section, we will consider the mathematical task of numerically solving a system of ordinary equations for given initial values:

$$y'(t) = f(t, y) \qquad y(t_0) = y_0 \in \mathbb{R}^n$$

The solution of this problem is a function y. A numerical method aims at computing good approximations, $y_i \approx y(t_i)$ at discrete points, the communications points t_i, within the interval of interest $[t_0, t_e]$. We collect the data that describes the problem in a class, as follows:

```
class IV_Problem:
    """
    Initial value problem (IVP) class
    """
    def __init__(self, rhs, y0, interval, name='IVP'):
        """
        rhs 'right hand side' function of the ordinary differential
                                            equation f(t,y)
        y0 array with initial values
        interval start and end value of the interval of independent
        variables often initial and end time
        name descriptive name of the problem
        """
        self.rhs = rhs
        self.y0 = y0
        self.t0, self.tend = interval
        self.name = name
```

The differential equation:

$$y'(t) = \begin{pmatrix} y_1'(t) \\ y_2'(t) \end{pmatrix} = \begin{pmatrix} y_2(t) \\ g/l \sin y_1(t) \end{pmatrix} \quad \text{with} \quad y_0 = \begin{pmatrix} \pi/2 \\ 0 \end{pmatrix}$$

describes a mathematical pendulum; y_1 describes its angle with respect to the vertical axis, g is the gravitation constant, and l is its length. The initial angle is $\pi/2$ and the initial angular velocity is zero.

The pendulum problem becomes an instance of the problem class, as follows:

```
def rhs(t,y):
    g = 9.81
    l = 1.
    yprime = array([y[1], g / l * sin(y[0])])
    return yprime

pendulum = IV_Problem(rhs, array([pi / 2, 0.]), [0., 10.] ,
                                        'mathem. pendulum')
```

There might be different views on the problem at hand, leading to a different design of the class. For example, one might want to consider the interval of independent variables as a part of a solution process instead of the problem definition. The same holds when considering initial values. They might, as we did here, be considered a part of the mathematical problem, while other authors might want to allow variation of initial values by putting them as a part of the solution process.

The solution process is modeled as another class:

```
class IVPsolver:
    """
    IVP solver class for explicit one-step discretization methods
    with constant step size
    """
    def __init__(self, problem, discretization, stepsize):
        self.problem = problem
        self.discretization = discretization
        self.stepsize = stepsize
    def one_stepper(self):
        yield self.problem.t0, self.problem.y0
        ys = self.problem.y0
        ts = self.problem.t0
        while ts <= self.problem.tend:
            ts, ys = self.discretization(self.problem.rhs, ts, ys,
                                                self.stepsize)

            yield ts, ys
    def solve(self):
        return list(self.one_stepper())
```

We continue by first defining two discretization schemes:

- Explicit **Euler** method:

```
def expliciteuler(rhs, ts, ys, h):
    return ts + h, ys + h * rhs(ts, ys)
```

- Classical **Runge-Kutta four-stage** method (**RK4**):

```
def rungekutta4(rhs, ts, ys, h):
    k1 = h * rhs(ts, ys)
    k2 = h * rhs(ts + h/2., ys + k1/2.)
    k3 = h * rhs(ts + h/2., ys + k2/2.)
    k4 = h * rhs(ts + h, ys +  k3)
    return ts + h, ys + (k1 + 2*k2 + 2*k3 + k4)/6.
```

With these, we can create instances to obtain the corresponding discretized versions of the pendulum ODE:

```
pendulum_Euler = IVPsolver(pendulum, expliciteuler, 0.001)
pendulum_RK4 = IVPsolver(pendulum, rungekutta4, 0.001)
```

We can solve the two discrete models and plot the solution and the angle difference:

```
sol_Euler = pendulum_Euler.solve()
sol_RK4 = pendulum_RK4.solve()
tEuler, yEuler = zip(*sol_Euler)
tRK4, yRK4 = zip(*sol_RK4)
subplot(1,2,1), plot(tEuler,yEuler),\
      title('Pendulum result with Explicit Euler'),\
      xlabel('Time'), ylabel('Angle and angular velocity')
subplot(1,2,2), plot(tRK4,abs(array(yRK4)-array(yEuler))),\
      title('Difference between both methods'),\
      xlabel('Time'), ylabel('Angle and angular velocity')
```

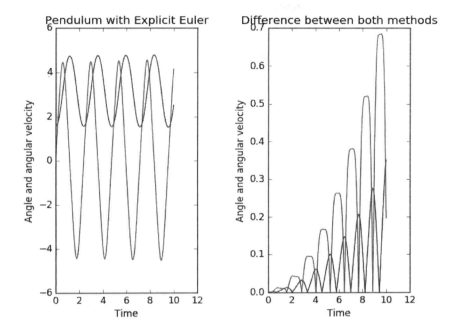

Figure14.4: Pendulum simulation with the explicit Euler method and comparison with the results of the more accurate Runge–Kutta 4 method

It is worthwhile discussing alternative class designs. What should be put in separate classes, what should be bundled into the same class?

- We strictly separated the mathematical problem from the numerical method. Where should the initial values go? Should they be part of the problem or part of the solver? Or should they be left as input parameter for the solve method of the solver instance? One might even design the program so that it allows several possibilities. The decision to use one of these alternatives depends on the future use of this program. Looping over various initial values as in parameter identification would be eased by leaving the initial values as input parameters for the solve method. On the other hand, simulating different model variants with the same initial values would motivate to couple the initial values to the problem.

- We presented for simplicity only solvers with constant and given step size. Is the design of the IVPsolver class appropriate for a future extension of adaptive methods, where a tolerance rather than a step size is given?

- We suggested earlier to use a generator construction for the stepping mechanism. Adaptive methods need to reject steps from time to time. Is this need conflicting with the design of the stepping mechanism in `IVPsolver.onestepper`?
- We encourage you to check the design of the two SciPy tools for solving initial values, namely `scipy.integrate.ode` and `scipy.integrate.odeint`.

Summary

Most of what we explained in this book is bundled into the three longer examples of this chapter. They mimic code development and give prototypes, which you are encouraged to alter and confront with your own ideas.

You saw that code in scientific computing can have its own flavor due to its strong relation with mathematically defined algorithms and that it is often wise to keep the relationship between code and formula visible. Python has techniques for this, as you have seen.

Exercises

Ex. 1 → Implement a method `__add__`, which constructs a new polynomial $p+q$ by adding two given polynomials p and q. In monomial form, polynomials are added by just adding the coefficients, whereas in Newton form, the coefficients depend on the abscissa x_i of the interpolation points. Before adding the coefficients of both polynomials, the polynomial q has to get new interpolation points with the property that their abscissa x_i coincides with those of p and the method `__changepoints__` has to be provided for that. It should change the interpolation points and return a new set of coefficients.

Ex. 2 → Write conversion methods to convert a polynomial from Newton form into monomial form and vice versa.

Ex. 3 → Write a method called `add_point` that takes a polynomial q and a tuple (x,y) as parameters and returns a new polynomial that interpolates `self.points` and (x,y).

Ex. 4 → Write a class called `LagrangePolynomial` that implements polynomials in Lagrange form and inherits as much as possible from the polynomial base class.

Ex. 5 → Write tests for the polynomial class.

15
Symbolic Computations - SymPy

In this chapter, we will give a brief introduction on using Python for symbolic computations. There is powerful software in the market for performing symbolic computations, for example, Maple™ or Mathematica™. But sometimes, it might be favorable to make symbolic calculations in the language or framework you are used to. At this stage of this book, we assume that this language is Python, so we seek for a tool in Python — the SymPy module.

A complete description of SymPy — if possible, would fill an entire book, and that is not the purpose of this chapter. Instead, we will stake out a path into this tool by some guiding examples, giving a flavor of the potential of this tool as a complement to NumPy and SciPy.

What are symbolic computations?

All computations we did so far in this book were so-called numeric computations. These were a sequence of operations mainly on floating-point numbers. It is the nature of numeric computations that the result is an approximation of the exact solution.

Symbolic computations operate on formulas or symbols by transforming them as taught in algebra or calculus into other formulas. The last step of these transformations might then require that numbers are inserted and a numeric evaluation is performed.

We illustrate the difference by computing this definite integral:

$$\int_0^4 \frac{1}{x^2 + x + 1}\, dx$$

Symbolically this expression can be transformed by considering the primitive function of the integrand:

$$\frac{2}{\sqrt{3}} \arctan\left(\frac{2x + 1}{\sqrt{3}}\right)$$

We now obtain a formula for the definite integral by inserting the integral bounds:

$$\int_0^4 \frac{1}{x^2 + x + 1}\, dx = \frac{\sqrt{3}}{9}\left(-\pi + 6\arctan\left(3\sqrt{3}\right)\right)$$

This is called a closed-form expression for the integral. Very few mathematical problems have a solution that can be given in a closed-form expression. It is the exact value of the integral without any approximation. Also no error is introduced by representing real numbers as floating-point numbers, which would otherwise introduce round-off errors.

Approximation and round-off come into play at the very last moment, when this expression needs to be evaluated. The square root and the *arctan* can only be evaluated approximately by numerical methods. Such an evaluation gives the final result up to a certain (often unknown) precision:

$$\int_0^4 \frac{1}{x^2 + x + 1}\, dx \approx 0.9896614396123$$

On the other hand, numerical computation would directly approximate the definite integral by some approximation method, for example, Simpson's rule, and deliver a numeric result, often with an estimate of error. In Python, this is done by these commands:

```
from scipy.integrate import quad
quad(lambda x : 1/(x**2+x+1),a=0, b=4)
```

They return the value *0.9896614396122965* and an estimate for the error bound *1.1735663442283496 10⁻⁰⁸*.

The following diagram shows the comparison of numeric and symbolic approximation:

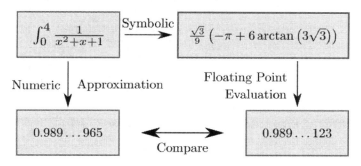

Figure 15.1: Symbolic and numeric quadrature

Elaborating an example in SymPy

To begin with, let's elaborate the previous example in SymPy which are explained the steps.

First, we have to import the module:

```
from sympy import *
init_printing()
```

The second command makes sure that formulas are presented in a graphical way, if possible. Then, we generate a symbol and define the integrand:

```
x = symbols('x')
f = Lambda(x, 1/(x**2 + x + 1))
```

x is now a Python object of type `Symbol` and f is a SymPy `Lambda` function (note the command starting with a capital letter).

Now we start with the symbolic computation of the integral:

```
integrate(f(x),x)
```

Depending on your working environment, the result is presented in different ways; refer to following screenshot (*Figure 15.2*) which represents two different result of SymPy formula in different environments:

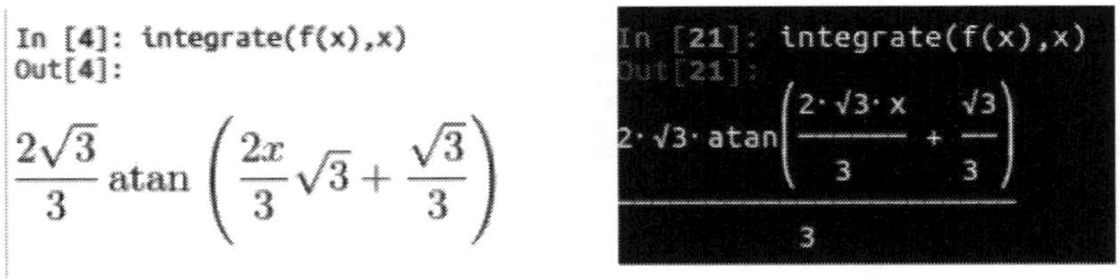

Figure 15.2: Two screenshots of a SymPy presentation of a formula in two different environments.

We can check by differentiation whether the result is correct. To this end, we assign a name to the primitive function and differentiate with respect to *x*:

```
pf = Lambda(x, integrate(f(x),x))
diff(pf(x),x)
```

The result obtained will be as follows:

$$\frac{4}{3\left(\frac{2x}{3}\sqrt{3}+\frac{\sqrt{3}}{3}\right)^2+3}$$

which can be simplified by using the following command:

```
simplify(diff(pf(x),x))
```

to

$$\frac{1}{x^2+x+1}.$$

The result we expected.

The definite integral is obtained by using the following command:

```
pf(4) - pf(0)
```

It gives the following output after simplification with `simplify`:

$$\frac{\sqrt{3}}{9}\left(-\pi + 6\arctan\left(3\sqrt{3}\right)\right)$$

To obtain a numerical value, we finally evaluate this expression to a floating-point number:

```
(pf(4)-pf(0)).evalf() # returns 0.9896614396123
```

Basic elements of SymPy

Here we introduce the basic elements of SymPy. You will find it favorable to be already familiar with classes and data types in Python.

Symbols – the basis of all formulas

The basic construction element to build a formula in SymPy is the symbol. As we saw in the introductory example, a symbol is created by the command `symbols`. This SymPy command generates symbol objects from a given string:

```
x, y, mass, torque = symbols('x y mass torque')
```

It is actually a short form of following command:

```
symbol_list=[symbols(l) for l in 'x y mass torque'.split()]
```

followed by a unpacking step to obtain variables:

```
x, y, mass, torque = symbol_list
```

The arguments of the command define the string representation of the symbol. The variable name of the symbol is often chosen identical to its string representation, but this is not required by the language:

```
row_index=symbols('i',integer=True)
print(row_index**2)  # returns i**2
```

Here, we also defined that the symbol is assumed to be an integer.

An entire set of symbols can be defined in a very compact way:

```
integervariables = symbols('i:l', integer=True)
dimensions = symbols('m:n', integer=True)
realvariables = symbols('x:z', real=True)
```

Similarly, symbols for indexed variables can be defined by using the following:

```
A = symbols('A1:3(1:4)')
```

This gives a tuple of symbols,

$$(A_{11}, \quad A_{12}, \quad A_{13}, \quad A_{21}, \quad A_{22}, \quad A_{23}).$$

The rules for the range of the indexes are those we saw earlier in this book when working with slices (refer `Chapter 3`, *Container Types* for more details).

Numbers

Python evaluates operations on numbers directly and introduces unavoidably rounding errors. These would obstruct all symbolic calculations. This is avoided when we `sympify` numbers:

```
1/3   # returns 0.3333333333333333
sympify(1)/sympify(3)   # returns '1/3'
```

The `sympify` command converts an integer to an object of type `sympy.core.numbers.Integer`.

Instead of writing 1/3 as an operation of two integers, it can also be represented directly as a rational number by `Rational(1,3)`.

Functions

SymPy distinguishes between defined and undefined functions. The term undefined functions (might be a bit misleading) refers to well-defined Python objects for generic functions that have no special properties.

An example of a function with special properties is `atan` or the `Lambda` function used in the introductory example of this chapter.

Note the different names for the different implementations of the same mathematical function: `sympy.atan` and `scipy.arctan`.

Undefined functions

A symbol for an undefined function is created by giving the `symbols` command an extra class argument:

```
f, g = symbols('f g', cls=Function)
```

The same can be achieved by using the `Function` constructor:

```
f = Function('f')
g = Function('g')
```

with undefined functions, we can evaluate general rules of calculus.

For example, let us evaluate the following expression:

$$\frac{\mathrm{d}}{\mathrm{d}x} f(xg(x))$$

This is symbolically computed in Python by using the following command:

```
x = symbols('x')
f, g = symbols('f g', cls=Function)
diff(f(x*g(x)),x)
```

When executed, the previous code returns the following as output:

$$\left(x \frac{d}{dx} g(x) + g(x) \right) \left. \frac{d}{d\xi_1} f(\xi_1) \right|_{\xi_1 = xg(x)}$$

This example shows how the product rule and the chain rule were applied.

We can even use undefined functions as a function in several variables, for example:

```
x = symbols('x:3')
f(*x)
```

which returns the following output:

$$f(x_0, x_1, x_2).$$

Note the use of the star operator to unpack a tuple to form *f* with arguments; refer to section *Anonymous functions,* Chapter 7, *Functions*

By using list comprehension, we can construct a list of all partial derivatives of *f* :

```
[diff(f(*x),xx) for xx in x]
```

This returns a list with the elements of ∇f (the gradient of *f*):

$$\left[\frac{\partial}{\partial x_0} f(x_0, x_1, x_2), \quad \frac{\partial}{\partial x_1} f(x_0, x_1, x_2), \quad \frac{\partial}{\partial x_2} f(x_0, x_1, x_2) \right]$$

The command can also be rewritten by using the `diff` method of the `Function` object:

```
[f(*x).diff(xx) for xx in x]
```

Another method is Taylor series expansion :

```
x = symbols('x')
f(x).series(x,0,n=4)
```

This returns Taylor's formula, together with the rest term expressed by the Landau symbol:

$$f(0) + x\,f'(0) + \frac{x^2}{2} \frac{d}{dx} f'(x)\bigg|_{x=0} + \frac{x^3}{6} \frac{d^2}{dx^2} f'(x)\bigg|_{x=0} + \mathcal{O}\left(x^4\right)$$

Elementary Functions

Examples for elementary functions in SymPy are trigonometric functions and their inverses. The following example shows how simplify acts on expression which include elementary function:

```
x = symbols('x')
simplify(cos(x)**2 + sin(x)**2)   # returns 1
```

Here is another example for the use of elementary functions:

```
atan(x).diff(x) - 1./(x**2+1)   # returns 0
```

If you use SciPy and SymPy together, we strongly recommend that you use them in different namespaces:

```
import scipy as sp
import sympy as sym
# working with numbers
x=3
y=sp.sin(x)
# working with symbols
x=sym.symbols('x')
y=sym.sin(x)
```

Lambda – functions

In section *Anonymous functions* of `Chapter 7`, *Functions*, we saw how to define so-called anonymous functions in Python. The counterpart in SymPy is done by the `Lambda` command. Note the difference; `lambda` is a keyword while `Lambda` is a constructor.

The command `Lambda` takes two arguments, the symbol of the function's independent variable, and a SymPy expression to evaluate the function.

Here is an example that defines air resistance (also called drag) as a function of speed:

```
C,rho,A,v=symbols('C rho A v')
# C drag coefficient, A coss-sectional area, rho density
# v speed
f_drag = Lambda(v,-Rational(1,2)*C*rho*A*v**2)
```

`f_drag` is displayed as an expression:

$$\left(v \mapsto -\frac{AC}{2}\rho v^2 \right).$$

This function can be evaluated in the usual way by providing it with an argument:

```
x = symbols('x')
f_drag(2)
f_drag(x/3)
```

which will results in given expression:

$$-2.0AC\rho \qquad -\frac{AC}{18}\rho x^2$$

It is also possible to create functions in several variables by just providing it with several arguments as for example:

```
t=Lambda((x,y),sin(x) + cos(2*y))
```

A call to this function can be done in two ways, either by directly providing several arguments:

```
t(pi,pi/2)   # returns -1
```

or by unpacking a tuple or list:

```
p=(pi,pi/2)
t(*p)   # returns -1
```

Matrix objects in SymPy make it even possible to define vector-valued functions:

```
F=Lambda((x,y),Matrix([sin(x) + cos(2*y), sin(x)*cos(y)]))
```

This enables us to compute Jacobians:

```
F(x,y).jacobian((x,y))
```

Which gives the following expression as output:

$$\begin{bmatrix} \cos(x) & -2\sin(2y) \\ \cos(x)\cos(y) & -\sin(x)\sin(y) \end{bmatrix}.$$

In the case of more variables, it is convenient to use a more compact form to define the function:

```
x=symbols('x:2')
F=Lambda(x,Matrix([sin(x[0]) + cos(2*x[1]),sin(x[0])*cos(x[1])]))
F(*x).jacobian(x)
```

Symbolic Linear Algebra

Symbolic linear algebra is supported by SymPy's `matrix` data type which we will introduce first.

Then we will present some linear algebra methods as examples for the broad spectrum of possibilities for symbolic computations in this field:

Symbolic matrices

We briefly met the `matrix` data type when we discussed vector valued functions. There, we saw it in its simplest form, which converts a list of lists into a matrix. To have an example, let's construct a rotation matrix:

```
phi=symbols('phi')
rotation=Matrix([[cos(phi), -sin(phi)],
                 [sin(phi), cos(phi)]])
```

When working with SymPy matrices we have to note that the operator $\star$ performs matrix multiplications and is not acting as an elementwise multiplication which is the case for NumPy arrays.

The above defined rotation matrix can be checked for orthogonality, by using this matrix multiplication and the transpose of a matrix:

```
simplify(rotation.T*rotation -eye(2))   # returns a 2 x 2 zero matrix
```

The previous example shows how a matrix is transposed and how the identity matrix is created. Alternatively, we could have checked whether its inverse is its transpose, which can be done as:

```
simplify(rotation.T - rotation.inv())
```

Another way to set up a matrix is by providing a list of symbols and a shape:

```
M = Matrix(3,3, symbols('M:3(:3)'))
```

This creates the following matrix:

$$\begin{bmatrix} M_{00} & M_{01} & M_{02} \\ M_{10} & M_{11} & M_{12} \\ M_{20} & M_{21} & M_{22} \end{bmatrix}$$

A third way to create a matrix is by generating its entries by a given function. The syntax is:

```
Matrix(number of rows,number of colums, function)
```

We exemplify the above matrix by considering Toeplitz matrix is a matrix with constant diagonals. Given a *2n-1* data vector *a*, its elements are defined as

$T_{ij} := a_{i-j+(n-1)}$ for $i, j = 0, \ldots, n-1$.

In SymPy, the matrix can be defined by directly making use of this definition:

```
def toeplitz(n):
    a = symbols('a:'+str(2*n))
    f = lambda i,j: a[i-j+n-1]
    return Matrix(n,n,f)
```

Executing the previous code gives `toeplitz(5)`:

$$\begin{bmatrix} a_4 & a_3 & a_2 & a_1 & a_0 \\ a_5 & a_4 & a_3 & a_2 & a_1 \\ a_6 & a_5 & a_4 & a_3 & a_2 \\ a_7 & a_6 & a_5 & a_4 & a_3 \\ a_8 & a_7 & a_6 & a_5 & a_4 \end{bmatrix}$$

One clearly sees the desired structures; all elements along subdiagonals and superdiagonals are the same. We can access matrix elements by the indexes and slices according to the Python syntax introduced in the section *Lists* of `Chapter 3`, *Container Type*:

```
a=symbols('a')
M[0,2]=0  # changes one element
M[1,:]=Matrix(1,3,[1,2,3]) # changes an entire row
```

Examples for Linear Algebra Methods in SymPy

The basic task in linear algebra is to solve linear equation systems:

$Ax = b$.

Let us do this symbolically for a 3 × 3 matrix:

```
A = Matrix(3,3,symbols('A1:4(1:4)'))
b = Matrix(3,1,symbols('b1:4'))
x = A.LUsolve(b)
```

The output of this relatively small problem is already merely readable which can be seen in the following expression:

$$\left[\frac{1}{A_{11}}\left(-\frac{A_{12}}{A_{22}-\frac{A_{12}A_{21}}{A_{11}}}\left(b_2-\frac{\left(A_{23}-\frac{A_{13}A_{21}}{A_{11}}\right)\left(b_3-\frac{\left(A_{32}-\frac{A_{12}A_{31}}{A_{11}}\right)\left(b_2-\frac{A_{21}b_1}{A_{11}}\right)}{A_{22}-\frac{A_{12}A_{21}}{A_{11}}}-\frac{A_{31}b_1}{A_{11}}\right)}{A_{33}-\frac{\left(A_{23}-\frac{A_{13}A_{21}}{A_{11}}\right)\left(A_{32}-\frac{A_{12}A_{31}}{A_{11}}\right)}{A_{22}-\frac{A_{12}A_{21}}{A_{11}}}-\frac{A_{13}A_{31}}{A_{11}}}-\frac{A_{21}b_1}{A_{11}}\right)+A_{13}\left(b_3-\frac{\left(A_{32}-\frac{A_{12}A_{31}}{A_{11}}\right)\left(b_2-\frac{A_{21}b_1}{A_{11}}\right)}{A_{22}-\frac{A_{12}A_{21}}{A_{11}}}-\frac{A_{31}b_1}{A_{11}}\right)}{A_{33}-\frac{\left(A_{23}-\frac{A_{13}A_{21}}{A_{11}}\right)\left(A_{32}-\frac{A_{12}A_{31}}{A_{11}}\right)}{A_{22}-\frac{A_{12}A_{21}}{A_{11}}}-\frac{A_{13}A_{31}}{A_{11}}}+b_1\right)\right.$$

$$\frac{1}{A_{22}-\frac{A_{12}A_{21}}{A_{11}}}\left(b_2-\frac{\left(A_{23}-\frac{A_{13}A_{21}}{A_{11}}\right)\left(b_3-\frac{\left(A_{32}-\frac{A_{12}A_{31}}{A_{11}}\right)\left(b_2-\frac{A_{21}b_1}{A_{11}}\right)}{A_{22}-\frac{A_{12}A_{21}}{A_{11}}}-\frac{A_{31}b_1}{A_{11}}\right)}{A_{33}-\frac{\left(A_{23}-\frac{A_{13}A_{21}}{A_{11}}\right)\left(A_{32}-\frac{A_{12}A_{31}}{A_{11}}\right)}{A_{22}-\frac{A_{12}A_{21}}{A_{11}}}-\frac{A_{13}A_{31}}{A_{11}}}-\frac{A_{21}b_1}{A_{11}}\right)$$

$$b_3-\frac{\left(A_{32}-\frac{A_{12}A_{31}}{A_{11}}\right)\left(b_2-\frac{A_{21}b_1}{A_{11}}\right)}{A_{22}-\frac{A_{12}A_{21}}{A_{11}}}-\frac{A_{31}b_1}{A_{11}}}{A_{33}-\frac{\left(A_{23}-\frac{A_{13}A_{21}}{A_{11}}\right)\left(A_{32}-\frac{A_{12}A_{31}}{A_{11}}\right)}{A_{22}-\frac{A_{12}A_{21}}{A_{11}}}-\frac{A_{13}A_{31}}{A_{11}}}$$

Again, the use of `simplify` command helps us to detect canceling terms and to collect common factors:

```
simplify(x)
```

which will result in the following output which looks much better:

$$\left[\frac{A_{12}A_{23}b_3-A_{12}A_{33}b_2-A_{13}A_{22}b_3+A_{13}A_{32}b_2+A_{22}A_{33}b_1-A_{23}A_{32}b_1}{A_{11}A_{22}A_{33}-A_{11}A_{23}A_{32}-A_{12}A_{21}A_{33}+A_{12}A_{23}A_{31}+A_{13}A_{21}A_{32}-A_{13}A_{22}A_{31}}\right.$$

$$\frac{-A_{11}A_{23}b_3+A_{11}A_{33}b_2+A_{13}A_{21}b_3-A_{13}A_{31}b_2-A_{21}A_{33}b_1+A_{23}A_{31}b_1}{A_{11}A_{22}A_{33}-A_{11}A_{23}A_{32}-A_{12}A_{21}A_{33}+A_{12}A_{23}A_{31}+A_{13}A_{21}A_{32}-A_{13}A_{22}A_{31}}$$

$$\left.\frac{A_{11}A_{22}b_3-A_{11}A_{32}b_2-A_{12}A_{21}b_3+A_{12}A_{31}b_2+A_{21}A_{32}b_1-A_{22}A_{31}b_1}{A_{11}A_{22}A_{33}-A_{11}A_{23}A_{32}-A_{12}A_{21}A_{33}+A_{12}A_{23}A_{31}+A_{13}A_{21}A_{32}-A_{13}A_{22}A_{31}}\right]$$

Symbolic computations becomes very slow with increase in matrix dimensions. For dimensions bigger than 15, there might even occur memory problems.

The preceding figure (*Figure 15.3*) illustrates the differences in CPU time between symbolically and numerically solving a linear system:

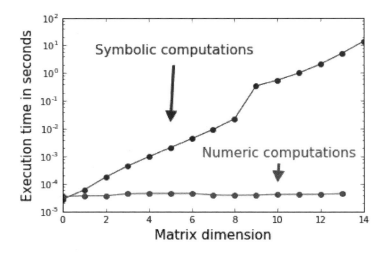

Figure 15.3: CPU time for numerically and symbolically solving a linear system.

Substitutions

Let us first consider a simple symbolic expression:

```
x, a = symbols('x a')
b = x + a
```

What happens if we set $x = 0$? We observe that b did not change. What we did was that we changed the Python variable x. It now no longer refers to the symbol object but to the integer object *0*. The symbol represented by the string 'x' remains unaltered, and so does b.

Instead, altering an expression by replacing symbols by numbers, other symbols, or expressions is done by a special substitution method which can be seen in following code:

```
x, a = symbols('x a')
b = x + a
c = b.subs(x,0)
d = c.subs(a,2*a)
print(c, d)    # returns (a, 2a)
```

This method takes one or two arguments:

```
b.subs(x,0)
b.subs({x:0})   # a dictionary as argument
```

Dictionaries as arguments allow us to make several substitutions in one step:

```
b.subs({x:0, a:2*a})   # several substitutions in one
```

As items in dictionaries have no defined order – one never knows which would be the first – there is a need for assuring that permuting the items would not affect the substitution result. Therefore in SymPy, substitutions are first made within the dictionary and then on the expression. This is demonstrated by the following example:

```
x, a, y = symbols('x a y')
b = x + a
b.subs({a:a*y, x:2*x, y:a/y})
b.subs({y:a/y, a:a*y, x:2*x})
```

Both substitutions return the same result, that is,

$$\frac{a^2}{y} + 2x .$$

A third alternative to define multiple substitutions is by using a list of old-value/ new-value pairs instead:

```
b.subs([(y,a/y), (a,a*y), (x,2*x)])
```

It is also possible to substitute entire expressions by others:

```
n, alpha = symbols('n alpha')
b = cos(n*alpha)
b.subs(cos(n*alpha), 2*cos(alpha)*cos((n-1)*alpha)-cos((n-2)*alpha))
```

To illustrate substitutions of matrix elements, we take the 5 × 5 Toeplitz matrix again:

$$\begin{bmatrix} a_4 & a_3 & a_2 & a_1 & a_0 \\ a_5 & a_4 & a_3 & a_2 & a_1 \\ a_6 & a_5 & a_4 & a_3 & a_2 \\ a_7 & a_6 & a_5 & a_4 & a_3 \\ a_8 & a_7 & a_6 & a_5 & a_4 \end{bmatrix}$$

Consider the substitution `M.subs(T[0,2],0)`. It changes the symbol object at position [0, 2], which is the symbol a_2. It also occurs at two other places, which are automatically affected by this substitution.

The given expression is the resulting matrix:

$$\begin{bmatrix} a_4 & a_3 & 0 & a_1 & a_0 \\ a_5 & a_4 & a_3 & 0 & a_1 \\ a_6 & a_5 & a_4 & a_3 & 0 \\ a_7 & a_6 & a_5 & a_4 & a_3 \\ a_8 & a_7 & a_6 & a_5 & a_4 \end{bmatrix}.$$

Alternatively we can create a variable for this symbol and use it in the substitution:

```
a2 = symbols('a2')
T.subs(a2,0)
```

As a more complex example for substitution we describe, how to turn the Toeplitz matrix into a tridiagonal Toeplitz matrix. This can be done in the following ways:
First we generate a list of those symbols that we want to substitute; and then we use the `zip` command to generate a list of pairs. Finally we substitute by giving a list of old-value/new-value pairs as described above:

```
symbs = [symbols('a'+str(i)) for i in range(19) if i < 3 or i > 5]
substitutions=list(zip(symbs,len(symbs)*[0]))
T.subs(substitutions)
```

This gives the following matrix as result:

$$\begin{bmatrix} a_4 & a_3 & 0 & 0 & 0 \\ a_5 & a_4 & a_3 & 0 & 0 \\ 0 & a_5 & a_4 & a_3 & 0 \\ 0 & 0 & a_5 & a_4 & a_3 \\ 0 & 0 & 0 & a_5 & a_4 \end{bmatrix}.$$

Evaluating symbolic expressions

In the context of scientific computing, there is often the need of first making symbolic manipulations and then converting the symbolic result into a floating-point number .

The central tool for evaluating a symbolic expression is `evalf`. It converts symbolic expressions to floating-point numbers by using the following:

```
pi.evalf()    # returns 3.14159265358979
```

The data type of the resulting object is `Float` (note the capitalization), which is a SymPy data type that allows floating-point numbers with an arbitrary number of digits (arbitrary precision).

The default precision corresponds to 15 digits, but it can be changed by giving `evalf` an extra positive integer argument specifying the desired precision in terms the numbers of digits,

```
pi.evalf(30)    # returns  3.14159265358979323846264338328
```

A consequence of working with arbitrary precision is that numbers can be arbitrary small, that is, the limits of the classical floating-point representation are broken; refer *Floating Point Numbers* section in `Chapter 2`, *Variables and Basic Types*.

Interestingly enough, evaluating a SymPy function with an input of type `Float` returns a Float with the same precision as the input. We demonstrate the use of this fact in a more elaborated example from numerical analysis.

Example: A study on the convergence order of Newton's Method

An iterative method with iterates x_n is said to converge with order q with $1 < q \in \mathbb{N}$ if there exists a positive constant C such that

$$\lim_{n \to \infty} \frac{|x_{n+1} - x_n|^q}{|x_n - x_{n-1}|} = C .$$

Newton's method when started with a good initial has order $q = 2$, and for certain problems, even $q = 3$. Newton's method when applied to the problem arctan$(x) = 0$ gives the following iteration scheme:

$$x_{n+1} = x_n - \frac{f(x_n)}{f'(x_n)} = x_n - \arctan(x_n) \cdot (x_n^2 - 1)$$

which converges cubically; that is $q = 3$.

This implies that the number of correct digits triples from iteration to iteration. To demonstrate cubic convergence and to numerically determine the constant C is hardly possible with the standard 16-digit float data type.

The following code, uses SymPy together with high-precision evaluation instead and puts a study on cubic convergence to the extreme:

```
x = sp.Rational(1,2)
xns=[x]

for i in range(1,9):
    x = (x - sp.atan(x)*(1+x**2)).evalf(3000)
    xns.append(x)
```

The result is depicted in the next figure (*Figure 15.4*) which shows that the number of correct digits triples from iteration to iteration.

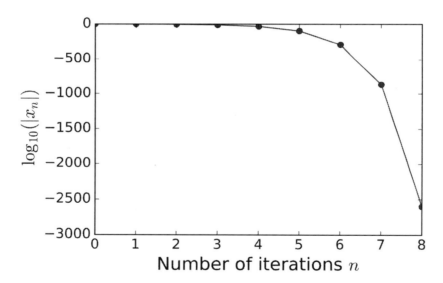

Figure 15.4: A study on the convergence of Newton's method applied to arctan(x)=0

This extreme precision requirement (3,000 digits!) enables us to evaluate seven terms of the preceding sequence to demonstrate cubic convergence in the following way:

```
# Test for cubic convergence
print(array(abs(diff(xns[1:]))/abs(diff(xns[:-1]))**3,dtype=float64))
```

The result is a list of seven terms which let us assume that $C = 2/3$:

```
[ 0.41041618, 0.65747717, 0.6666665,  0.66666667, 0.66666667, 0.66666667,
0.66666667]
```

Converting a symbolic expression into a numeric function

As we have seen the numerical evaluation of a symbolic expression is done in three steps, first we do some symbolic computations and then we substitute values by numbers and do an evaluation to a floating point number by `evalf`.

The reason for symbolic computations is often that one wants to make parameter studies. This requires that the parameter is modified within a given parameter range. This requires that an symbolic expression is eventually turned into a numeric function.

A study on the parameter dependency of polynomial coefficients

We demonstrate a symbolic/ numeric parameter study by an interpolation example to introduce the SymPy command `lambdify`.
Let us consider the task to interpolate the data $x = [0, t, 1]$ and $y = [0, 1,-1]$. Here, t is a free parameter, which we will vary over the interval [-0.4, 1.4].
The quadratic interpolation polynomial has coefficients depending on this parameter:

$$y(x) = a_2(t)x^2 + a_1(t)x + a_0.$$

Using SymPy and the monomial approach described in gives us closed formulas for these coefficients:

```
t=symbols('t')
x=[0,t,1]
# The Vandermonde Matrix
V = Matrix([[0, 0, 1], [t**2, t, 1], [1, 1,1]])
y = Matrix([0,1,-1])  # the data vector
a = simplify(V.LUsolve(y)) # the coefficients
# the leading coefficient as a function of the parameter
a2 = Lambda(t,a[0])
```

We obtain a symbolic function for the leading coefficient a_2 of the interpolation polynomial:

$$\left(t \mapsto \frac{t+1}{t\,(t-1)} \right)$$

Now it is time to turn the expression into a numeric function, for example, to make a plot. This is done by the function `lamdify`. This function takes two arguments, the independent variable and a SymPy function.

For our example in Python we can write:

```
leading_coefficient = lambdify(t,a2(t))
```

This function can now be plotted, for example, by the following commands:

```
t_list= linspace(-0.4,1.4,200)
ax=subplot(111)
lc_list = [leading_coefficient(t) for t in  t_list]
ax.plot(t_list, lc_list)
ax.axis([-.4,1.4,-15,10])
```

The preceding figure (*Figure 15.5*) is the result of this parameter study, one clearly sees the singularities due to multiple interpolation points, (here at $t = 0$ or $t = 1$):

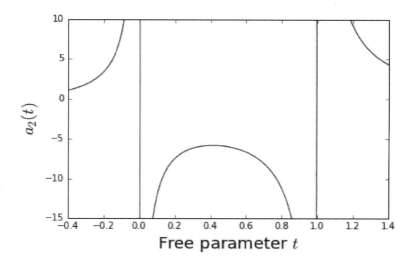

Figure 15.5: The dependency of a polynomial coefficient on the location of an interpolation point.

Summary

In this chapter you were introduced in the world of symbolic computations and you got a glimpse of the power of SymPy. By guiding examples you learned how to set up symbolic expressions, how to work with symbolic matrices, and you saw how to make simplifications. Working with symbolic functions and transforming them into numerical evaluations built finally the link to scientific computing and floating point results. You experienced the strength of SymPy as you used its full integration into Python with its powerful constructs and legible syntax.

Consider this last chapter as an appetizer rather than a complete menu. We hope you became hungry for future fascinating programming challenges in scientific computing and mathematics.

References

1. M. Abramowitz and I.A. Stegun, *Handbook of Mathematical Functions with Formulas, Graphs, and Mathematical Tables*, U.S. Department of Commerce, 2002. ISBN: 9780486612720.

2. *Anaconda – Continuum Analytics Download page.* URL: `https://www.continuum.io/downloads`.

3. Michael J. Cloud, Moore Ramon E., and R. Baker Kearfott, *Introduction to Interval Analysis*, Society for Industrial and Applied Mathematics (SIAM), 2009. ISBN: 0-89871-669-1.

4. *Python Decorator Library.* URL: `http://wiki.python.org/moin/PythonDecoratorLibrary`.

5. Z. Bai E. Anderson, C. Bischof, S. Blackford, J. Demmel, J. Dongarra, J. Du Croz, A. Greenbaum, S. Hammarling, A. McKenney, and D. Sorensen, *LAPACK Users' Guide*, SIAM, 1999. ISBN: 9780898714470.

6. *fraction – Rational Numbers Library.* URL: `http://docs.python.org/library/fractions.html`.

7. Claus Führer, Jan Erik Solem, and Olivier Verdier, *Computing with Python*, Pearson, 2014. ISBN: 978-0-273-78643-6.

8. *functools – Higher order functions and operations on callable objects.* URL: `http://docs.python.org/library/functools.html`.

9. *Python Generator Tricks.* URL: `http://linuxgazette.net/100/pramode.html`.

10. G.H. Golub and C.F.V. Loan, *Matrix computations*, Johns Hopkins studies in the mathematical sciences. Johns Hopkins University Press, 1996. ISBN: 9780801854149.

11. Ernst Hairer and Gerhard Wanner, *Analysis by its history*, Springer, 1995.

12. *Python versus Haskell.* URL: `http://wiki.python.org/moin/PythonVsHaskell`.

13. *The IEEE 754-2008 standard.* URL: `http://en.wikipedia.org/wiki/IEEE_754-2008`.

14. *Interval arithmetic.* URL: `http://en.wikipedia.org/wiki/Interval_arithmetic`.

15. *IPython: Interactive Computing.* URL: `http://ipython.org/`.

16. H.P. Langtangen, *Python scripting for computational science* (Texts in computational science and engineering), *Springer*, 2008. ISBN:9783540739159.

17. H.P. Langtangen, *A Primer on Scientific Programming with Python* (Texts in Computational Science and Engineering), Springer, 2009. ISBN: 9783642024740.

18. D. F. Lawden, *Elliptic Functions and Applications*, Springer, 1989. ISBN: 9781441930903.

19. M. Lutz, *Learning Python: Powerful Object-Oriented Programming*, O'Reilly, 2009. ISBN: 9780596158064.

20. *NumPy Tutorial – Mandelbrot Set Example.* URL: `http://www.scipy.org/Tentative_NumPy_Tutorial/Mandelbrot_Set_Example`.

21. *matplotlib.* URL: `http://matplotlib.sourceforge.net`.

22. *Standard: Memoized recursive Fibonacci in Python.* URL: `http://ujihisa.blogspot.se/2010/11/memoized-recursive-fibonacciin-python.html`.

23. *Matplotlib mplot3d toolkit.* URL: `http://matplotlib.sourceforge.net/mpl_toolkits/mplot3d`.

24. James M. Ortega and Werner C. Rheinboldt, *Iterative solution of nonlinear equations in several variables*, SIAM, 2000. ISBN: 9780898714616.

25. *pdb – The Python Debugger*, documentation: `http://docs.python.org/library/pdb.html`.

26. Fernando Pérez and Brian E. Granger. IPython: a System for Interactive Scientific Computing." In: Comput. Sci. Eng. 9.3 (May 2007), pp. 21–29. URL: `http://ipython.org`.

27. Michael J.D. Powell. "An efficient method for finding the minimum of a function of several variables without calculating derivatives." In: Computer Journal 7 (2 1964), pp. 155–162. doi: `doi:10.1093/comjnl/7.2.155`.

28. Timothy Sauer, *Numerical Analysis*, Pearson, 2006.

29. L.F. Shampine, R.C. Allen, and S. Pruess, *Fundamentals of Numerical Computing*, John Wiley, 1997. ISBN: 9780471163633.

30. Jan Erik Solem, *Programming Computer Vision with Python*, O'Reilly Media, 2012. URL: `http://programmingcomputervision.com`.

31. *Python Documentation – Emulating numeric types.* URL: `http://docs.python.org/reference/datamodel.html#emulating-numeric-types`.

32. *Sphinx: Python Documentation Generator.* URL: `http://sphinx.pocoo.org/`.

33. J. Stoer and R. Bulirsch, *Introduction to numerical analysis. Texts in applied mathematics*, Springer, 2002. ISBN: 9780387954523.

34. *Python Format String Syntax.* URL: `http://docs.python.org/library/string.html#format-string-syntax`.

35. S. Tosi, *Matplotlib for Python Developers,* Packt Publishing, 2009. ISBN: 9781847197900.

36. Lloyd N. Trefethen and David Bau, *Numerical Linear Algebra,* SIAM: Society for Industrial and Applied Mathematics, 1997. ISBN: 0898713617.

37. *visvis – The object oriented approach to visualization.* URL: `http://code.google.com/p/visvis/`.

38. The full list of built-in exceptions can be found at `http://docs.python.org/library/exceptions.html`

Index

%

%matplotlib command 123

3

3D plots
  creating 145, 148

A

AGM iteration 201
allclose command 70
Anaconda
  about 13
  installing 13
annotations
  about 141
  example 141
anonymous functions
  about 165
  Lambda construction 166
arguments
  about 154
  default arguments 157
  immutable arguments 155
  modifying 155
  mutable arguments 155
  passing, by keyword 154
  passing, by position 155
  variable number 158
arithmetic geometric mean 201, 203
array functions 88
array type casting 76
array views
  about 97
  copy operation 99
  example 97
  reshape operation 98
  slices operation 98
  transpose operation 98
arrays
  about 56
  altering, with slices 79
  as functions 71
  broadcasting 110
  broadcasting, issues 110
  comparing 99
  constructing, with functions 79
  creating, from lists 76
  dimensions 72
  dtype property 75
  elementwise operations 71
  entries, accessing 77
  in NumPy 71
  indexing 102
  overview 67
  properties 75
  shape 72
  shape property 75
  silent type conversion 76
  slicing 77, 78
  strides property 75
  syntax 76
  type 75
arrow properties 142
assertion tools 253
attributes
  about 174, 176
  bound method 182
  class attributes 182
  class methods 183, 185
  dependency 180
  methods 176, 178
  property function 181, 182
  reference, example 174

unbound methods 182
automatic Boolean casting 39
automatic testing
   about 246
   bisection algorithm, testing 247
axes object
   about 139
   annotations 141
   areas, filling between curves 142
   line properties, modifying 140
   ticklabels 144, 145
   ticks 144, 145

B

banana function
   displaying 133, 135
banded matrices 115
basic data types
   about 18
   Boolean expression 20, 21
   lists 19
   numbers 18
   strings 18
   variables 19
bisection method 169
Boolean arrays
   about 99
   indexing 102
   operators, using 101
   where command, using 103
Boolean casting 38
Booleans
   about 37
   and integers 40
   and operators 37
   and operators, return value 39
   automatic Boolean casting 39
   not operators 37
   or operators 37
   or operators, return value 39
bound method 182
break keyword 196
broadcasting, examples
   columns, rescaling 113
   functions, of two variables 113

rows, rescaling 113
broadcasting
   about 106
   arrays 110
   constant functions 107
   conventions 110
   functions, building of variables 108
   mathematical view 106
   mechanism 108
   shape mismatch, with arrays 112
bugs 223
built-in exceptions
   ImportError 216
   IndexError 216
   IOError 216
   KeyError 216
   LinAlgError 216
   NameError 216
   ValueError 216
built-in universal functions 86

C

call stack 223
characteristic polynomial 265
Chebyshev polynomials 161, 170, 189
class attributes 182
class methods 182, 183, 185
classes
   _init_method 173
   about 172
   as decorators 189, 191
   syntax 173
closures
   using 165
code refactoring 246
code
   encapsulating, by functions 23
color map 137
columnstack function 84
companion matrix 265
comparison operator 100
compiled code 104
complex numbers
   about 34
   conjugate part 34

imaginary part 35
in mathematics 34
j notation 34
real part 35
symbol 18
compressed sparse column (CSC) format 118
compressed sparse row (CSR)
about 116
data array 116
indices array 117
indptr array 117
concatenate method 84
conditional statements 22
constant functions 107
container
conversions 62
types 49
context manager
about 221
using 259, 260
context managers 223
continuation line 17
continue keyword 196
contour command
used, for displaying level curves 133
contours
3D plotting 145
about 132
and images 138
convergence acceleration 203, 204
cubic splines 94

D

de Moivre's formula 44
debug commands 226
debugging 256
default arguments
about 157
mutable default arguments 158
default value 157
degree of sparsity 167
diagonal matrices 115
dict command 59
dictionaries
about 59

altering 59
creating 59
looping over 60
differential equation
solving, with one-step method 185
docstring 163
dot function 69, 70
dot operations 73
dot product 74
dubugger tool 223

E

elementary functions
about 288
Lambda command 289, 290
elementwise multiplication
versus matrix multiplication 74
elliptic integral
about 202
computing 213
empty list [] 53
empty set 61
encapsulation 188
equations
solving, numerically 276, 279
escape sequence 41, 131
Euclid's algorithm 170
Euclidean 2-norm 157
Euclidean vector 91
Euler method 278
exceptions
about 215, 217
bugs 223
catching 218, 220
context manager 221
context managers 223
debugging 227, 228
principles 217
Python debugger 224, 226
raising 217, 218
stack 223
user-defined exceptions 220
execution time, measuring
about 256
context manager, using 259

magic functions, using 257
Python module timeit, using 258
Explicit Euler 185
exponent 30

F

Fibonacci sequence 201
figure command 125
file handling
  about 237
  file modes 239
  files, interacting with 237
  files, iterating 239
filling areas
  displaying 143
float comparisons 253
floating point numbers
  about 30
  in NumPy 33
  infinite 31
  not-a-number 31
  representation 30, 31
  underflow 32
for loop
  about 195
  break keyword 22
  else keyword 22
  indentation 21
  used, for repeating task 21
for statement 195
formatting 132
  with plot() function 129
FORTRAN 75
Frobenius norm 157
full adder circuit 47
functional test 255
functions
  array functions 88
  arrays, constructing 79
  as decorators 167
  as objects 164
  basics 153
  documentation 163
  partial application 164
  recursive functions 161

return values 160
types 85
universal functions 85
used, for code encapsulation 23
variables, accessing 156
vectorizing 106
functools 169

G

Gauss elimination method 89
Geany 12
generator expression 207, 208
generators 198
global variables 156, 157
greatest common divisor
  computing 170
Greek letters 145

H

half adder circuit 46
hashable objects 61
heaviside function 86
hist command 130
hstack function 84

I

ImageMagick 150
images
  and contours 136, 138
  reading 243
  writing 243
imaginary number 34
immutable arguments 155
immutable list 58
implication 45
import command 25
imshow command 137
in-place modification 161
indexing 69
inf floating-point number 31
infinite iterations
  about 210
  recursion 211
  while loop 210
infix notation 74

inheritance 171, 185, 187
initial value problem 185
instantiation 171
integers
  about 29
  and Booleans 40
  plain integers 29
interpolation 137
interpreted code 104
IPython
  about 14
  modules 234
  plotting commands, using 123
  using 15
iterable object 55, 197
iterator object 209
iterators
  about 197
  arithmetic geometric mean 201, 203
  as lists 207
  generator expression 207, 208
  generators 198
  recursive sequences, generators 201
  reusing 199
  tools 199
  zipping 208

J

j notation 34
Jacobians
  computing 290
Jupyter notebook 7, 15, 16

K

k-means clustering algorithm 273
key/data pair 59
keys 59

L

Lambda command 289, 290
lambda keyword
  about 165
  construction 166, 167
LAPACK 89
LaTeX 130, 145

least common multiple
  computing 170
legend function
  about 125
  optional arguments 126
len command 50
Lena test image 151
lexicographical order 42
LIL format
  about 119
  matrices, altering 119
  matrices, slicing 119
line joining
  explicit line joining 17
  implicit line joining 17
linear algebra functions
  sl.cholesky 92
  sl.det 92
  sl.eig 92
  sl.inv 92
  sl.lstsq 92
  sl.lu 92
  sl.norm 92
  sl.pinv 92
  sl.qr 92
  sl.solve 92
  sl.solve.banded 92
  sl.svd 92
linear algebra methods
  common methods 92
  least square problem, solving with SVD 91
  linear equation systems, solving with LU 89
linear algebra
  about 67
  linear system, solving 70
  operations 69
list comprehension 55, 56
list methods
  list.append(x) 54
  list.count(x) 54
  list.expand(L) 54
  list.insert(i,x) 54
  list.pop() 54
  list.remove(x) 54
  list.reverse() 54

list.sort() 54
lists
   about 19, 49
   altering 53
   elements, determining 53
   filling, with append method 205
   from iterators 205, 206
   generated values, storing 206
   in-place operations 54
   merging 55
   operations 20
loadtxt method 240
local variables 156
logical operators 101
loglog function 128
loop variable 195
loops
   flow, controlling 196
   used, for replacing statements 21
LU factorization 89

M

machine epsilon 32
magic functions 15, 257
Mandelbrot contour image 151
Mandelbrot fractal, example 136, 152
mantissa 30
manual testing 245
Maple 281
Mathematica 281
Matlab data files
   reading 243
   writing 243
matplotlib
   about 123
   objects 138
matrices 67
   about 67
matrix slicing 77
memoization 162
Mencoder 150
meshgrid
   about 132
   banana function, displaying 135
   Rosenbrock's banana function, displaying 133

methods
   reverse operations 178, 179
Midpoint Rule 185
modules, IPython
   about 234
   magic command 234
   main variable 234
modules
   about 232, 233
   and script 24
   creating 24
   simple modules 24, 25
   using 25
modulo operation 39
modulu function 151
monomial representation 263
movies
   creating, from plots 149, 150
moving average, array 94
mutable default arguments
   modifying 158

N

namespace
   about 229, 230
   using 25
nan floating-point number 31
Newton polynomial class
   defining 270, 271
numeric computations 281
numeric function
   symbolic expression, converting to 299
numeric types 28
NumPy
   about 67
   arrays 71
   float types 33
   loadtxt method 240
   savetxt method 240

O

object-oriented approach 138
operator overloading 177
out-of-bound slices 51
overflow 31

P

parameters 154
parent class 187
partial application
  about 164
  closures, using 165
pendulum
  period, computing 203
permutation matrix (P) 90
pickle module 241, 242
plain integers 29
plotting
  with plot() function 123, 125, 128
polyfit command 125
polynomial class
  designing 266, 268, 270
polynomials
  about 263
  designing 263
  Lagrange representation 264
  Newton representation 263
  programming tasks, formulating 265
polyval command 125
post-mortem analysis 224
Powell's method 135
program flow 16, 17
program
  about 16
  comments 17
  line joining 17
property function 181, 182
Python debugger (pdb)
  about 224, 226
  commands 226
Python interpreter 25
Python modules
  contextlib 235
  datetime 235
  functools 235
  itertools 235
  matplotlib 235
  numpy 235
  os 235
  pickle 235
  re 235
  scipy 235
  shelves 235
  sympy 235
  sys 235
  time 235
  timeit 235
Python shell 14
Python
  configuration 12, 14
  performance 104
  requisites 12

R

range command 50
raw strings 41
recursion 211
recursion depth 162
recursive functions 161
recursive sequences
  generators 201
reduction operation 74
reserved keywords 28
reshape method
  about 81
  transpose 83
reverse addition 178
reverse operations 178, 180
Rosenbrock's banana function
  displaying 133, 135
row-based linked list format 118
Runge-Kutta 4 185
Runge-Kutta four-stage method (RK4) 278

S

sanity test
  performing 254
savefig command
  about 132
  transparent parameter 132
savetxt method 240
scipy.sparse module 116
SciPy
  about 14, 89
  linear algebra methods 89

scope, variable 157, 230, 231
script
  about 24
  executing 15
sets 60, 61
shadowing 233
shape
  accessing 80
  modifying 80
  number of dimensions, obtaining 81
  reshape method, using 81
  shape function 80
shelves 242
Sieve of Eratosthenes 212
singular value decomposition (SVD)
  about 91
  least square problem, solving 91
slices
  about 77
  used, for altering arrays 79
slicing
  about 50, 51, 52, 69
  rules 79
  strides 52
sparse matrices, formats
  about 116
  compressed sparse column (CSC) 118
  compressed sparse row (CSR) 116
  LIL format 119
  row-based linked list format 118
sparse matrices
  about 115
  generating 119
  methods 120
spectral clustering 272, 273, 275
spline arc, arrow 142
Spyder 12
stacking 84
star operator 187
statements
  replacing, with loops 21
  syntax 17
strides 52
string, raw 131
strings

about 40
braces 44
formatting 43
list, joining 42
methods 42
operations 42
searching 42
splitting 42
subclassing 185, 187
subplots_adjust command 132
substitutions 294, 295, 296
sum function 88
surfaces
  3D plotting 145
symbolic computations
  about 281, 282, 283
  SymPy, example 283, 284, 285
symbolic expressions
  converting, to numeric function 299
  evaluating 296, 297
  examples 297, 298
  parameter dependency study, of polynomial
    coefficients 299, 300
symbolic linear algebra
  about 290
  examples 292, 294
  symbolic matrices 291
symbolic matrices 291
symplectic permutation, example 85
SymPy
  basic elements 285
  example 283, 284, 285
  functions 286
  numbers 286
  symbols 285, 286
  undefined function 287, 288

T

Tab key 15
Taylor polynomial 171
Taylor's formula 288
tests
  discovering 256
  parameterizing 251
three-term recursion 161, 179

throw-away variables 274
timeit module 258
title command 125
transpose 83
triangular matrix (L) 90
tuples 58
type checking 168

U

unbound method 182
underflow
  machine epsilon 32, 33
unit test 255
unittest package
  for identifying errors 223
  setUp method, testing 250
  tearDown methods, testing 250
  using 249
universal functions
  about 85
  built-in universal functions 85
  creating 86
user-defined exceptions 220

V

Vandermonde matrix 94
Vandermonde system 266
variable
  about 27
  scope 230, 231
  type, checking 63
vectorization 105, 106
vectorize function 87
vectors
  about 67, 68
  stacking 84
views 97
visvis module 149
vstack function 84

W

where command 103
while loop 210

Y

yield keyword 198

Z

zero-based indexing 49
zip function 55

Made in the USA
San Bernardino, CA
31 May 2018